WORKING TOGETHER

Workplace Culture,
Supported Employment,
and
Persons with Disabilities

DAVID HAGNER AND
DALE DILEO

Brookline Books

Library of Congress Cataloging-in-Publication Data
    Hagner, David.
      Working together : workplace culture, supported employment, and people with disabilities / David C. Hagner, Dale DiLeo.
         p.   cm.
      Includes bibliographical references and index.
      ISBN 0-914797-88-3 (paper) : $27.95
      1. Vocational guidance for the handicapped--United States.
    2. Handicapped--Employment--United States. I. Dileo, Dale, 1953-
.
    II. Title
    HV1568.5.H34   1993
    331.5'9'0973--dc20   93-25052
                                                  CIP

Printed in the USA by Thomson-Shore, Dexter, MI.
Second printing, 1995.

Distributed in the U.K. by:
Drake Educational Associates
St. Fagans Road, Fairwater, Cardiff CF5 3AE, Wales
A CIP record for this title is available from the British Library.

Published by
Brookline Books
P.O. Box 1047, Cambridge, MA 02238-1047

Table of Contents

Foreword

In the autumn of 1976 I was responsible for helping a young man with disabilities learn his job at a company in Portland, Oregon, that manufactured brass pull knobs for furniture. I understood my role quite clearly: teach Roger to do his job quickly, safely and independently. Naturally, I stayed close to Roger in order to provide assistance on productivity, quality and staying on schedule. One evening during Roger's shift, while I was engaged in my support role, an older woman who worked on the machine next to Roger's leaned toward me and said: "You can go on, son, he'll do just fine here. We'll help him."

That woman knew then what people concerned about supported employment are discovering now. The issue of community employment for people with severe disabilities is an issue of helping people be a part of the fabric of the community, the fabric of the workplace. It is a matter of helping shape connections, personal networks and opportunities. It is not about having paid professionals providing all of the assistance that every person with a significant disability will ever need. The Supported Employment Initiative emerged in the early 1980s with a firm belief that all people with severe disabilities could work if needed supports were provided. In those days it was easy to assume that the support provided would come from the same kinds of people who had provided support to people in activity centers and workshops, but now they would be called job coaches or employment training specialists. What has emerged is the amazing capacity of large and small companies to include people with disabilities in the community and the workforce. If we define our role as *supporting inclusion of individuals with disabilities*, rather than providing all of the assistance to individuals, we perhaps move closer to the goal of full participation in the things that are the best things about community life.

In this book, David Hagner and Dale DiLeo explore in detail the idea that we can assist the business world and the community to include people with disabilities in typical ways. In reading this book you will notice several things. It is a book about people you know, and places you have worked. It is about the stories that make so many workplaces enjoyable places. It is about companies doing business in ways that place value in the people that work there without regard for a disability label. It is a book about community. It is a book about ways that people with disabilities can get the same kind of supports in the workplace that other employees get. It is a book about making supported employment for people with disabilities less special as a human service, and more typical of anyone else's employment in the community.

Working Together: Workplace Culture, Supported Employment and People with Disabilities begins with a thoughtful discussion of the emergence of supported employment and the importance of understanding the culture of the workplace. This discussion sets the stage for reconsidering the entire process of developing jobs and providing supports for people with severe disabilities. The third chapter explores the value of career planning, introducing ideas for individualized planning that puts the person with disabilities in the role of decision maker.

Chapters 4 through 8 discuss, in a refreshing way, the processes of job searching and negotiation, employee training and supports, joining the culture of the workplace, and supporting coworker involvement. To these processes Hagner and Dileo bring sound concepts and good examples of new ways to support the inclusion of people with disabilities.

Finally, the authors revisit the overriding issue of careers. For more than a decade, as a field we appear to have been consumed with the notion of just getting access to community jobs. It is past time to begin thinking of a job for anyone with a disability as one job in a career path filled with choice.

This is a book for many audiences. Interested readers should include the friends and families of people with disabilities, as well as the people who spend every day trying to figure out meaningful employment for people with disabilities. It will be of interest to students preparing for a variety of roles in supporting people with disabilities in the community and their instructors. Readers should also include school personnel who are preparing students to be members of the community.

This book provides an opportunity to rethink our roles in the lives of people with disabilities, to listen to the people in the community and in the workplace. I wish that I had listened more clearly in 1976 to the message of the older woman in the manufacturing plant in Portland, Oregon, about support for employees with disabilities. And I hope you will listen clearly to the message provided by David Hagner and Dale DiLeo in this book.

David Mank
University of Oregon, February 1993

Preface

This book is the product of our efforts to bring together and systematize ideas and approaches to supported employment and career assistance for individuals with severe disabilities that have been evolving over the past several years. Our central concern is with understanding workplaces as social environments, forming collaborative partnerships between businesses and vocational services, and achieving social inclusion for employees with disabilities. Support resources internal to the business world are emphasized over those imported from the outside by "job coaches." Training and other behavior change strategies, the dominant theme in much existing supported employment literature, are considered within the context of a wider perspective. We try to make the case that the success of training and any other aspect of employment depends on how well inclusion and partnership issues are addressed, not the other way around.

It is a book of practical information, stories and strategies, based on our work with supported employment over several years in a variety of different roles. Our primary method has been to "analyze success" by searching out the best examples of successful employment, observing what is going on, and talking with the people involved. Formal research findings, more informal anecdotes and practitioner tips, and to some extent ideas from business management, personnel psychology and the job hunting literature have been collected and organized into a coherent approach to employment.

The first two chapters present the background and conceptual base for our approach. The remaining chapters can be read in order or can be used as a sort of "desk reference," to obtain information about specific issues related to facilitating successful employment in whatever order those issues arise. Although the information is practical, we do not present a method, a model or a recipe for supported employment. With the right attitude and approach, the correct recipe can be developed from the ingredients at hand in each situation.

This manuscript owes a great deal to John Butterworth and Pat Rogan, whose critique of an earlier draft was of immeasurable value. We are also grateful to Kim Milliken for her guidance, inspiration and assistance in developing many of the ideas. The illustrations are the work of Joannie Berriman, whose creative energy is matched by her tolerance. Thanks also to Milt Budoff and Bill Kiernan for making our work possible.

Some of the stories and examples throughout the book are based on the work of Nancy Clarke, Susan Moreno, Ellen Zamanski, and other skilled and dedicated professionals. We acknowledge their contribution and dedicate this book to the supported employees, employers, and service providers who work together and make it happen.

David Hagner
Dale Dileo

CHAPTER 1

Employment Support in Perspective

"As we extend the realm and reign of our consciousness and competence we will find ourselves moving farther and farther from home."
— Judith Viorst

Being employed in our society means many things. In part it fulfills a social expectation for people to be productive, get paid what they are worth, and make their own way. Beyond survival, work has always been a means for status, self-definition, and personal accomplishment. A great percentage of our waking hours for a large part of our lives is spent at work. People who work use their employment as one of their key social roles. In fact, one of the first things we seek when meeting someone new is to find out "what they do." Working is an integral aspect of our participation in our community.

Many individuals with disabilities have been arbitrarily isolated from full participation in society and have found their participation in the workforce seriously restricted. Unemployment rates for individuals with disabilities are four to five times higher than for individuals without disabilities (U.S. Bureau of the Census, 1985). A system of special services and programs developed to offer specialized assistance has had the paradoxical effect of furthering the social isolation of many individuals from the mainstream of the community. The result has been a lowering of the expectations both of society and people with disabilities themselves, and an exaggeration of the perception of differences brought about by disability.

Restricted participation in the workforce is not confined just to one sphere or domain of an individual's life. Our work, our recreational and leisure pursuits, our friendships, our membership in our community, all of these are linked to one another. What happens in one area affects the others. We use our personal relationships to find jobs, and use our jobs to develop personal relationships.

Leisure interests develop out of our relationships, and employment provides the income to pursue them. A relationship or a leisure interest may spark a job or a career change. What we earn affects where we live; what we do affects how we are viewed in the community and who we are. We might analyze our lives into separate bits and pieces, but we live life whole.

Isolation and paternalism for people with disabilities have not only limited the quality of life for these individuals, they have cost society greatly. Businesses cannot compete as effectively when employers are denied access to an important pool of reliable and productive workers at a time when a dwindling supply of labor is becoming an increasing concern (Johnston & Packer, 1987). The corresponding loss of tax revenues reduces the overall tax base and places an additional burden on taxpayers to provide public benefits and services to involuntarily and needlessly unemployed individuals. Further, the costs of specialized programs and facility-based services have grown at astronomical rates, with the most restrictive and outmoded services costing the most.

But the past few decades have also seen dramatic, and it is even fair to say, revolutionary changes in the way we view and respond to someone with a disability. This has had less to do with changes in what individuals can do, and more with an evolution in the way we view disability. In vocational services, a key development indicative of this major shift in approach has been the emergence of *supported employment*.

Supported employment is a simple concept. It refers to a process whereby people traditionally denied career opportunities due to the perceived severity of their disability are assisted to obtain jobs in the community and provided support for as long as needed. Developed over the past few years from small demonstration projects, supported employment has emerged as an important service available to people with severe disabilities.

One result of this new service has been some 73,000 persons in supported jobs in the U.S. in 1991 (Virginia Commonwealth University Rehabilitation Research and Training Center, 1991). These jobs have dramatically changed the lives of many individuals who had previously been denied access to employment or found employment only in sheltered workshops.

Some have welcomed supported employment, others have adapted to it, and still others have tried to resist or contain what they believed was too radical a change. People closely involved in developing and marketing a new product or service tend to emphasize how "new" and "improved" the product or service is. Supported employment is no exception. So it is worthwhile to take a brief look at the history of vocational services for people with disabilities and see what is new and what is a continuation of past practices. The development of supported employment and support practices prevalent today needs to be understood in context. Emerging lessons, both from a service agency perspective and from a business perspective, are setting the stage for new approaches to employment support.

A LOOK BACK AT EMPLOYMENT AND PEOPLE WITH DISABILITIES

Until the middle of the present century, most adults whom we might today label as severely disabled either lived with their families or were placed in large institutions. Those who lived with their families, the vast majority, often pitched in with the work on the family farm or business. And community employment, with employers providing needed accommodations and supports, was viewed as perfectly natural for at least some individuals with disabilities. For example, Dugdale (1877) noted in his study of the family he called the "Jukes," that several members of this family worked for a local employer, including some who apparently had intellectual disabilities. This employer provided help to the employees in money management and in dealing with social difficulties, made sure that instructions were clear and stuck to a set work routine. Dugdale noted that these supports were not provided out of charity but were simply good business. "He has not taken up his work as a 'mission', but strictly as a business-man who, finding himself placed where he must employ the laborers of his locality, deals with them on the sound and healthy basis of commercial contract, honestly carried out and rigidly enforced" (p. 64).

Individuals in institutions often worked at various trades and occupations, weaving fabric and making clothing, tending livestock, or growing vegetables. Often this work was performed without pay, and many institutions operated as virtually self-sufficient communities. Work without pay was one of many indignities and abuses endured by the residents of these institutions, and the practice was eventually banned by the courts.

Thus, institutions became places of idleness, to be later "corrected" with what professionals called "active programming." This programming often consisted of simulated "work-like" exercise, such as stuffing envelopes with blank paper, or sorting various kinds of hardware into bags. Nearly all of these activities, however, were vocationally meaningless. Such simulated work activities were developed not because people were believed incapable of work, but as the easiest way to implement court decisions requiring that institutional residents receive habilitation services.

With the establishment of the state-federal vocational rehabilitation program, first in 1918 for veterans of World War I and then for civilians with physical disabilities in 1920, a system of formal services developed to assist people with disabilities to obtain employment. In 1943, vocational rehabilitation services were extended to individuals with mental retardation and mental illness.

The predominant model of services to people with severe disabilities served by the vocational rehabilitation system became the sheltered workshop, a separate work facility offering work contracted from businesses for people with disabilities. Sometimes work-related activities, such as telling time or classes in managing money were also provided. Wages were usually less than the usual federal minimum wage, requiring special certificates authorized by the U.S. Department of Labor.

Sheltered workshops were originally modelled after the workhouses created for orphans and other populations in the early days of industrialization in England. The originators of the workshop concept, generally families, philanthropists and social reformers, were simply trying to fill an unmet need. They saw that large numbers of people with disabilities were unemployed, but able and willing to work. There was no particular motive to segregate people with disabilities from the rest of the workforce. The problems disability professionals now know to be inherent in segregated services were not well understood during this time. Nor were the early pioneers claiming that workshop employees were "not ready" for work in the community, any more than others were claiming that the orphanages they founded were for children who were "not ready" to live with regular families. The facility-based solutions of early reformers were simply the solutions that occurred to them in the context of the times and culture.

As the years went by and the values and social trends of our country shifted, the rationale for sheltered work and other facility-based services shifted more and more to one of professional specialization and segregation. The original rationale for segregation was not that the disabilities of workers were too severe or their behavior was inappropriate such that they needed to be apart of the mainstream of the community. It was more to keep tight control over a segment of the population believed to be disposed towards crime and other social vices, and especially to curtail the reproductive freedom of people believed to be "genetically defective."

In fact, during all of this time it was known that employees with severe disabilities were capable of working in the community with the appropriate supports. For example, several residents in one state institution were placed in employment in a Massachusetts rubber factory during World War I when rubber production was sorely needed for the war effort (Bigelow, 1921). These projects came to an end because wartime production stopped and because returning veterans were viewed as more deserving of the remaining jobs, not because there was any problem with the arrangement or the employees.

Development of the Service Continuum

Eventually, advocates, families and some professionals began to criticize sheltered workshops for a number of shortcomings. These included offering low pay, providing relatively simplistic and meaningless work, supplying few or no employment benefits, demonstrating little opportunity for advancement, and finally, because workshops relegated people with disabilities to their own subculture separate from the rest of society (Gold, 1972; Greenleigh Associates, 1975).

People began to search for alternatives, and some (e.g. Riscala, 1974) began to question whether sheltered workshops were really needed at all. The principle of "normalization" (Wolfensberger, 1972), or providing persons with opportunities for social roles which a community will value, was becoming widely adopted and efforts began to introduce its principles in vocational services. In employment, this meant a movement towards real work in the community, away from a segregated facility.

One alternative form of employment support that developed involved groups of individuals, supervised by agency staff, working in industrial settings. These alternatives were called "work crews" (Hansen, 1969) or "work stations in industry" (McGee,1975) and later, "enclaves" and "mobile work crews" (Mank, Rhodes and Bellamy, 1986). Providers of vocational services to individuals with psychiatric labels developed a number of other service designs for community employment support, including the "clubhouse" model and worker-owned businesses (Fairweather, Sanders, Maynard, Cressler, & Black, 1969; Lamb, 1971).

Another alternative used advances that had been made in teaching techniques for people with disabilities (Gold, 1980) to teach community jobs on an individual basis. In an early description, Wehman (1976) described the main ingredients of this approach: analyzing a job into small steps, systematic instruction in each step, collecting data, and gradually fading instruction. (Wehman also advocated involving co-workers early and fully in the training process, a point missed by many who adopted the approach.)

Rather than segregate persons with disabilities into a facility for skill training of this kind, services would be provided where they would be most needed — at the job site itself. The notion of individual placement with job training provided at the setting where the work would be performed was a revolutionary leap in service delivery. But the presence of a human service professional remained integral to the success of the placement. This professional is usually called a "job coach" or an "employment specialist," and the approach has become known as the "individual supported jobs" model or the "job coach" model.

As new options were developed, the older approaches continued in existence. A system called the "continuum of services" was developed (Taylor, 1988). Within vocational services, sophisticated procedures of assessment and placement within this system developed, using standardized evaluations of readiness for placement in and movement from each "program model". The "readiness" rationale for segregated work was invented.

Within vocational services the continuum of services specifically designed for persons with disabilities in its present form consists of:

- *Non-vocational Day Treatment or Habilitation Services*

  A program, usually facility-based, that focuses on therapies and skill training related to daily living, such as hygiene, cooking, shopping, etc.

- *Partly Vocational Day Activity Services*

  A program which incorporates part-time training for daily living skills, along with some part-time practice of vocational experiences in a simulated environment, usually related to sorting, assembly, or cleaning functions.

- *Sheltered Work*

  Paid employment usually based on productivity time studies in which the employee with a disability is paid "per piece" in a facility which procures sub-contract work, generally "benchwork" such as sorting or assembly.

- *Semi-sheltered Group Enclaves or Work Crews*

  Small groups, usually up to eight, of employees with disabilities perform paid work for real businesses under the supervision and auspices of a human service agency, which generally has a contract agreement with the "host site" and bills the business.

- *Individual Supported or Transitional Jobs*

    Paid employment in which the employee is hired and directly supervised by the business, with ongoing support of a human service agency.

- *Competitive (unsupported) Employment.*

    Paid employment in which the employee is hired and directly supervised by the business, with only initial support from a human service agency.

The Advent of Supported Employment

The mid-eighties saw the establishment of the concept of supported employment as a viable service option in the rehabilitation system. The Office of Special Education and Rehabilitative Services funded a number of states to create "systems change" to incorporate supported employment in rehabilitation services. This funding helped initiate policy changes and interagency collaboration at the state and local levels so that more employment options would become available to people historically denied them.

In 1986 the Rehabilitation Act (PL 99-506) was amended to add supported employment as a legitimate rehabilitation outcome. Not only did the Act give it a clearer definition, it made funds, known as Title VI(c) funds, available to all states exclusively for supported employment. In addition, PL 99-506 authorized the use of Title I "case service" dollars, money used for individuals traditionally served by vocational rehabilitation, for supported employment services.

These changes opened new avenues for those persons who were in the past often left out of funding eligibility for employment services. Supported employment revolves around the idea that meaningful employment should be an option for everyone, regardless of label or perceived deficits. This idea is in direct contradiction to traditional vocational rehabilitation services which centered on the idea of employability. Employability implies that some people are "ready" for employment while others are not. Most persons in the traditional rehabilitation paradigm are considered in need of preparatory training on a wide variety of vocationally related skills to overcome disability-related deficits.

What makes supported employment different is that there is a presumption of employability for everyone in some sort of job related to a person's interests and skills. What remains is to figure out the types and level of support to ensure success in a meaningful job that leads to a satisfying career for the individual.

We are enmeshed in a paradox. On the one hand, the concept that everyone has a productive skill and could be meaningfully employed has always been with us and we have always understood it. Yet, on the other hand, we have scarcely begun to realize the promise of supported employment.

LOOKING TO THE FUTURE:
THE BUSINESS-REHABILITATION PARTNERSHIP

Early supported employment efforts were human service-controlled. Workers with disabilities often worked together as a group, usually with no or minimal social contact other than with their peers or their staff supervisor. The supervisor was usually a staff member of the vocational agency, rather than an employee of the business. Further, the workers were usually employed by the agency under its "sheltered workshop license" rather than truly being company employees. In individual supported jobs, workers were employees of the company but the "job coach" took care of all of the training and most personnel issues for supported employees.

As supported employment has evolved, people with disabilities have consistently exceeded expectations. They have proved themselves not only valuable, but often *invaluable* assets to industry. At the same time, the need for hiring groups of people in a more rigid program or model has begun to be seriously questioned (Brown, et al., 1990; Conte, Murphy & Nisbet, 1989). As a result, more and more employers are hiring individuals with disabilities to fill specific labor needs, basing their hiring decisions on what a person can accomplish, with appropriate accommodation and support. This has built a strong relationship between business and vocational services.

A progression is evident away from the provision of artificial environments and heavily staff-controlled supervision of employees with severe disabilities. The perspectives of human service staff are evolving in several different ways.

Changing Human Service Perspectives

A trend is evident towards greater utilization of the capacity of a community to provide support to all of its members, with a greater emphasis on "functional" skills. The same evolution has taken place in other domains, such as education (Lipsky & Gartner, 1989) and residential supports (Ford & Knoll, 1987). This has amounted to what some have called a conceptual revolution (Karan, 1993) in which the role of caretaker has been supplanted by the role of a facilitator.

As service providers become more familiar with businesses and work environments, they are coming to trust that some of the expertise they thought they alone possessed is also available in the community. For example, many supported employment programs have imported into business settings some of the behavior management techniques and technology that had been successful in building skills and modifying behavior in human service settings. In doing so they have learned that not all of these strategies transfer smoothly or are in fact necessary. For example, the use of behavior programs, data sheets, reinforcement schedules, and token systems impart an unnecessary clinical atmosphere to the setting where the supported employee works. Not only that, the natural work setting often has informal approaches to skill building, behavior change, and accommodation that work quite well and fit more smoothly into the existing culture.

They are also realizing that some of their beliefs about the limitations of people with severe disabilities and their need for ongoing professional "care" and human service supervision has been artificially created. These beliefs have been fostered by the way services were designed rather than real inherent characteristics of the people being served. As they reached out to use the community, they crossed a threshold into environments which human services did not create and do not control.

These realizations have led to a new emphasis in vocational services to build mutually beneficial partnerships with business. As successful employment experiences have taken hold in company after company, these successes have led to a willingness to try new approaches and question old assumptions.

Transition through the continuum has not proved successful. Sheltered work and other simulated training experiences have not shown themselves equal to the task of preparing people for work in the community. Primarily, they prepare people to be better "clients" and sheltered workers within the artificially created service system. In an ethnographic study of sheltered employment, Turner (1983) pointed out that the work behavior of sheltered employees did not improve over time, but did become less noticeable and less disruptive to the staff. One national study found that it would take the average individual with mental retardation in an adult activity program over 47 years to progress through the various levels to competitive employment (Bellamy, Rhodes, Borbeau & Mank, 1986). A study in California projected an even greater number of years (Zivolich, 1991). It turns out that sheltered environments "prepare" people best for sheltered environments.

Human service intervention can restrict community participation. The view that all services are positive cannot be maintained. The longer people remain as "clients" of traditional services, the fewer their connections to the community (Wesiolowski, 1987) and the more deviant their work experiences (Richardson, Koller & Katz, 1988). Lowered expectations, fewer demands, and greater reliance on paid support people are among the reasons. When professionals design "interventions" to assist someone, the interventions themselves have to fit not just the needs of that individual, but the needs of the setting as well (Aveno, Renzaglia & Lively, 1987).

Providing employment services by grouping people according to disability is counterproductive. Such common human service practices as grouping people with disabilities together into specialized programs is so stigmatizing as to overwhelm the capacity of businesses to adapt and deal effectively with each employee as an individual (Conte, Murphy & Nisbet, 1989). Common sense says that placing an increasing number of people together who share perceived differences from others in the population will only magnify those differences to others. In addition, opportunities for having effective models for learning are diminished, as one's peers often share impoverished experiences and difficulties with learning and/or behavior.

Integration is not a passive process. To date, practices and policies aimed at achieving integration have largely focused on trying to make sure that persons with disabilities are present where other non-disabled people work. While presence is a necessary condition for social inclusion, it is not sufficient by itself. Sometimes workers become included and develop strong working relationships on their own, but other times assistance is required to facilitate inclusion. Supported employees can easily be stereotyped as "clients," "students," "objects of charity," or "robot-workers," (Olson and Ferguson, 1992) and left out of work cultures. Facilitating social inclusion at the workplace is now seen as an active process that cannot be left to chance.

The intrusiveness of human service involvement can be radically diminished. As service providers began to experiment with less intrusive services (e.g., developing enclaves for employees who were once thought to require sheltered workshops; developing individual jobs for workers who were once thought to require enclaves; enlisting co-workers to provide support once thought to require specialized staff) they experienced overwhelming success. Each success has led to higher expectations and, more importantly, to an attitude of experimentation with less intrusive forms of support. The "rule of diminishing feedback" that Marc Gold (1980) once taught as an instructional technique for skill-building has been extended to the organizational and systemic level. When one approach is found to work, service providers try to figure out how to provide support in a way that is even more indirect and even less intrusive.

The basic premise of rehabilitation has shifted to empowerment and equality. The message on one advocacy poster: "You gave us your dimes; now we want our rights" speaks of the shift that has occurred from viewing assistance to people with disabilities as a charitable enterprise based on benevolence to one of guaranteeing equal access and participation for a group of citizens facing discrimination. Today rehabilitation services are grounded in a belief in equality (Rubin & Millard, 1991). The Americans with Disabilities Act (PL 101-336) has formalized these principles into law. It provides a far-reaching national mandate to end discrimination based on disability in employment, public accommodations, telecommunications, transportation and the activities of state and local governments.

Businesses are another "client" of vocational services. The rehabilitation community has begun to recognize the critical importance of meeting the needs of businesses as they meet the needs of people with disabilities. If businesses are not well served, people with disabilities are not well served. This has led to a recognition that businesses as well as individuals with disabilities can be considered "clients" of vocational rehabilitation (Garvin, 1985). Also, as people with disabilities are entering employment at a younger age, families are being recognized as an important team member and a source of information, career planning, job development, and support.

Many human service functions are already in place in businesses. Businesses already have in place mechanisms for training new employees and for evaluating employees. For example, businesses in the United States spend more on employee training than the combined budgets of all US public colleges and universities (Sonnenfield, 1985). Employee assistance programs for all workers are in place in many organizations that can meet some of the personal needs of individuals with disabilities (Kiernan & McGaughey, 1992). Personnel staff within these organizations who work with all workers are potentially available to work with those with disabilities. There is, in fact, no need to duplicate or impose training practices for job success. Rather, human service professionals need to be able to adapt, modify or bridge people and their unique skills and learning styles to those existing practices, using local resources in the organization as frequently as possible.

Funding resources are not inexhaustible and must be used wisely. The need to use public resources wisely and effectively has become an increasing concern. Waiting lists for employment services for people with disabilities are not uncommon across the United States. For vocational service programs to duplicate the training and support functions that businesses already do, and usually can do better, is an ineffective use of scarce resources (Rhodes, Sandow, Mank, Buckley & Albin, 1991).

Changing Business Perspectives

In the process of maintaining sheltered workshops, businesses were asked for occasional subcontracts, such as a piece of an operation or a temporary job that required some extra workers or extra space, to bring into a segregated facility. Agencies billed companies for work performed, including an "overhead" amount that partially subsidized the training and supervision of the workers on the subcontract and the operation of the facility.

When vocational service agencies developed enclaves and work crew programs, businesses were asked to make their facilities available to groups of individuals with disabilities, while the agency controlled the selection, employment and supervision of the workers. With individual supported jobs programs, businesses are being asked to directly hire individuals with significant disabilities, with assistance from an agency job coach. Part of the marketing strategy includes selling the business on the idea that the agency will take care of all the training and handle many of the personnel problems of the employees (Rhodes, Sandow, Mank, Buckley & Albin, 1991).

SOME OF OUR BEST DISCOVERIES ARE MADE BY MISTAKE

Over the years Mideastern University had worked with a local human service agency and had hired several employees with disabilities to work in student dining halls. During the summer, two employees with seniority were retained but were assigned to a new dining hall. The food service administrator became concerned that the these employees might need assistance adapting to a new site and summer schedule. He requested, as a precaution, that the agency assign someone to assist them.

The agency hired a college student with "job coach" experience to work at the new dining hall for a few weeks. The job coach assumed that the dining hall manager knew who the supported employees were, but in fact the dining hall manager had not been told.

The job coach reported to the dining hall manager and asked which employees needed help with their jobs. The manager directed the job coach to an employee with a quick temper who had difficulty getting along with co-workers. The job coach observed this employee's work, talked to her, and made suggestions about how to modify the job to remove sources of conflict between this individual and her co-workers. Several days later, the job coach discovered that this individual had no connection with the human service program. Two other workers in the dining hall were clients of the agency.

This breakdown in communication taught the food service administrator, the dining hall manager and the supported employment agency two important lessons. First, they learned that they had been identifying and treating certain employees as "employees with disabilities" who apparently needed no more support than was routinely available to any employee. At least from a manager's perspective, there was no particular relationship between being associated with a human service program and needing help and support to do well at work.

The second lesson was that the supportive assistance developed for and usually provided to employees with disabilities could be applied to employees in general. The job coach did indeed help the dining hall become a pleasanter workplace for the rest of the summer.

When asked, many businesses have given subcontracts to sheltered workshops. When asked, many businesses have opened their doors to work enclaves. And when asked, many businesses have worked in partnership with job developers and job coaches. By and large, the business community has shown a level of understanding and flexibility that is nothing short of remarkable in the face of confusing program models and contradictory messages.

For their part, businesses are beginning to experience a change in their view of disability in response to growing demands for equality and non-discrimination. Estimates of approximately 43 million Americans with disabilities translates to a significant consumer and labor market. Like other citizens, business managers and supervisors are increasingly finding that their neighbors, members of clubs and organizations they belong to, classmates and friends of their children include people with disabilities. The fears and misconceptions of the past are eroding. And as successful employment experiences have taken hold in company after company, successes have led to a willingness to try new approaches and then to further successes. Several realizations have led to new understandings, resulting in a stronger emphasis on partnerships with vocational services.

Employing people with disabilities is not different from employing anyone else. Supervision, training, and employment of employees with disabilities generally involve at most minor extensions or modifications of the same familiar practices that work for any employees (Pati, 1985). Managers report that employees with disabilities rate as well as other workers in productivity, performance, and cost of employment (Parent & Everson, 1986). The cost of most job accommodations has proven to be remarkably low (Harold Russell Associates, 1982). When productive and well matched to the job, no employee is "handicapped."

Businesses benefit when they exercise ownership and control over the employment process. When practices foreign to the business world are brought in by an agency, businesses experience them as "tacked on" and mysterious. The business remains dependent on the outside expert and loses the sense of control and ownership. While some specialized expertise may be essential (Parent & Everson, 1986), too much takes away control. Employee training is one example. About 40% of employers surveyed report that they would rather do their own training (McConaughy, Curl, & Salzberg, 1987) with assistance and support than have the training done for them by an outside agency. Some vocational service agencies report that their first experimentation with utilizing the pre-existing training and support functions of the work setting was at the insistence of the company (Hagner, Rogan & Murphy, 1992). Employers such as Pizza Hut, Inc., MacDonalds, the Marriott Corporation and others have initiated their own efforts to hire and support people with disabilities using internal company resources (Fabian & Luecking, 1991; Laabs, 1991; Zivolich, 1990).

Strategies and techniques available from supported employment programs are useful in working with other employees. There are many useful applications of human service skills that can transfer well into the business world. For example, the training techniques of job analysis, systematic instruction, self-management of behavior, and others are valuable skills for company supervisors and managers (Mank, Oorthuys, Rhodes, Sandow & Weyer, 1992). Technology developed to break down complex skills and systematically teach skills to people with a variety of personal learning styles is precisely what many companies need. Thomas (1990) asks businesses to test every policy and practice by asking "Is this something artificial, for only one group, or something that benefits everybody?"

Investment in human resources is the most important investment a business can make. Personnel represents the largest and fastest growing cost for most businesses. Supporting employees has been recognized as an important investment in human resources. Developing and maintaining a capable workforce is best accomplished by businesses themselves (Pinebrook & Bissonet, 1992). All employees work better when their unique needs are respected and valued. This includes a recognition that coaching and mentoring are important management functions (Evered & Selma, 1989; Orth, Wilkinson & Benfari, 1987).

Managing a diverse workforce is an increasingly critical business function. The older concept of disability management has evolved into diversity management (Thomas, 1990). Progressive companies have found that diversity is not only inevitable but a healthy and positive phenomenon (Solomon, 1989). Over 85% of workers entering the work force during the 1990s will, paradoxically, be minorities, that is, members of traditionally underrepresented and disenfranchised groups: women, racial minorities, older workers, and workers with disabilities (Solomon, 1989). The customer base is experiencing the same shift, leading companies to value the input of a diverse workforce as they try to attract and accommodate to the needs of new markets, including some of the 43 million American consumers with disabilities who respond best to those businesses sensitive to their needs.

A convergence of interests is evident. Both within vocational rehabilitation and within the business community, each has seen the benefits of working together.

SUMMARY

Isolated instances of successful employment of individuals with severe disabilities, even in the complete absence of any disability-related services or expertise, are as old as work itself. But throughout most of this century, in industrialized countries, a system of separate services and restricted opportunities for individuals with significant disabilities has created a vicious circle. Individuals with disabilities have become largely unconnected to and apprehensive about the world of employment and employees, and employers have become largely unconnected to and apprehensive about individuals with disabilities.

Supported employment has played a major role in challenging and reevaluating this traditional system, opening new doors to meaningful employment for individuals who previously could receive assistance only in sheltered workshops, "day habilitation" centers or other segregated facilities.

As supported employment has grown and developed, human service professionals have gained increasing respect for both the capacities of people with disabilities and the capacities of work settings to work together. "Staff" roles are evolving away from traditional caretaker functions towards more facilitating functions. Businesses have experienced similar changes, becoming more confident in their ability to manage a diverse workforce, more cognizant of the potential contributions of workers with disabilities, and more interested in obtaining expertise and resources to get the job done than in having their role dictated by others.

CHAPTER 2

Workplace Culture and Social Integration

"Before we start experimenting it would be wise to
find out what occurs in the natural situation."
— Seymour Sarason

All of us live in a complex web of interdependent relationships. We depend on other people for support, enjoyment, company, compassion, and even survival. Some relationships are formal, based in social structures, while some are rooted in friendship, family, or shared goals. *Social belonging* is one of the ways we define the quality of our lives. The people around us influence our perceptions of success and failure, and even reflect back whom we seem to be as a person.

Wherever people regularly interact together, social organization is found. Workplaces are no exception. Work is an essentially interdependent social activity. The unique groups of individuals who come together regularly to produce some product or service come to know each other and respond to each other as individuals, develop patterns of interaction with one another, and develop a shared sense of community.

Management studies have shown that, depending on the type of work and work setting, most workers spend between 35% and 90% of their work time interacting with one another, and about half of all workers spend "a good deal of time" talking to their co-workers at work (Henderson and Argyle, 1985).

Some of these interactions are required to do a job. For example, a waitress may call food orders in to the short-order cook. But the vast majority of interactions at work are not really required by the employer. They are extra, "surplus" (Peponis, 1985), or informal interactions. For example, the tired waitress who humorously calls in a order to the kitchen for "a quiche and a back massage" is combining a formal, job-related interaction with an informal social comment.

While the amount and type of social interaction vary widely across workplaces, some types of workplace social interactions are found almost anywhere. Henderson and Argyle (1985) found that the most common types, in order, were:

- joking,
- teasing,
- helping with work,
- chatting casually,
- discussing work,
- having coffee or meals together,
- discussing personal life,
- asking for or giving personal advice, and
- teaching a work task.

Interactions are more likely to occur among workers with interdependent job tasks (Peponis, 1985). Formal interactions are usually required by interdependent jobs, and these interactions have a way of spilling over into informal interactions. In addition, workers with shared responsibilities have common experiences, frustrations and accomplishments to talk about.

Another important set of stimuli for workplace interactions are problems on a job and breaks in a routine. Interruptions, unplanned occurrences and problems require communication. The need to negotiate job boundaries, or the "rough edges" of a job, where it is not exactly clear who will do what, also precipitates interaction at work (Hagner, 1989).

Many work settings have "peaks and valleys" in the daily work routine, times of intense productivity, and slower times. Informal interactions may sometimes be concentrated in these slower times, between tasks or between peak work periods. For example, the workers at a restaurant may be busy until about 2:00 pm; then as business calms down, they have time to talk to one another socially.

Either the beginning of a shift or the end of a shift may be a more social time as well. At the beginning of a shift, people greet each other — Deal and Kennedy (1982) call these "howdy rituals" — touch base regarding non-work social topics, and may plan any unique features of that day's work, such as a special task needed that day or reassigning work if someone is out sick. At the end of a shift, people may "wind down" by tending to socialize a little more, discuss their non-work plans, and say "good-bye." A work week may have a similar rhythm, with socialization more common on Mondays (or the first day) and Fridays (or the last day). Often, employees use "It must be Friday" as an excuse to act sillier or accomplish less.

Over time, working relationships develop among workers as they interact to complete assignments, solve problems and share frustrations. Of course, not every worker forms the same kind of relationship with every co-worker. Many different kinds of working relationships are possible. Coworkers may be:

- *Social friends*, with whom an employee spends some non-work time,

- *Work friends*, with whom an employee interacts informally and during free time at work,

- *Workmates*, with whom an employee interacts regularly at work but usually regarding work topics, or

- *Conflict relationships*, with someone an employee may have confrontational interactions with or tries to avoid.

Management theorists recognize the importance of informal social interaction and relationships at work. They refer to the shared social customs, norms and expectations that develop among the workers in a work organization as the "culture" of the workplace. Probably "subculture" would be a better term, since workplaces are embedded within the larger culture of the community, but the terms "workplace culture" and "organizational culture" have caught on and are widely used.

This chapter examines the concept of workplace culture in detail. Implications of workplace culture for the employment of people with disabilities are outlined. Some of the current practices in supported employment are analyzed from a workplace culture perspective, laying the groundwork for a new approach to employment and support.

YOUR CULTURE OR MINE?

Workplace cultures revolve around shared values and attitudes and the shared experiences that validate them. A culture includes everything that is learned and shared by its members: its social heritage and rules of behavior, its own customs and traditions, jargon and stories (Smircich, 1983). To work at a job means being a part of a social group, joining and being "included" as a member of the culture of a workplace, as someone who belongs.

The formal documents and official management policies of a work organization express some facets of its culture. For example, the organizational chart depicts who reports to whom, and job descriptions may outline some of the ways people interact. The company may sponsor an annual picnic in the summer. But these formal aspects of an organization are only the tip of the cultural "iceberg."

As they spend time in the same setting together and interact together on a daily basis to produce some good or service, solve problems, and experience events together, workers form the rest of the "iceberg" and develop norms and expectations of behavior. This is done over time, in small increments, without anyone writing it down, and without the direction, or sometimes even the knowledge, of company management. It's not something anybody has to try to do or even be conscious of. Regular patterns of behavior and regular expectations simply evolve whenever and wherever people gather regularly. Several key elements define most workplace cultures. All of us have probably been a part of a workplace culture, and many of these elements may sound familiar.

Social customs — "Whose turn is it to make the coffee?"

Every workplace has its share of informal social customs. At about 2:00 this afternoon, once the lunch crowd has thinned out, the waitresses at the Downtown Diner will sit at one particular booth — the one closest to the ice machine — and take a break. They never think of sitting at another booth. If customers are still sitting there, they take their break later!

At about the same time, someone at the Security Mutual insurance company down the street will go around the office and ask if anyone wants anything from the soda machine upstairs, collect money, and "make a run" to the machine. If someone's door is closed, they knock once then stick their head in. At the Quick Print Shop, most people work right through the afternoon because anyone who stops for an afternoon break is considered a "dead end" employee. And if an employee there knocks on someone's office door, he or she only opens the door after they hear the person answer. At Firstbank, on the other hand, a closed door means "don't knock," period.

In short, at every work site, a great deal of social behavior, what people wear and where they hang their coats, what they say and who says it first, is governed by social customs. Following these customs determines whether or not you are considered a part of the culture.

Many social customs revolve around food and drink. Most work shifts include one or more break and/or meal times. These are important social times. There are usually traditions governing when and where food is eaten and beverage breaks are taken and how food and drink is prepared and purchased. At one setting, everyone contributes to a coffee fund and people take turns making coffee and cleaning the cups. At another setting, a group of employees go out for lunch on pay day.

The power of food and drink customs can be noted by simply recalling what happens to any of us when we make poor coffee. This event will often become the center of attention for the day, week or month, with teasing or threats of banishment made to the offending party.

Failure to understand the power of this particular norm and the depths of its practice can indeed lead to social difficulty. One new supported employee, learning of a custom of buying donuts, volunteered to bring in donuts for the following day. Unfortunately, her fellow employees were less than impressed with her attempt. It seems she bought the donuts from the "wrong bakery" and failed to get the customary six jelly donuts and four chocolate covered ones! Respecting the prevailing social customs of a workplace is one of the strongest indicators that one is on the "inside" rather than a merely marginal or "token" member.

Stories and Roles — "Did we ever tell you about how John went to the board meeting and..."

People who share adventure and misadventure, stress, humor, danger, success or failure learn to rely on each other. This in turn creates a strong bond that can endure for years, often outlasting changes and time. This network of bonds can evolve into specific roles, based on how people performed: counselor, planner, doer, muscle, organizer, deliverer, staller, negotiator, clown, etc.

The role of storyteller is an ancient and venerable one which is still very much alive and well in many work settings. Most cultures hand down stories of events that have happened along the way. Anecdotes about co-worker escapades, crises lived through and humorous events help define the atmosphere of the workplace.

Many workplaces have their heroes; some have their villains. Stories remembered and retold recall an organization's history and communicate its values (Langton, 1992). Whether it is humble beginnings, or how an outside threat was handled, or personal/natural catastrophes lived through, these stories tend to shape the values of the setting. Values may be implicit in how the story is told, what is emphasized, who the characters are and what happens to them. For instance, a story about how a last-minute proposal was worked through and submitted, only to be awarded, may subtly support a freewheeling, shoot from the hips style that values quick thinking and action rather than deliberate planning.

At the Financial Services company, new employees are told about the time someone started their first day on the job in jeans, only to be sent home to change. This story informs new members of the culture about dress expectations, and teaches using past events, without having to put people through the pain of making a cultural "faux pas."

At the offices of Smith and Jones, a high-pressure architectural firm, the story is often told about the time Mr. Jones (with a reputation of forgetfulness) rushed off to a critical meeting wearing a three-piece suit, but without the pants! He actually did this on purpose, running around to the back door to grab his pants before rushing off to the meeting. Staff who saw him off howled with laughter. They understood that this was his way of providing humor to defuse the tension. At this particular work setting, humor was valued and necessary. Moments of lightness helped to keep everyone more relaxed and productive, and the ability to tease, play light-hearted jokes, and still get the work done was highly valued in this culture. Learning to understand the message of stories and fables, and what these imply about work roles and behaviors, is a key element in job success.

Language and Symbolism — "Fourth and long, time to punt"

Lawyers, doctors, and other professionals, including human service professionals, have been accused of speaking their own private language (e.g. "legalese"), incomprehensible to outsiders. For example, supported employment personnel talk about service plans, behavior programs, fine motor skills and fading. Speaking and understanding this language is partly what identifies them to each other as "insiders" in the supported employment field.

Specialized jargon or "argot" (as anthropologists call it in *their* jargon) isn't limited to technical or professional terms. We all have worked in places where a certain phrase, word or expression has a private meaning to insiders. In the Discount Department store stockroom, whenever a truck arrives, the stock team yells "truck-ho!" This yell is repeated with variations throughout the process of unloading ("next box-ho!"; "broken case-ho!") and has even been extended to a form of expression covering other aspects of work, so that at the end of the shift the secretary will say "quitting time-ho!" Insiders are identified by their use of the expression.

At Supersaver food store, all the staff say "make my day" in their best Clint Eastwood impression whenever crises occur. At the Moonlight Inn restaurant, difficult customers are referred to by the waitresses as "bozos". The boss at the State Planning office is a big sports fan and always uses football metaphors. All the staff have picked this up, and a staff meeting is filled with expressions like "Let's throw the bomb," "Run up the middle," and "15-yard penalty on that one."

Sometimes the culture has evolved its language such that it has become a critical part of getting the job done. To work at the Downtown Diner, for instance, one might need to know that:

Get me a shimmy!	=	(an order of jello)
Pierre on a slab!	=	(french toast)
A bucket of mud!	=	(a dish of chocolate ice cream)
Clean the kitchen!	=	(an order of hash)

Being part of a work team requires understanding and using the unique language and gestures of a work setting. A new employee in particular needs time to assimilate this information and present it in the right contexts.

Social Activities — "Pizza and beer, coffee and cake, softball and card games"

The business lunch or after-work cocktail has become a tradition for many businesses with detailed rituals around participation. There have even been self-help books noting how to succeed at "power lunches." Business executives know the importance of the golf game or dinner invitation to relationships on the job. Shared social activities outside of work time are a part of many workplace cultures. Social events can range from organized recreation teams to impromptu card games or pizza nights on Friday.

At one setting, several co-workers use their lunch time on Tuesdays to attend an aerobic exercise class. These activities cement work friendships in more relaxed surroundings, where people can drop some of the formality of their employment roles and behaviors.

At the Colonial Publishers book packaging department, most workers spend their break time playing cards. The participants are in two groups, each with its own subculture. One group is very serious about keeping track of game scores over time. Another group keeps no track of who's winning. Often it is the card game that dominates social conversation during work. Those who don't know what's going on have little to share with cardplaying co-workers.

As people come to learn more about each other, they build trust, warmth, and a personal history. This carries over to interactions on the job. When an employee needs advice, help or support, there is an established network of people to turn to. Participation in social activities builds and strengthens this network.

Work Space — "My desk has always been here, and that's where it's staying!"

Each member of a culture occupies a predetermined amount of "personal space." At work, our office, cubicle, work station, desk, or locker may be our territory. This space has social meaning. When our space is invaded, we take offense and employ measures to fend off the intruder.

Everyone has experienced the importance of territory to co-workers. Just think back to the last time your place of work shifted offices. Even a casual announcement of impending space changes can produce hysteria. As one employee put it, "a lot of things can happen that won't ruffle anyone here, but switch around where people work and all hell breaks loose."

Work space is often symbolic of status, power, or influence. Offices with windows are guarded. Spacious areas are worth as much as a raise in salary to many people. Space can connote prestige, comfort and convenience. An employee with no personal space is usually at the bottom of the workplace "pecking order."

Understanding the importance of space is critical for professionals in supported employment. For example, some employees with disabilities may need environmental modifications. The social impact of a rearrangement of space, even something as seemingly trivial as moving someone's desk a few inches to widen an aisle, must be considered along with its physical impact.

Power and Influence — "Who's in charge here, anyway?"

Cultures have organized relationships based on power and influence as far back as history has been able to record. Some social relationships are defined by a deliberately created structure. At the workplace, this is called the organizational chart, a diagram that purportedly demonstrates who reports to whom and who has responsibility for what.

These charts rarely tell the whole story about how the organization truly runs. For example, there frequently are aspects of organizational "politics" occurring behind the scenes. An administrative assistant may have the real decision-making power on certain issues, or there may be romantic affairs in progress which affect what can be said to whom.

Levels of supervision, size of management structure and rigidity of exchange also influence communication and thus cultural norms. Subcultures can also arise in different departments, with opposing norms and struggles or dominance.

Many new employees find workplace politics frustrating. They usually try to link up with "people in the know" to avoid missteps and political errors.

Style of Leadership — "Bambi meets Godzilla"

The manner in which management informs, directs and supervises produces a certain climate throughout an organization. Whether the style of management is authoritarian and controlling, participatory and consensus building, or a "laissez-faire," anything-goes approach affects what people say and what they do.

For example, one factory gives out a bonus each month for the best suggestion about work methods improvement, and workers sometimes use their break time to experiment with or talk over a new idea. The style of management may either encourage and mesh with the informal culture or clash with it and drive the culture "underground," so that a great deal of informal social behavior comes to involve complaining about, making fun of, or subverting managerial initiatives.

Management generally directs a wide variety of work-related issues and thus has a great deal of influence over the work culture. But this is not just a matter of exercising power and authority, although these certainly can affect culture. It is also the style used in exercising power.

Authoritarian bosses tend to limit flexibility, restrict behavioral norms to tighter limits, and limit input to how the workplace functions. This leads to a culture with less informal behavior and reduced creativity. Bosses who abdicate decision-making, on the other hand, foster a culture where people are confused about the norms. This is typified by the employee who shakes his or her head when something goes wrong, saying "isn't that typical of this place?" In between are a wide variety of styles, including use of humor, delegation, management by objectives, "bottom-line, no-nonsense" approaches, and many others.

Each leadership style affects the relationships and interactions within the setting. New employees need to learn how management operates and how to deal with supervision, evaluation and communication expectations.

Tone of Interactions —
"It's not what she said, it's how she said it"

Interactions between co-workers and others can range from congenial to cut-throat. Although they may vary from day to day or person to person, there may also be a predictable pattern within a company or department. At some companies it is important to always appear in a hurry. Failure to "get to the bottom line" quickly is considered rude, whereas in other companies it is rude to start a work conversation without easing into it by asking how the co-workers' weekend was or making some other social comment. In some environments swearing is a mandatory part of any utterance. Other cultures prescribe sarcasm as a way of conveying information.

Companies involved in international business have become keenly aware of the need to consider cultural differences. For example, American business people may be viewed as impolite and impatient in countries which expect ritualistic social courtesies to be extended before the business at hand is discussed.

The level of expected productivity and the formal and informal norms around acceptable breaks, on-task time, and output contribute to the pace of work and the tone of co-worker interactions. Taken together, the tone of interactions helps define the "atmosphere" of a setting. Learning to read the tone of interactions and to fit in with the accepted communicative style will influence successful work inclusion with co-workers and supervisors.

Gathering places —
"See you at Marge's office for break?"

Almost every work setting has its "gathering places" (Sundstrom, 1985). These are the settings where people tend to congregate when they are on break or between tasks, or when work is slow. These places become important elements of the culture. When a designated break room or conference room is not available for this purpose, employees improvise: a particular office, the water cooler or soda machine area, the space in front of the elevator, the mail room, or some other area will be commandeered as a gathering place.

Sometimes workers create their own informal gathering places even though one is officially provided. On a tour of Community Medical Clinic, a visitor asked about a door with a sign labeled "Lunch Room". The tour guide seemed to notice the sign for the first time as she explained simply, "Oh we never go in there." Part

Figure 2.1: The Gathering Place

"Get back to what? On Friday afternoon?
You must be new here."

of the process of inclusion in a work setting consists in learning the appropriate times and places as well as the rules for informal socializing.

Celebrations —
"We're collecting for a gift for Sally's baby shower."

People take joy in celebrating special events. The event may be personal, such as someone's birthday, wedding or anniversary. It may be work related, based on someone's achievement or promotion. Or the event could involve the work group, as when the company softball team toasts a victory Some celebrations may have meaning only within the particular culture: "ice cream day," "wear purple day," or the anniversary of some significant event in the company's history.

In many ways, celebration defines the essence of community (McKnight, 1987). Celebrations vary from the very simple, such as giving a card which everyone has secretly signed, to the more elaborate, with presents, "belly-grams," and flower deliveries. At Southern Fried Chicken restaurant, the workers have flowers delivered to women co-workers on their birthdays. The presence and nature of these celebrations provide an important clue to the social nature of the work setting. Generally, cultures which organize celebrations do a good job of helping people feel a sense of belonging. Shared events that are rewarding and personal strengthen bonds of reciprocal support.

Company Image —
"Our name means quality."

Organizations have letterhead, logos, company and department names, slogans and other symbols. These symbols convey an image of what the organization is about. It may make a great deal of difference whether an organization is "clean-cut," places a premium on friendliness to customers, or is trying to attain some other social image within the community.

One key aspect of image is standards of dress and appearance. Fitting in with the preferred style of dress, from jeans to business suits, can be a strong influence on gaining workplace acceptance and even job advancement. Even minute details of grooming or "accessorizing" can be important, and workers try to "dress for success" by choosing the right kind of outfit to make the best possible impression on those who can advance one's career. The recent popularity of "image consultants" in corporate America also attests to the degree of seriousness people invest in projecting the right personal image.

Employees are expected to learn to fit in and dress and act in such a way as to project the correct image for the particular business culture. Management rewards are partially linked to an employee's ability to project the correct image.

IMPLICATIONS OF WORKPLACE CULTURE

The cultural aspects of a workplace affect every aspect of work: who stays, who goes, what's accepted and what gets done. It is virtually impossible to overestimate the importance of culture.

At one time, company managers and organizational theorists did ignore, for the most part, the informal, cultural aspects of work settings or saw them as something problematic. These managers saw themselves as interested only in production, and many aspects of the social culture do not necessarily involve activities that managers viewed as productive. It was not atypical to hear a manager say, "I don't have time for this nonsense. People need to worry about one thing — getting the work done." Managers were also sometimes suspicious of a force that could influence productivity, quality and employee behavior but that they could not directly control.

Successful managers no longer ignore or fight against the informal culture, but recognize both its inevitability and its utility for the organization (Lebas & Weigenstein, 1986). Effective managers support and appreciate the role of workplace culture. Positive and nurturing workplace cultures can:

- Improve morale and job satisfaction, leading to better job retention and productivity;
- Streamline organizational communication; and
- Provide a source of stability and behavioral organization.

Clearly an understanding of culture is no less important to people who are interested in assisting people with disabilities to take their rightful places in the workforce. The fact that workplaces have a "culture" has enormous implications for helping people with severe disabilities to achieve quality employment outcomes, as well as for employers wishing to better utilize diverse and traditionally untapped sources of labor. The better we understand the dynamics of workplace cultures, the better we will be able to assist employees, including those with disabilities, to become socially included at work. The clues to inclusion are found in understanding the culture.

What's the Password?

Becoming successful at a job does not consist solely in learning to perform a sequence of tasks (although that is certainly an important part). It also involves entering or gaining admission to the culture of the setting and becoming a member of a social group.

In learning an isolated task such as using a stapler or an automatic teller machine, or learning to interact in formal or impersonal social situations, such as crossing an intersection or calling for directory assistance, once the list of steps or formal rules have been correctly followed, the task is complete. Joining a social group is different. It is more like joining a club. If you have ever gained admission to a social club or similar informal association, you may remember that there are important considerations besides having skills. It often helps if someone who is already a member will "sponsor" your membership. If that isn't possible, it's important to hook up fairly quickly with someone on the inside who can give you some inside information and help introduce you to what's going on.

As a new member, you can also expect to be "checked over" in the beginning, possibly teased or "hazed" as a sort of initiation ritual or test. These same considerations apply whenever you start a job.

No matter how many skills a new employee arrives with, he or she never knows exactly what to do in any particular setting when he or she is new to setting. This applies not only to social customs but also to work tasks themselves. Where items are stored, how machines work, how various jobs mesh with one another, how materials are procured and disposed of, and other information, all have to be told or shown to each new employee.

Because bringing new people on board is a recurring need in work settings, and because joining the culture is important, workplace cultures usually include traditions for passing on the culture to newcomers. For example, an experienced worker may act as a "mentor" (Zey, 1988) for a new employee and guide the socialization of the new employee into the informal understandings and customs of the organization. The process of initiation of new members is an aspect of workplace cultures that is important for the insiders as well as for the newcomer (Sutton & Louis, 1987).

This is How We Do It Here

Because each workplace culture develops separately and with roots in a particular physical setting, each culture is unique. At one setting, you have to talk softly; at another, people are boisterous. Each work setting has what Deal and Kennedy (1982) call "ways of doing things around here." Even in two different buildings that are part of the same company doing the same work, or two franchises of the same fast food chain at different ends of the same town, differences can be found in their cultures (Amsa, 1986; Peponis, 1986).

It is rarely possible to apply what is known about the culture of one setting to another. The culture of each workplace must be examined individually. Because cultures are unique, we should question anyone who claims to have a list of which behaviors are appropriate or inappropriate, in general, at any work setting.

The culture of a workplace cannot usually be gleaned from a brief observation or conversation. Even though they follow them, the members of a culture cannot say what all of the informal social customs are at a setting. Cultures evolve informally, unofficially, and even to some extent unconsciously, and people just follow the customs without thinking about them. To make matters even more complex, there may be a rule within a culture about not discussing a particular custom.

Managers may have an especially limited awareness of informal social customs. They may not be directly present in the work area consistently enough to be included in some of the customs and are usually only aware of selected aspects of the culture that are important to them. Also, some social customs may be deliberately hidden from managers because these activities would not be permitted. For example, at one setting the workers listen carefully as the supervisor assigns each to a specific task, then as soon as the supervisor has left the area they renegotiate assignments among themselves based on personal preferences.

Gabarro (1985) and Hirszowicz (1982) have both emphasized that some of the details of work cultures can be so subtle as to be "invisible" to a casual observer. Sathe (1983) recommended that in order to understand the culture of the workplace, some of the techniques of ethnographers be employed. Ethnographers seek to understand a culture through careful observation, conversations with a variety of different members, and sometimes studies of documents and other physical objects ("artifacts") created within the culture. By keeping careful records and testing out various ideas, a picture of the culture can be constructed. Techniques for analyzing workplace cultures and assisting people with disabilities to become included in the cultures of workplace settings are covered in Chapter 7.

THE CASE OF THE MISSING NOTICES

Sally organized and filed paperwork for a department in the state office building. There was a long-standing tradition at this office of going out for pizza on Friday after work. Since there were some seven local pizza restaurants, they would vary their visits, and someone would usually decide on a place by 2:00 or so that Friday. Usually five or six people would make it to the restaurant on any given Friday, but everyone participated over time.

The office was busy, and many times people would be away from their desks. The way that people were informed of the gathering place decision was for the decision-maker to leave a slip of paper on the chair at the person's desk. This was the surest way for people to get the message, as the mailboxes were down the hall, in-boxes on desks were often full, and some people's desktops had large piles of papers and materials on them.

The only problem for Sally in this ritual was that she used a wheelchair. When she was away from her desk, so was her chair. As a result, she was often inadvertently left out of the message loop.

A simple cultural accommodation remedied the situation. By informally discovering how the message notice worked, Sally was able to get her message, too. She simply cleared a special space at her desk every Friday and put out a little empty Pizza box. The box served two purposes. First, it reminded people that Sally wanted to know where they were headed and not to forget her. Second, it provided a clear spot for her message that no one could confuse or forget. Ultimately, several other workers decided to use the Pizza Box technique when they missed their messages because the paper had fallen off their chairs and was thrown out by someone.

Joining In and Helping Out

Most workplace cultures include norms related to giving and receiving support. Asking for and giving help are among the most valued social rules at work (Henderson and Argyle, 1986).

The support provided by co-workers and supervisors can be surprisingly rich and varied. Workers may complete each others' work, give reminders or "cover" for a mistake, change their jobs to accommodate the needs of a co-worker, provide transportation, help with apartment or house hunting, give medical and dieting advice, arrange dates, and provide literally countless other forms of support to one another. Support goes beyond practical help or *instrumental support* and also includes expressions of solidarity and emotional, or *affective support*. For example, a co-worker may tell a joke to defuse a stressful situation, or back up a fellow worker who feels unfairly treated.

Workers do not regard supporting one another as a big deal or as anything special, nor do they consciously dole out only a certain quota of support and that's all a person can get. Under most conditions, support is flexible, open-ended, and individualized. Some give and take is expected when others need help, but reciprocity does not have to be equal (Morey & Luthaus, 1991).

Workers also receive support from their supervisors. Kaplan and Cowen (1981) found that industrial supervisors spent an average of about 2.5 hours per week helping workers with personal problems. One of the roles supervisors assume towards their subordinates is the role of a "coach" (Evered & Selma, 1989), assisting with improving work performance and with career growth.

Everyone makes mistakes and faces problems on the job. Making a mistake or having a problem can be thought of as making a withdrawal on our "account" with our employer. The balance in the account at any one time consists of the "capital" we have accumulated. If our account is overdrawn we risk losing the source of our support, and ultimately, the job.

According to Sathe (1986) two different kinds of "capital" can be deposited in our account: *technical capital* or expertise at the job and *social capital*, or co-worker relationships and social network connections in the workplace. We probably need some of each kind of capital but, as Sathe points out, social capital is the more important of the two. This is because if we are well connected with our co-workers, they will help us through difficulties, cover for our mistakes and teach us what we need to know. But if we are isolated and not accepted, we may never accumulate enough technical capital to make it through the day.

Feldman (1977) found a similar phenomenon when he interviewed workers about when they felt competent at their jobs and when they felt accepted by their co-workers. He found that most workers begin to feel accepted first, and competent second. There are some important reasons why acceptance is primary. Because most work involves more than one person, acceptance into the work group opens the door to information and help essential to doing a job well.

But even more important, information about how a person is doing on his/her job is social information (Thomas & Griffin, 1989). We get feedback on how we are doing and which aspects of our work are the most important, not from our internal sense of these things but from the people around us. Membership in the culture provides the feedback mechanism. Co-worker supports and relationships are indispensable for successful employment.

How Was Your Day at Work?

People work for many different reasons, but social relationships and participation in the social culture of a workplace are an important part of job satisfaction for most workers. When one large company split up into two smaller plants, the company asked each employee which of the two was his/her first choice to work in. Researchers asked the workers about their decision. The single most important consideration was the preservation of established social relationships (Miller & Labowitz, 1973). In fact, some management experiments to redesign jobs and allow workers greater autonomy resulted in failure (e.g. Lawler, Hackman & Kaufman, 1973) precisely because the redesign disrupted patterns of social interaction. Workers did not necessarily want more "autonomy" if it meant less opportunity to talk to familiar co-workers or go to the supervisor with a problem.

It is important to keep in mind that at least two key parties have to be satisfied in the employment relationship: the employer and the employee. Workers who are dissatisfied because they are not included socially may take a number of different paths. They may either lose or leave their jobs because they receive inadequate support and information, produce less work, get into difficulties on the job, or become a problem for both management and any support agency involved. Least fortunate in many ways are those employees who remain marginally employed, socially isolated and unhappy, with no opportunity to express their dissatisfaction or obtain assistance to change jobs. Career development and assessment of job satisfaction are covered in Chapter 9.

"This is Not My Real Job"

The concept of a workplace culture applies to any work setting. Even workplaces with the highest levels of employee turnover can't turn over fast enough to avoid the patterning and structuring of behavior and formation of relationships among workers, and exhibit a remarkable amount of stability in their social customs.

However, workplaces do seem to vary in what we might call the "strength" of their cultures. In one work setting, numerous social customs are evident, meaningful social friendships form, workers can tell you each others' birthdays and about their families, and have a strong sense of each person's needs and strengths. In another setting, workers may greet each other and exchange small talk and there may be some customary ways of doing things, but no strong social bonds or relationships seem to exist. We can refer to the former situation as a "strong culture" and the latter as a "weak culture."

As a general rule, weak cultures tend to be concentrated in settings where wages are low, benefits and working conditions are poor, and jobs turn over quickly. Both employees and employers in these situations may consider each other "disposable" — to be used temporarily then thrown away — and the commitment by either party to the other is not very great. Higher turnover, of course, reduces the amount of time that any given group of employees spend together and therefore inhibits the formation of social bonds and customs. Even more importantly, workers within these lower status jobs tend to put less of themselves, as it were, into their work. The jobs present less personal meaning or "engagement" to them (Kahn, 1990). Some may even distance themselves from their jobs with comments like "This is not my real job."

The connection between lower status, menial jobs and weak cultures is only a rule of thumb. Many other factors, such as a company's style of management, influence the strength of its culture. And even entry level jobs can hold status for employees. As their careers develop, employees for whom social interaction is rewarding eventually try to gravitate towards settings with stronger cultures and values and norms they feel comfortable with.

WORKPLACE CULTURE AND THE MEANING OF INTEGRATION

Supported employment developed as an alternative service to the exclusion of people with severe disabilities from the labor force and their resulting segregation into special work facilities and "day programs." A central value in supported employment is the achievement of *integration*.

Facilitating integration is usually counted among the tasks of supported employment personnel. A topic called "advocacy" can be found in many supported employment training manuals with a few points about helping people succeed socially. But the section on advocacy is usually very brief and embedded in a context that is overwhelmingly behavioral and task-acquisition oriented. Integration must be understood and approached in a more coherent way in supported employment, and in fact should be reassigned as a priority. It is important to be clear about the *what*, *when*, and *how* of integration at work.

What is Integration?

Sometimes integration is thought of as merely the physical presence of a worker with a disability on a job site in the community. But while this in itself is a large step forward for many individuals, physical integration alone is incomplete. Although it is true that physical presence is a *necessary* condition for social belonging to a diverse community, it is not a *sufficient* one. An individual may be working in a physically integrated environment and yet be very lonely and socially uninvolved, or even actively teased and rejected.

When integration is thought of as mere presence and defined, for example, as a number like "no more than eight" or a ratio like "no more than one percent," something is missing. We are forgetting that integration is a social rather than a numerical phenomenon, and low numbers or low percentages are only either *signs* that integration may take place or *conditions* under which it may happen. They are not integration itself.

Social integration is also sometimes misunderstood to mean something like "interactional equality." Some researchers count how many times people with and without disabilities engage in various kinds of interactions to see if they are the same or different in a statistical sense. And proponents of this view often advocate teaching people social skills so they will come closer to acting the way others act. But this type of "equality" is not the same thing as social integration.

Socially, two people may interact differently yet still be equal, and the reverse can be true as well. Social philosopher Ronald Dworkin (1977) pointed out that there is a difference between treating people equally and treating people as equals. For example, if a family has two children, one of whom has poor vision, treating the children as equals would mean obtaining eyeglasses for the child with poor vision.

Social integration works the same way. If one worker likes to talk less than others, or needs more encouragement or learns more slowly, engaging in the statistically same type and amount of interaction would be *unequal* treatment of that person, a sign of a lack of integration. It is not possible to treat this as an issue of simply counting frequencies. There will be some regularities and some "irregularities" in behavior across individuals in a work setting and to know which behaviors are important is to understand the culture.

Another way people sometimes think of social integration is that people are integrated only when nobody notices or refers to another person's disability — when disability disappears from awareness and people are "just people" or "just individuals."

This phenomenon does occur and is a wonderful ideal. But most workers even in the most socially integrated settings remain conscious that a co-worker has a disability, although it does cease to be the primary defining characteristic of the person. And these workers may treat the employee differently from others precisely because of the disability. Yet it is common for co-workers in socially integrated workplaces to say that they treat their co-worker with a severe disability "just like anyone else" (Hagner, Cotton, Goodall & Nisbet, 1992) even when the treatment is not in fact the same. For example, one supervisor who stated that she treated her supported employee "like anyone else" also reported that she sometimes came in on her day off to check on how the employee was doing, something she did not do for her other employees. What, then, do co-workers mean by saying that the individual is treated "like anybody else?" Are they confused or mistaken?

We can use the concept of a workplace culture to understand "treatment as an equal" and the related concept of social integration. It has been argued that the essence of equality consists in participation in those key aspects of a culture that symbolize inclusion (Baer, 1983; Fullinwider, 1980). Social integration can be defined in the same way. It means being included as an insider in the social group and participating in the customs and rituals that symbolize membership. It means that differences are considered, accommodated for, and channelled into the most productive and meaningful means. Integration occurs when a disability does not block inclusion into important aspects of the culture. In a supported employment context, being treated "like anyone else" means being treated as an individual in the context of being *a member of* or *as an insider in* the culture of a workplace.

When do we Think About Integration?

We have seen that gaining acceptance, participating in a support network, and earning "social capital" are critical elements of job success. It follows from this that being socially included cannot be regarded as a fancy option in supported employment. Nor should it be a feature of a job that is attended to after the new employee gets settled. The reality is that the employee can never "get settled" without it. Integration, a feeling of social belonging, and participation as a member of the work culture has to be considered up front, from the very start.

In supported employment, therefore, it is necessary to consider social integration, or inclusion in the culture of work settings, in every aspect of program design and implementation. The parameters for inclusion are sometimes established, for better or worse, in the initial contact between an employer by the individual developing the job (Hagner & Daning, 1991).

Some agencies have added supported employment as a new service option onto their existing system of services. These agencies tend to view supported employment as one more level on a continuum, rather than as an alternative to the continuum of "day program" models. Continued reliance on a continuum of services makes it easier to put off thinking about real social integration until some time in the indefinite future. Manuals for "job coach training" that include only a few pages about advocating for integration in supported employment, and conferences and seminars that have a session at the end about "facilitating natural support" sometimes reinforce this misleading view of integration. A better approach is to plan for people to become included in the cultures of their work settings right from the start in all aspects of career planning, job development, job design and every other aspect of supported employment.

How do we Achieve Integration?

The process by which we go about trying to achieve something is sometimes as important as the result. Indeed, it generally determines the result. It is easy to be misled by the term "supported employment" because, as a label for a type of service to workers with disabilities, it seems to suggest that only workers with disabilities need support to succeed at a job and that support to a worker with a disability is something that outside agencies provide. It makes job support a professional service.

We have seen that support is a natural phenomenon, a part of every workplace culture. It is not something that has to be imported from outside, as an intervention. However, this does not mean that we should just "keep everything natural" or that human service activity and intervention are unnecessary or wrong. Sometimes the support that is naturally available in a work setting has to be adapted, shaped or supplemented in various ways, perhaps significantly, for an employee with a disability to succeed. After all, the "natural" state of affairs seems to be that too few people with severe disabilities participate effectively in the workplace.

From the perspective of workplace culture, two considerations need to be kept in mind in designing workplace "interventions:"

- The intervention should not subvert or bypass whatever natural support processes are available at the setting, and

- The intervention should fit in with the setting as well as with the needs of the employee (Aveno, Renzaglia & Lively, 1987).

When support is already available, it makes little sense to duplicate it from an external source. When latent support resources are present that can be adapted or augmented, working with those latent resources is more effective and more culturally normative than importing an external support model. The human service activity that makes sense within human service settings may not be simply transposable to other contexts. The effects that outside intervention may have on the culture and on the participation of the employee in the culture should be carefully monitored and understood. Some of the difficulties that can thwart the efforts of support services which are designed without attention to workplace cultures are outlined in the following section.

TAKE TWO VERBAL PROMPTS
AND CALL ME IN THE MORNING

The most familiar and widely used supported employment service for individualized employment is sometimes known as the "job coach model." Job coaches provide support to an employee at a community work site by analyzing the job to be performed, directly teaching each task to the employee using a prompt hierarchy or similar instructional method, and then gradually fading their presence at the site as the employee masters more and more of the job, keeping data to monitor progress.

Job coaches, or employment specialists using this direct instruction method, are also expected to advocate for social acceptance and inclusion. But the results of this effort have been mixed. One study, for example, found that workers were more integrated the *less* time job coaches spent with them (Udvari-Solner, 1990). While job coaches are often effective at teaching the job tasks, becoming a member of a workplace culture only partly consists of learning job tasks. Job coaching can interfere with the socialization process if careful attention is not paid to the workplace culture.

Maintaining Rigid Task Structures

In teaching employees to do the required, or formal job tasks, job coaches can downplay the importance of the informal tasks that are important to social inclusion. For example, greeting co-workers or helping make the coffee may be missing from a job analysis because they are not formally required to do the job. As a result, the supported employee does not learn these work behaviors. But these may be those that make the biggest difference to successful social inclusion.

Many times a job coach's list of tasks to teach are derived solely from the description given by the supervisor. But the supervisor may not even know all of the important social customs, or may not realize how important they are.

A lot of the informal social interaction at work will be stimulated by a problem or interruption, such as when there is a special rush order to complete, or when someone calls in sick and the work has to be divided up differently. These can be key times for the formation of social bonds. When job coaches analyze a job into a set routine, they can be communicating that the employee can only follow the established task list. This decreases the employee's value to the employer, who usually appreciates a little flexibility. It also leaves supported employees out of a lot of opportunities to interact and build relationships.

Workers also interact to negotiate the details of how their jobs relate to one another on a day-to-day basis. Their jobs aren't designed perfectly, leaving "rough edges" to be smoothed out through interaction. Which one of us will go to the storeroom? Do you wheel the cart to my area or do I come to your area and get it? Employees work these details out among themselves.

Job coaches may regard it as their job to structure every step and every movement of a supported job. Perhaps they do this to record data more accurately and precisely, or perhaps the funding source expects that type of service. Perhaps they believe the employee would not know how to work things out with their co-workers. This may be more myth than reality. In one study of time management skill training (Martin, Elias-Burger, & Mithaug, 1987), workers with severe disabilities were able to interrupt their usual routine to handle a special task or respond to a disruption and then return to the routine with no problem. Some job coaches appear to structure jobs rigidly simply because that's what they were taught to do. In any case, overstructuring task performance on-the-job can restrict the potential for growth and socialization. And in doing so, they may be robbing supported employees of interaction opportunities.

Replacing the Mentor

Pairing a new worker with an experienced co-worker mentor for initial training is a common method for helping new employees learn their jobs. This "mentor" teaches the job and the social customs important to inclusion, and typically forms a relationship with the trainee. Job coach training is a different type of pairing, one that is often substituted for co-worker mentoring. Some supported employment organizations specifically promise, as part of their marketing of services to employers, that they will take responsibility for employee training. This substitution can deny access to informal social customs and tricks of the trade for supported employees. It also blocks the formation of a potentially longer-term supportive relationship with the mentor.

Job coach training also has a way of communicating that, with very little preparation, the job coach can learn a job well enough to teach it to someone else. This message can deny or demean the expertise that employees develop at a setting. Co-workers may even be inclined to try to sabotage such efforts.

Creating the Mystique of the Expert

As specialists in training employees with disabilities, job coaches may inadvertently project the message that it takes special skill or training to teach, support, or interact with an individual with a disability. If special behavioral or data collection procedures are used, they may appear mysterious and foreign to those at the setting. Any social distance or hesitation that co-workers or supervisors may initially feel towards a worker with a different background or unfamiliar characteristic is legitimized and reinforced in this way. Individuals within the natural environment may come to feel that important decisions about assignments, work methods, and the like should be left to the perceived expert in these matters, the job coach. Then, when a problem occurs, everyone will turn to this expert to "fix it." This "take two verbal prompts and call me in the morning" approach disempowers and mystifies the natural setting.

Exaggerating Deviance

Because they come from the human service world, some of the perspectives and language of job coaches are different from those prevalent in the business world. For example, one job coach, sitting at lunch with the supported employee and two or three co-workers, tried to help an employee engage in social conversation by asking, "How are things at your group home?" This question probably seemed perfectly natural to the job coach, but it projected to the employee's co-workers a sense of difference rather than commonality. More than this, the mere fact that a human service worker was sitting next to the employee at lunch, despite the fact that the person was quite capable of eating lunch without assistance, implied

---

WORKSITE COMPETENCE CAN BE OVERLOOKED

The manager at the Moonlight Inn restaurant explained to a visitor that a job coach had carefully taught Bill his job prior to fading from the site. Because Bill had trouble with task sequencing, the job coach had made a picture book depicting the sequence of Bill's job tasks. The manager explained that Bill referred to his book whenever he became confused, and thus was able to do the job.

Inspecting the pictures carefully, the visitor noticed that they did not match what Bill was doing. When asked, Bill said he never looked at the pictures.

As it turned out, the manager had introduced a number of changes into the job in the months since the job coach had left, and taught each one to Bill. For example, Bill now was responsible for polishing brass railings in the lobby, and the way stock was put away had changed. The manager himself had taught each of these changes, and yet attributed Bill's success to a job coach's special training strategy.

something was different about this employee.

At another setting the supported employee often forgot to do the last two of his tasks each day. His co-workers had an obvious explanation for this behavior: he was trying to get out of some work. This was something they could all identify with. The job coach, however, in designing an intervention to help the employee, explained to his co-workers that the employee needed a special accommodation because of a traumatic brain injury. The issue is not whether the employee needed assistance to learn about completing work expectations. It was more in explaining to his co-workers why the learning needed to occur.

Regardless which explanation was more accurate, this intervention had the effect of creating social distance between the employee and his co-workers. Some supported employees are very much conscious that the presence of a job coach stigmatizes them as deviant and will use strategies such as working very poorly in the presence of the job coach (Hagner, Cotton, Goodall & Nisbet, 1992) to express their displeasure.

Overemphasizing Independence

Whereas supervisors and co-workers place a high priority on mutual support and interdependence, job coaches tend to be guided, or misguided, by a concept that is often considered the hallmark of success in human services, "achieving independence."

This emphasis leads to designing isolated, single-person jobs in situations where jobs are typically much more interactive and co-dependent. This cuts employees out of the workplace communication network. Many times supported jobs are deliberately designed to afford less social interaction than other jobs within a setting. A fear that employees will have difficulties handling social interaction, and the practical difficulties of handling the unpredictable and complex world of social interaction within the behavioral framework of task analysis and training, seem to play a role in this process.

Clearly, agency personnel can inhibit the process of joining the culture of a workplace at the same time that they help an employee learn his job. What is needed is a common-sense middle way between the extreme of interfering in the natural processes of relationship formation and social support at work on one hand, and the extreme of non-intervention and non-support of a worker with a disability who needs it on the other. What must occur are strategies of providing

---

WORKING IN PAIRS

One of the authors assisted with a job coach training seminar on a college campus which included a session on task analysis using real janitorial tasks in the building. Several job coach trainees were asked to analyze and then teach the task of buffing the floor of one of the classrooms. They were having a difficult time with the steps involved for a person to move a heavy oak table to one side of the room. It was suggested that the trainees might ask the people who normally perform the task as the best source of information on the most efficient process. This happened to be the building janitors, who, happy to have the job coach trainees do some of their work, were drinking coffee downstairs.

When one of the janitors was asked how he moved the heavy table, he responded, "Well, one person never cleans those rooms. Two people work together, and they both take an end and move the tables." The trainees were being trained to analyze and teach as isolated single-person jobs an operation that in the real world was not done in isolation.

---

extra or individualized assistance which augments and supplements the support that is naturally available. These include strategies for encouraging maximum use of the "natural support" potential of work settings. We must provide as much assistance as people need, but no more. And when we add "special" supports, we must find ways of doing this that are:

- as indirect as possible, and

- as unobtrusive and non-disruptive to the work place culture as possible.

This can be summed up by thinking of supported employment not as supporting employees with a severe disability, but as supporting *relationships* between employees and employers. Working together means being a member of a social group, giving and receiving support, and being included in the culture of a workplace.

In practice, most job coaches and other employment specialists have found ways to avoid many of the above pitfalls and have developed techniques for facilitating the natural processes of relationship formation and admission to the culture. Primarily, they have developed these techniques in isolation from one another and without much guidance from the available supported employment literature. What is now needed is a way of collecting these techniques and systematizing them as much as possible so they can be shared, expanded upon, and tested. The following chapters present a comprehensive approach to employment services and assistance which supports people with and without disabilities working together.

SUMMARY

Work takes place within a social context, and efforts to intervene and insure success for a worker with a disability must be based on a thorough understanding of this context. The social side of work is best understood through the concept of workplace culture: The unique set of norms, roles and expectations shared by the employees in a given work setting. Aspects of work rules, language, dress, work speed, the use of space, celebrations, and numerous other facets are all part of the culture of a workplace.

Most work cultures have norms for giving and receiving support among workers, including established mechanisms for initiating and socializing newcomers into the culture. Many aspects of culture appear to be stronger in more valued and higher-status work settings, weaker in settings characterized by lower-status, menial work. The specific culture of each work setting has to be discovered anew, a process made more difficult by its informality and the tendency to "hide" some facets of a culture from outsiders.

Because inclusion in the culture is critical to job success, supported employment professionals need to invest time to better help employees to become full-fledged, accepted members of the culture of the worksite. This requires active facilitation strategies, but strategies developed and applied in a way that respects and fits in with the culture of the workplace. Support strategies developed within special human service settings may need to be reexamined or modified to better reflect the needs and the possibilities of workplace cultures.

CHAPTER 3

Career Planning

"All the complicated structures we create are built on sand.
Only our relationships to other people endure."
— Harold Kushner

Where do you start in assisting a person to find employment? How do you decide what kinds of jobs to explore? What information do you need? What if the person expresses no preference, says yes to everything, or wants something that seems unrealistic?

Ideally, career planning should be part of secondary education for each of us. But today human service agencies are responsible for the career planning of many individuals who have had no secondary education or an inadequate one, and many who have worked in segregated settings for many years or been offered only non-vocational, "activity programming." Regardless of previous experiences or services, "it's never too early; it's never too late" (Mount & Zwernick, 1988) to begin the process of career planning.

The response by human service agencies to the career planning needs of individuals with disabilities has taken a number of routes.

- Sometimes people with severe disabilities are "placed" into jobs without much career planning. A placement professional may canvass the employment market, find employers interested not in a specific person but in "hiring someone from our agency," and then try to match someone to the job order.

- Human service agencies sometimes start the placement process with a survey of the business community to identify the high-demand, high-turnover occupational areas in their community. Individuals with disabilities are then assessed to see which of these high-demand occupations they would be best suited for.

- A program may have a few different training programs in a fairly narrow range of occupational areas and individuals receiving services select from among the available options. Convincing a person to accept one of the available options may be called "counseling" the individual to "accept your disability" or "be realistic."

- Finally, some employment services administer tests and collect information about an individual's aptitudes, abilities, disabilities and interests. Then the professionals interpret the resulting information and arrive at a suitable occupational goal for the individual.

All of these approaches miss the central fact that the starting point for career planning has to be the individual job seeker. To really be of assistance to an individual who has been labeled as disabled and denied employment opportunities, we first need to explore and discover the individual's dreams for the future and gifts they have to offer.

When we start by trying to understand the individual's career aspirations or "dreams", we start with an enormous advantage:

- Job seekers are more invested and involved in a process centered on their deeply felt aspirations and dreams. Using information about people in a clinical way, even when interests are included as "data," does not empower the person to be at the center of the process. Life goals and dreams are personal things.

- Employer contacts based on helping actualize a person's life dreams are broader in scope and more creative. Information about skills, aptitudes, and even tested interests is all information about the past, and an individual with a severe disability is likely to have had a narrow, restricted range of past experiences. The highest-turnover jobs in a community will usually be lowest-status, lowest-paying jobs, the ones people don't want or want to leave quickly.

- When a job has elements that match an individual's dreams, the individual is more motivated to succeed and keep the job. Conversely, ignoring a person's life dreams or only considering those dreams as one of many equally relevant factors will eventually backfire and lead to a situation in which enormous amounts of effort have to be poured into trying to "save the job."

- Job-hunting based on a person's life dreams is more individualized, leading naturally to an employer contact strategy based on personal networking. As a result, discussions with potential employers are also more personal.

- When a job search and discussions with employers are more personal, the chances that an employee will be socially included and receive individualized support on the job are increased.

- Jobs that are developed based on approaching a person's dreams are more likely to be uniquely tailored to the individual.

Only after we have come to discover some of the uniqueness of a person can we begin to be of assistance. And the individual's own perspectives and viewpoints must be taken seriously, not merely as a set of data about aptitudes, skills and measured interests, but as the guiding and expressed vocational direction given by the person. Only then can we plan supports and directions not *for* but *with* him or her.

As a vision of the future and plans begin to take shape, career goals must be considered in the context of an individual's lifestyle, including living arrangements, social relationships, supports, hobbies and leisure activities. Career planning thus is part of a comprehensive process which will assist an individual to move toward his or her vision.

The following core values (Dileo, McDonald, & Killiam, 1991) should be shared by people involved in assisting individuals with disabilities to design meaningful careers.

Person-centered. The person who receives services should be the central driving force in determining the kinds of supports, training, settings, activities, etc. that are utilized. People should not be "placed" or grouped together on the basis of label, functioning level or service provider convenience.

Focus on capacities. Individuals should be provided opportunities to develop skills of interest and use in their lives by discovering and expressing their unique gifts and capacities.

Choice and control. Persons should receive options related to their interests and desires in life, actively participate in the planning process and exercise control and autonomy over their life's direction.

Social connectedness. We often call upon others who are important in our life for guidance and assistance in making difficult decisions and plans. The people in an individual's informal social network should, depending on the wishes of the individual, be an important part of the career planning process.

Holistic perspective. Efforts to provide a holistic and integrated life service support should be made. Individuals should have consistent service and community opportunities which connect to the fabric of work, home, family, social and recreational interests.

This chapter presents a number of strategies for helping an individual explore his personal dreams or the future and turning these into career goals. As a starting point, we take a closer look at some of the traditional vocational assessment approaches, and consider the issue of whether a job in the community is right for everyone.

TESTING MAY BE HAZARDOUS TO YOUR CAREER

A great deal of time and effort in the field of rehabilitation is devoted to testing and other types of assessments of people with disabilities. The purpose of these assessments is to uncover and define an individual's skills, aptitudes and interests and aid in the process of selecting an occupational objective. Four vocational assessment procedures are commonly used.

Psychological tests are generally "paper and pencil" formats, although a variety of other means have been developed. For example, oral administration is usually available and many tests have been adapted or specially designed for administration by computer keyboard or "mouse." A wide variety of tests of aptitudes, skills, and interest is available. These tests are usually administered in an office or evaluation center.

Work samples are tasks designed and standardized to simulate some of the major features of particular occupations or work fields. For example, a clerical work sample may consist of zip-coded envelopes and corresponding mail slots into which they must be sorted. An evaluation center usually is divided into several work stations consisting of different work samples. An individual "works" at each sample for several minutes to several hours.

Situational assessments are brief tryouts of jobs, usually in a rehabilitation facility, ranging from a couple of days to a couple of weeks. A detailed report on productivity and work behavior is completed following the assessment period.

On-the-job evaluations are brief tryouts of actual jobs in the community. Sometimes the first few weeks of a job are considered an evaluation period, after which the employee and employer decide whether to continue the relationship and the support agency uses the information to plan support services. Other times the relationship is designed to be temporary, and ends with completion of a performance report.

It is important to examine these strategies very carefully and to be aware of their potential to restrict options and deny opportunities. All of the above procedures, with the exception of on-the-job evaluations using actual jobs, are in one way or another artificial. The usefulness of artificial strategies, especially for people with more severe disabilities, has been questioned for many years (Gold, 1980; Rogan & Hagner, 1990; Schalock & Karan, 1979). Problems with artificial assessment are numerous and serious:

1. Even the most "realistic" work samples capture small, arbitrarily isolated pieces of real jobs, with no real proof that the correct pieces have been sampled or that it makes sense to project from performance on a sample to performance on the whole job. Even the pieces, the work sample equipment and supplies, become worn and changed as they are re-used so that the task becomes either artificially easier or artificially more difficult, by some unknown amount, than the task it is supposed to resemble.

2. Work environments affect behavior (Kazdin, 1977; Sundstrom, 1986). Artificial assessment environments lack the production pressures, co-worker interactions, and the sights and sounds of real work places. Even most short-term on-the-job evaluations are artificial in that the tasks are not critical to the functioning of the workplace. There is no valid way to predict performance in real environments from performance in artificial environments.

3. Some individuals adapt slowly to a new environment or routine. Moreover, they may be unfamiliar or uncomfortable with the social context and significance of "being tested". These individuals are at a serious disadvantage when asked to perform tasks for brief periods of time and predictions from brief time samples will underestimate long-term performance.

4. When participants aren't paid during an assessment, a primary reinforce-

ment for working is absent from the situation. It is difficult to believe that anyone could seriously consider performance of a task without reinforcement as a "sample" of performance with reinforcement.

5. Many organizations performing assessments receive funding to serve the individual subsequent to his or her assessment. These centers are involved in a serious conflict of interest which may interfere with the impartiality of their findings and recommendations. They have an enormous incentive to recommend the services of the organization, especially the ones with "slots" available, as the ones the person needs. That is exactly what studies have found (Murphy & Hagner, 1988).

6. Assessment results are usually matched to standard lists of the skills and interests of people in various occupations to generate recommendations. Much of the occupational information used in this process is outdated, inaccurate, and influenced by political interests (Rugg, 1984). Moreover, "occupations" are themselves artificial constructs, and their utility has been questioned (Abbott, 1989). As we will see, a career vision is often not an occupation name but a more personal set of specifications and criteria.

7. Two decades of research have established almost no relationship between vocational assessment results and eventual success on a job (Vandergoot 1984). At best, an evaluation may be able to predict success in a particular agency's program (Cook, 1983), but not success in the world of work.

8. Vocational evaluators receive more feedback about false positives, find out about things they recommend that don't work out, than about false negatives, things they don't recommend that *would have* worked out. The reason for this is that their negative recommendations are used to deny people access to the latter options. Over time, with far more risky decisions in a positive direction appearing to be incorrect, their recommendations become more and more cautious.

The fact is that nobody has come up with an effective way to match the abstracted traits of a person to the abstracted factors of an occupation. Historically, vocational evaluation has served as a "scientific" means of objectifying what for the rest of the population is a highly personal, emotional, and, like it or not, learn-as-you-go process.

For people with severe disabilities, vocational assessment has served as a gatekeeping device to deny vocational services and opportunities. To cut off an individual's opportunity to be a productive member of the community and reach for his or her dreams in life based on an inadequate testing experience is nothing short of tragic. In order to avoid low expectations and artificial ceilings on opportunity, a creative process far different from traditional vocational evaluation is needed for career planning.

WHO IS READY FOR EMPLOYMENT?

We can effectively assist anyone to plan and implement career goals, regardless of his/her disability. But sometimes access to employment in the community is limited by such artificial concepts as "feasibility" and "employability" or "job readiness." We need to examine these concepts and make sure they do not get in the way of appropriate services to people who need them.

Feasibility

Many individuals with disabilities will receive or expect to have some of the services they need funded by their state office of Vocational Rehabilitation (VR). This includes initial training and adjustment services towards a supported employment goal. To be eligible for VR funding, an individual must have a disability that hinders his/her employment, and there must be a "reasonable expectation" that the individual will benefit from services, a criterion often called "feasibility." As a result of recent amendments to the Rehabilitation Act, applicants for services are now presumed to be eligible, unless it can be demonstrated otherwise by clear and convincing evidence.

Denials of feasibility are seldom legitimate. The success of supported employment has demonstrated that people with all types and all degrees of disability are successfully working in the community. For anyone at risk of being determined "not feasible" there is an individual with the same or greater severity of disability who is successfully employed.

It is also important to note that there is no requirement in the current Rehabilitation Act that people served must prove that they can become employed or "employable" to receive services, only that they "benefit in terms of employability." And any goods or services that can reasonably be expected to benefit an individual in terms of employability are allowable as part of a rehabilitation plan. Clearly, if the vocational services a person needs are provided, then the person will benefit in terms of employability.

Employability

A second problematic concept that can get in the way of effective services is the idea of "employability," sometimes called "job readiness." This premise requires people to start out in segregated settings such as sheltered workshops or day treatment centers and gradually earn the right to work in the "real" business community as their skills improve. People are told, in effect, "Work in this place with other people considered unemployable, doing things you may not be interested in. If you do real well, we'll help you find a real job."

The notion of employability as a property of the individual job seeker is just plain wrong. Employment is a contract between a buyer and a seller of labor, and as such who is employable depends as much on the employer and the nature of the work and workplace, as it does on the worker. There are criteria for employment in specific positions at specific times, but no such thing as "criteria for employability" or "readiness to work in the community" in general.

Employers tolerate different behavior to different degrees. Perceived assets may outweigh any particular perceived deficit. A study of interpersonal conflict at work by Volkemma and Bergmann (1989) found that workers reported engaging in all sorts of behavior people generally consider inappropriate — yelling, screaming, hitting, stealing, sabotaging co-workers' work, and others — to solve problems at work.

While we certainly are correct in considering these behaviors inappropriate and in encouraging people to decrease them, we are not correct if we use the presence of these behaviors to screen people out of the work force. Workers with these behaviors have other assets which employers are willing to pay for. In fact, it may be that every time an individual is denied the chance to obtain help finding a job based on some behavior considered evidence of "unemployability," a successful employee is engaging in that same behavior somewhere at that moment. In place of the misleading notions of feasibility and employability, the governing principle for career services should be the "universal hiring rule."

The Universal Hiring Rule

Employers exchange wages for the labor of employees because employers predict that they can exchange the resulting goods or services produced by the employees for more than they cost to produce. Hiring decisions are based on a projection that an applicant is likely to produce more than he or she will cost. Thus the market for employment operates on what Jackson (1991) refers to as the "universal hiring rule: "*Any employer will hire any individual who he or she believes will produce more than they cost.*" A true businessperson will not fail to make an investment that he or she is convinced will pay dividends in the future.

Employment is a long-term relationship. The benefits of one's work to the employer, one's productivity, must be understood broadly, encompassing all of the contributions a worker makes to the total productivity of a company over time. This may include:

- The quantity of work produced,

- Attention to the quality of work,

- The dependability and reliability of the worker to work when scheduled,

- A positive work attitude and contribution to workplace morale,

- Care in following workplace rules and safety procedures,

- The stability of the worker in filling a position,

- Care in bringing problems to the supervisor's attention, and

- Contribution to customer relations, such as courtesy in dealing with customers.

The total package is what the employer "purchases" from a worker. (This is why, to anticipate an issue discussed in Chapter 5, it is unfair to determine a wage solely on the basis of work quantity and quality.)

Costs of an employee should likewise be understood broadly, including:

- The wages paid to the worker,

- Payments to health insurers and others on behalf of the worker,

- Lost productivity due to time off for vacations, sickness, etc.,

- The cost of training and lower production during initial training,

- The cost of supervision and other personnel management,

- Space within the building (and possibly parking lot),

- Material waste and equipment repair due to errors, vandalism or theft, and

- A negative work attitude or influence on workplace morale, or conflict with co-workers.

Costs are considered relative to benefits in a specific context. Depending on the job, some characteristics of job applicants benefit an employer, some might cause the employer to incur costs, and others are irrelevant. And the relative importance of each factor varies across employers.

A person's attributes, out of context, are neither positive nor negative. Attributes become assets, or deficits, depending on the situation. Any characteristic can be tolerated, if not actually valued, somewhere in the world of work. This includes attributes which might be associated with disability or deviance. Whether a person makes socially unusual or inappropriate noises, for example, is generally irrelevant for wilderness trail maintenance or in a factory with a high noise level. And there are contexts in which attributes we label "disabilities" are assets.

In a supported employment context, a third factor, the support services the human service agency is able to provide, including training assistance, incentives like Targeted Jobs Tax Credits, and many others, becomes another factor influencing a hiring decision. Instead of employability as a property of job seekers, we can look at employability as the convergence of three sets of factors:

- The characteristics of job, setting and priorities of the employer,

- The attributes of the job seeker,

- The support services available through supported employment.

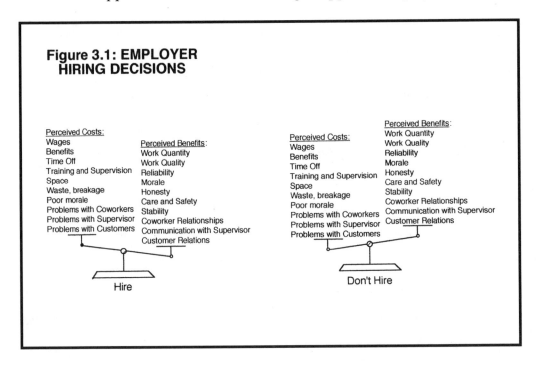

Figure 3.1: EMPLOYER HIRING DECISIONS

THE CONTEXT DETERMINES WHAT ARE ASSETS

A college instructor noticed that the department secretaries spent a fair amount of time photocopying for the faculty. The instructor inquired whether it wouldn't be a good idea to hire someone to do the photocopying.

"We used to have work-study students do it," the department chairperson said, "but it didn't work out. All the copying of tests is done here in the office and it was too tempting for the students to sell the tests. We couldn't trust them. So the secretaries have to do it."

The instructor then asked whether it would work out if the person doing the photocopying couldn't read and so would never know the content of the documents. "That would be ideal," the chairperson replied, "but how can a person who can't read use a copy machine?"

The instructor explained that a person could match the shape of the number on a photocopy order form with the shape of the numbers on the machine and learn which button was for starting, and so forth. This conversation eventually resulted in the college hiring a recent special education graduate as a clerical assistant.

Figure 3.2: WORKER, JOB AND SUPPORT "READINESS"

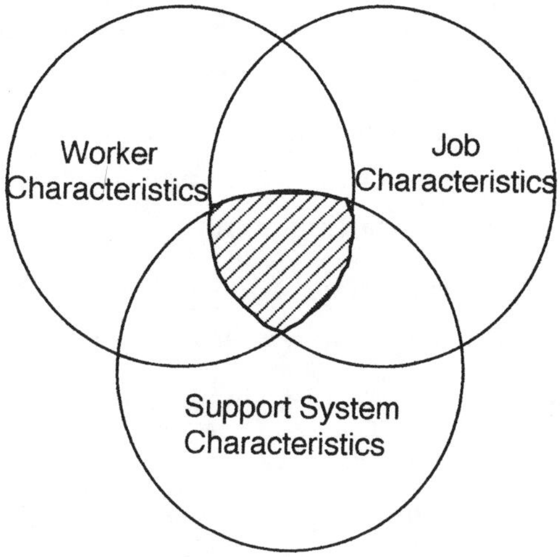

If these three work together, employment will be successful. Which jobs are suited for which job seekers, with which supports, is the only relevant issue. Therefore, thoughtful career planning is a critical part of a successful employment process.

To begin this process, those responsible for vocational support for someone have to find out quite a lot about that person. Movement through a program continuum, or assessing employability, readiness, or any other preparatory concept, merely distracts us from our real work. All of our time and effort should be directed towards one thing: assisting each individual to achieve a satisfying career.

BUILDING A PERSONAL PROFILE AND CAREER VISION

We all have ideas about what we want to achieve in life and how we eventually want our lives to look. They may be vague visions of careers and lifestyles, or more specific blueprints for what we want to be or do. These goals and dreams often relate to what we would like to change in our current situation, and they flow from who we are as a person and how we see ourselves.

Today's relationships, living situations, jobs and other factors influence how we want the future to be. Listening to and learning about a person and possibly even helping the person discover who he are and what his dreams are is the first step in helping the person plan a career.

The process can be thought of as having two parts: The first consists of a personal profile, answering the question "Who is the person?" The second is that of a career vision, answering the question "What kind of work would be satisfying to the person?" In practice, it is not always easy or necessary to make a clear distinction between the two.

Although creating a folder of assessment results is a lot tidier, the best ways to learn about a person are unstructured. The following three methods of information collection can be used as a starting point:

(a) Meeting with or interviewing the individual, his friends and family, and previous co-workers and employers;

(b) Spending time with the individual in his home and in a variety of community settings; and

(c) Conducting a group career planning meeting. Any combination of these approaches with other means of gathering information can be helpful.

Personal Interviews

Some people know what they want. Ted was clear: "I want to be a sports announcer." Lisa knew what she wanted as well: "I want to work where I can visit my grandmother easily." Both these individuals were definite about their career specifications, and constructing a career goal was no more complex than incorporating these wishes into a job search.

Other people may not be so certain of what they want. Many people with disabilities have few career or community experiences to draw from, and need assistance to explore and define what they want. Through spending time together, helping the person to access various career settings, asking questions in various ways and discussing career issues over time, a picture of a person's ideal job may emerge.

One strategy is to begin with manageable chunks of information. "What job do you want?" may be too difficult, but answering a smaller question might begin to piece together the bigger picture. Some helpful questions:

- "What do you like to do after school?"
- "What part of your day is the most interesting?"
- "Where would you like to go on a vacation?"
- "If you could buy anything you wanted at the store, what would it be?"
- "What is the best part of your day?"

Many successful job developers spend time talking with an individual before they ever open a file or look at a referral. They seek out clues to understanding what is important to the individual in many different domains: work, people, fun, settings, health, nutrition, and so on.

It is important that talks be informal and relaxed, rather than creating a formal "interview" situation. An office or conference room may be too threatening or unnatural an environment. Alternatives that are familiar to the individual help him or her relax and build trust. The person's home, for instance, is the most common location for discussion. Or interviewing can be combined with spending time together in the community.

If an individual has had past work or work training experiences, he or she may be able to discuss the positive and negative aspects. Photographs or even a videotape may also be used to keep a record of a job and viewing these may be the basis for discussion. It is a good idea to collect photographs of school work training sites and of each job, for use in planning for the next.

When options are presented to an individual, the order in which they are presented should be varied to avoid a situation in which the individual selects the first or last in a sequence. Let a particular subject wander a bit, then come back to it in a somewhat different way. It's important to be neutral about various statements and options to avoid a situation in which the individual says only what appears to meet with your approval.

Spending Time Together in the Community

Along with talking with an individual, spending time in a variety of community settings is an excellent strategy for getting to know the person (McLaughlin, Garner & Callahan, 1987). One can choose interesting places to visit, perhaps by asking what places the person has heard of or would like to see. What an individual chooses when he feels comfortable and free of constraints gives a clue as to what he enjoys. A few ideas:

- A walk in the neighborhood.
- Having coffee or a meal at a restaurant.
- Giving a ride to or from his present job or accompanying the person on the bus.
- Errands to the store, bank or post office.
- Visiting the library or employment service office.

A variety of settings offers a wealth of experience and stimuli. While in these community settings, observe the individual's reactions and behavior. Does the individual prefer structured environments? Environments with a lot of activity? Indoor places? Social settings?

Community visits give valuable information and a context for discussing work-related values with the person. They also represent a time commitment by the individual which is both an investment and some ownership of the exploration process. Some surprising results can come out of these visits. For example, while at a library, Joyce seemed interested in a computer. With a little bit of instruction, she quickly was able to use the computer for typing. The person with her asked others about Joyce and computers. Her mother recalled that Joyce really loved some informal computer training she received by a family friend on his own computer. This bit of knowledge wasn't in any of her records. The more settings visited, the greater the chance that an individual's skills, interests, and personal connections will reveal themselves.

Community visits can be easily combined with occupational exploration and job hunting. Filling out job applications, discussing the various jobs people have, and other interactions can lead to productive information and job possibilities. Informational interviews with employers can lead to a tryout on a job.

Interview Significant Others

One of the best ways to discover a person's interests, needs, experiences and aptitudes is through a sensitive exploration of life history, experiences and social relationships. A good source of information is from individually interviewing those who know a person.

The individual should select who is to be interviewed or, if that is not possible for some reason, consent to the list before interviews begin. The individuals interviewed should be (a) people with knowledge about the person either in general or in a specific context which might be relevant, and (b) people who care about the person. These may include:

- Immediate family members,
- Extended family members,
- Others the individual lives with,
- Friends,
- Current or former teachers, and
- Current or former co-workers or work supervisors.

Interviews can be held one at a time and then the information brought back to the individual for discussion. In the case of those who are not able to easily communicate about their career ideas, ideas from others can be synthesized into potential career goals. These can then be developed into a job or a series of job tryouts for the person. Another option is to hold a group meeting with the individuals selected to help plan the career. Career planning meetings are discussed in the next section.

Developing a Personal Profile

The personal career profile presents a "snapshot" of an individual and tries to capture most of what is important to him or her in life. This information needs to be thought about in relation to prospective community settings, social situations, employment, recreation, and other contexts.

Callahan (1990) notes how profiles are different from traditional vocational evaluation. A profile:

- Consists of existing information from the person's life and not a sample of performance solely for evaluation,

- Is used only as a guide,

- Considers it more important for a match to make sense in relation to a person's life than to predict failure or success,

- Does not rely on norm-referenced tests to prove readiness,

- Is open-ended and in a narrative format, and

- Involves and empowers the individual, family and friends rather than relying on professional judgment.

The following domains can be used as a guide for helping to write a vocational profile. While there is no rigid formula, it is a good idea to think about each area to be certain you have fully explored the individual's life.

Places and Activities. Where does the individual spend his/her day? What does a typical day look like? Which places and activities does the individual like best, and least? What is it about these things that the person likes or dislikes? How will the individual's living arrangement affect different career possibilities?

Relationships/Belonging. Who are the people that the individual is closest to? Who will be involved in helping the individual find and maintain a career? Are there others the individual would like to know better?

Work. What jobs, volunteer work, and/or work training has the individual had? What were the positive and negative features of each? What type of career, hours, position, location, setting, does the person prefer?

Personal Interests/Leisure Pursuits. What does the individual do for fun? What hobbies or special interests does the person have? What clubs or groups is the individual a member of? How will the individual incorporate motivating interests, hobbies into meaningful activities and participation, and how or should this relate to a vocation?

Personal Growth. What competencies does the person wish and need to develop to realize the goals stated?

Health. What areas of healthy living will need support?

The process of developing an understanding of what a person is looking for from his career can take as short as a half hour or as long as several months. At some point, though, enough information is collected so that you and the individual are both satisfied that there is a vision of what kind of career would be satisfying and what direction to take in job hunting.

A career vision is like a hypothesis that remains to be tested. Sometimes people get into a situation they thought they wanted, and find it doesn't suit their needs. The next hypothesis is then formulated based on that experience. Career development through a series of jobs is discussed in Chapter 9.

CAREER PLANNING MEETINGS

An especially effective tool for career planning is to take the interview process a step further and convene a group meeting of the important individuals in a person's life. Career planning meetings are based on strategies variously known as lifestyle planning (O'Brien, 1987), MAPS (Vandercook, York, & Forest, 1988), and circles of friends (Mount & Zwernick, 1988). These strategies share a common focus on a careful exploration of life history, experiences and social relationships which emphasizes ability rather than deficits. Each process draws upon the knowledge and contributions of an individual's network of community support people.

O'Brien (1987) described a way to work toward a desirable future for an individual with a disability called *lifestyle planning* or *personal futures planning*. A team works with the person to decide on a schedule of activities and supports that will organize available resources to move toward that future.

The process involves answering the following questions:

- What is the quality of the person's present life experiences?

- What is changing for the person or in the surrounding environment that is likely to influence the quality of the person's life?

- What are the most important threats and opportunities to better quality life experiences for the person?

- What is our image of a desirable future for the person?

- What are the most critical barriers to our moving toward the desirable future we have described?

- How will we effectively manage these critical barriers and move toward the future we've defined?

- What are the next steps?

- Based on our discussion, do we want to make any statements about necessary changes in the capabilities of the service system?

The *McGill Action Planning System* (MAPS) (Vandercook, York & Forest, 1988) assists a team to creatively dream and plan, in order to further the inclusion of individuals with disabilities into the activities, routines, and environments of their community. Although designed with students and school environments in mind, the process works with any age or setting.

MAPS planning typically occurs in one or two sessions. Participants are arranged in a half circle, with the facilitator positioned at the open end of the circle. The information and ideas generated are recorded on large chart paper and are based on seven questions:

- What is the individual's history of milestones and accomplishments?

- What are the life dreams for the future for the individual?

- What are life nightmares for the individual which the team must work hard to keep from happening?

- Who is the person ?

- What are the individual's strengths, gifts, and abilities?

- What are the individual's needs?

- What would the individual's ideal day look like and what must be done to make it happen?

A *circle of friends* is a group of people who meet regularly to help a person with a disability accomplish personal goals (Mount & Zwernick, 1988). The individual asks a number of people to work with her/him to overcome obstacles and to open doors to new opportunities. Circle members provide support to the person and take action on her/his behalf.

The person and his/her spokesperson determine the membership, setting, and frequency of meetings. The circle process follows the guidelines for personal futures planning outlined above:

- Discover capacities,
- Find directions for change,
- Generate strategies,
- Make commitments, and
- Reflect on what we are learning together.

These three processes are fairly similar to one another and are far different from traditional service planning meetings. A key to understanding the differences is recognizing that the membership of a career planning team is chosen directly by the individual, professional standing being not particularly relevant; and that the resulting plan is the person's plan, not an agency's.

Not everyone wishes to be the focus of a meeting of his or her friends, family and professionals. Some people find this intrusive and uncomfortable. Other people find a group meeting energizing and supportive. Each person will have his/her own level of comfort with group meetings or more individualized planning meetings. Group career planning sessions are ideal in situations where:

- Numerous people are involved in an individual's life from different perspectives and there is a danger that each one individually misses the wider perspective,
- The focal person has difficulty articulating his/her experiences and ideas, and
- An array of supports and a team of people will probably be needed to implement a plan.

Assembling the Group

There is no fixed membership for a career planning team other than the individual who needs support and the person responsible for helping coordinate it. Partici- pants can be friends, family, guardians, service providers, co-workers or profes- sionals, all depending on the wishes of the individual. Professionals at a career design session should be clear that they were invited because the individual trusts and respects them personally, and because they have technical expertise and access to resources that are useful. Professionals are not there to dictate the course of the meeting or represent an agency.

Invitations should be from the person, not from the organizer. A note or phone call from the individual to the effect that "I'd like you to come to a meeting and help me with some planning for my future career" sets the tone for participants from the start.

The meeting can be held in an individual's home or in another community location. A library or community center sometimes has rooms ideal for this purpose, and sometimes a restaurant may be chosen. Even picnics and barbecues may be the occasion for a career planning session. An agency building is not the preferred location since so much "program history" and expectations are associ- ated with agencies.

Make sure a time is selected that is good for most people. To keep the meeting informal and positive, snacks and drinks should be provided. Effective meetings can be held around a dinner table with a meal served. A flip chart or other paper and markers will be useful for recording the discussion points. Or, if a more informal process is desired, a simple notepad will do.

Facilitating Career Planning Meeting

Each meeting needs some sort of facilitator to guide the flow of conversation and write down what is said. The facilitator can be the individual who helped organize the meeting or someone else. A trusted friend or a community person who has experience in facilitating groups, or who facilitates career planning or career counseling in the community for people without disabilities, may be enlisted to serve as a facilitator.

The role of the facilitator is to ensure everyone is comfortable, introductions are made, and discussion and ideas flow. People should attend the meeting prepared with their knowledge of the person, along with ideas for next steps and how assistance may be provided.

Meetings should not be too long or focused on only one issue. The facilitator must be able to keep discussion moving so that each area of the person's life can be attended to.

The facilitator should set the stage by explaining the rules and values of the meeting, how long it will last, and any other particulars. A procedure that works well, though it is only one of several possibilities, is to hold two meetings, a few weeks apart, about an hour and a half each in length. The first meeting develops the personal profile, and the second creates the career vision. Whatever process is chosen, the participants need to know what to expect.

One key rule is to keep the focus positive, remaining centered around capacities rather than deficits. Everyone should be made aware that this is not the time to state obstacles or limitations; there will be plenty of time for these later. This meeting, in fact, is probably the only time in the year a few hours will be focussed on possibilities for the future for this person. Although seemingly simple enough, many people have enormous difficulty in not jumping to why a possible idea "isn't realistic." But for a meeting such as this one, keeping everyone geared toward the possibilities first requires a ground rule of "no obstacles for now."

Other ground rules can also be helpful, such as "free thinking." Whatever comes to mind can be said, no matter how unusual it may seem, providing it is respectful. Still another rule is to respect and listen to others' opinions. Creativity means some risk-taking in public, so the participants must feel comfortable with the setting and each other.

It is helpful if the meeting is divided into sections, by means of an agenda. Some facilitators structure the discussion by life areas: home, work or school, leisure, and relationships. Others break down the discussion in a more functional way: the past, the current situation, what works best and what doesn't work, and what the future should look like. A page for each topic on flip chart paper creates a visual structure for the agenda.

The facilitator should be committed to keeping the meeting focused properly and that time is used effectively. This includes:

- Keeping to the set time limit,

- Making sure all participants have a chance to speak,

- Writing down every idea a participant generates (even if it seems offbeat or redundant),

- Asking follow-up questions to explore ideas in more detail For example, "*Why* do you think she enjoys visiting the library?"
- Keeping the wishes of the individual as the center of planning, and
- Helping maintain creativity rather than dwelling on obstacles or "what is available."

If participants seem stuck in old expectations and roles for the person, the facilitator should try to stimulate thinking by asking questions that frame issues differently. Here is a partial list:

- If John received $10,000 and he had to spend it right away, what do you think he would spend it on? Why?
- If John could take a vacation anywhere in the world, where would it be? Why?
- If John could pick a famous person to live with, who would it be? Why?
- If you had to describe John in just two words, what would they be?

By answering questions out of the typical context, participants become freer to explore. This in turn will lead to creative ideas for career plans. The career profile topics in the previous section can serve as organizing topics for the personal profile part of a career planning process.

It is up to the facilitator to try to build a consensus around major themes. The facilitator should do this by taking cues from the individual (and family/guardians), either from previous discussions or opinions expressed at the meeting. Differences of opinion are not necessarily bad. They often can lead to a more diverse and creative array of possible support. If a team can be open to wide-ranging ideas, a fuller exploration of resources may be possible.

An effective facilitator keeps everyone meaningfully involved. This may mean redirecting a dominating team member, or asking someone who has been quiet for his/her opinions and thoughts. If specialized technology is discussed, the facilitator should make sure professional jargon is translated. Sometimes friends or family members are intimidated by human service professionals. The facilitator should demystify the opinions of professionals, with all due respect, as partners in a process with a useful perspective to offer.

If the discussion seems to be losing direction, the process should be put on hold or the discussion moved to another topic. Finally, if the meeting is getting bogged down in a conflict or differences of opinion, the facilitator may wish to suggest adjourning for a week or two, so more facts can be explored.

Developing Action Plans

A career vision should be one or two brief paragraphs which project the "best guess" of the type of activities, settings, times or other factors that would come closest to realizing the individual's dreams for his or her employment future. Not all dreams for the future will be met through employment. But specifications for one or more types of employment which would bring the individual closer to aspects of his or her vision should be a central outcome of the planning process.

Once a person's "career planning team" has listened, learned, and documented what it knows about an individual, the next step is to help the person project some concrete directions in his or her career. With thoughts written down about future career areas the person wants to change, emphasize or maintain, the team can then focus on a "travel route" to get there.

A travel route is a useful analogy. One can take many different routes to get to a goal. Some take longer, but may be more enjoyable along the way. Others are more direct and perhaps speedier. The choice of routes is of as much importance as the goal itself. Sometimes the journey matters even more than realization of the goal. That is why we should take seriously the responsibility of developing specific service support strategies.

An important feature of good facilitation is to be sure the closure of the meeting results in clear action steps. Steps to achieve a goal include:

- Actions the individual can take,
- Steps others at the meeting can take,
- Steps participants will ask others in the community to take, and
- Steps participants will ask human service agencies to take.

The facilitator will need to identify major themes which develop over the course of a meeting. Each theme can be reframed as a goal-directed statement. For example, if music is a strong theme, the planning team may want to explore how music relates to the person's career. This might mean an examination of relationships, resources, and potential opportunities. There may be connections with a neighbor, the local record store, or a brother-in-law who teaches piano. Each of these can suggest numerous action steps towards realizing the vision.

The group can decide when to meet again. If plans are made a certain number of months in advance, a meeting can be scheduled at that time to review what has happened. It can also be left to the individual when to reconvene a meeting. And it may be a slightly different group of people next time. There may be individuals willing to help with parts of a plan but who can't or don't want to come to a meeting.

A career goal is not always an occupation name. It can be something the individual wants to get out of his job: a sense of completion, for example, or a feeling of contributing to social improvement. It can be a type of setting: outdoors, for example, or businesslike and organized. It can be a particular social context: around crowds and excitement, for example, or a relaxed and quiet setting. Or it can be a particular location: downtown, for example, or near enough to visit grandmother on the way home. A person's vision can be to work with certain kinds of tools or equipment, wear certain kinds of clothing, or contribute towards a certain type of product or service.

The idea that what people want are occupations — "I want to be a teacher", "I want to be a mechanic", and so forth — is somewhat contrived. Contemporary economies are so fluid that many occupations people have did not exist when those people graduated from high school. The conventional clustering of job positions into groups called "occupations" is to some degree artificial (Abbott, 1989). What people want should be considered broadly, and from their perspective, not squeezed into an occupation label unless the label really does describe the essence of what the person wants.

WHAT ABOUT "UNREALISTIC" CAREER GOALS?

All too often, an individual with a disability has a vision which professionals or others dismiss as "unrealistic." How can he or she possibly be a singer, a boss, an artist, a doctor? It is a mistake to dismiss these visions out-of-hand. They communicate important information on how employment relates to the person's life.

We all make compromises, but there are various types and degrees of compromise. A vision for someone to work "in a parade", for example, might not be reasonably achievable as an ongoing career goal. The person may join the town Independence Day Parade Committee, but that is a short-term volunteer job. So

A CAREER PROFILE: SHARON

My name is Sharon. I am twenty years old and have recently moved to a new town and live in an apartment with my parents. I graduated from high school last June and work part-time at a bakery.

IMPORTANT THINGS ABOUT MYSELF:
- I have a friendly disposition and like to help others.
- Social relationships are very important to me. I send notes through the mail, telephone and visit my friends and family a lot.
- I enjoy trying new things, and like to learn new jobs and skills. I learn best if someone explains what to do and then shows me.
- I am neat, precise and orderly. I like to clean and organize my room.
- After I learn a job, I like to change how it is done to suit my own style. I still finish my work, but sometimes my supervisor thinks my way is not efficient and I make mistakes doing it my way. My supervisor would like me to have a more cooperative working style.
- I like drawing and writing, playing card games and watching movies. I do not like to be bored.
- I like working and receiving praise from people I care about.

IMPORTANT PEOPLE IN MY LIFE:
- My parents
- My two brothers
- George, a friend and staff member at an agency
- Don, my supervisor at work

MY CAREER VISION AND JOB SPECIFICATIONS:
I like being "on my own" and "my own boss." My dream is to become a professional singer. In the next year or two I would like to:
- Change jobs to something related to music and with people who share my love of music,
- Work as close to full time as possible at prevailing wages,
- Work in a setting with many other people,
- Have some autonomy to do a job my own way,
- Work fairly close to home so transportation isn't a big expense.
- Have a job where I can use my organizational skills.

they may have to compromise. But there is a big difference between compromising by working as Assistant Equipment Manager for the high school band, which has connections to music, uniforms and marching, and being told "There's no such thing as working in a parade. You can either be a dishwasher or do small parts assembly." There are several questions to ask in approaching career visions that seem difficult to attain.

What is the bottom line? While a life dream may not be achievable as stated, the essence of the dream, what it is that fundamentally intrigues the individual, may be attainable. For example, if an individual cannot actually work as a musician, he or she could seek creative ways to enter a field in which music is involved. Working in a music store, in a theater or at a radio station may bring the individual close to his or her dream.

Sometimes the atmosphere or trappings of a particular type of work are what is meaningful to the person — a uniform, keys, tools, or working downtown. These same things draw non-disabled people to various kinds of work. If the career planning process is truly exploratory, not just asking "what do you prefer?" but "why do you prefer that?", the essence of a person's dream will emerge. And the essence is very often achievable.

Where did it come from? Exploring how a person came to have a particular goal is relevant to understanding what it is in its essence. An individual who wants to be a surgeon, for example, got that idea from somewhere. Is someone he or she admires a surgeon? Did a surgeon save someone's life who is close to them? Does high-tech equipment fascinate the person? Each of these can lead down new paths. For example, other people whom the individual admires equally can perhaps be emulated more realistically.

How close can we get? If the goal is not a single statement but a series of items or a range of options, it is usually possible to achieve some of what is on the list, if not all or the main one. We can think of buying a car as an analogy. We may have style, low price, high gas mileage, safety, and good resale value on our list of considerations, but life being as unfair as it is, we can't have them all. So we pick the best combination we can get. Careers and the jobs within them are much the same. If the best effort has been made to achieve some of what is important, people can live with that.

Where do you start? Many dreams are for high-status careers that require preparation or a series of steps. People don't generally "start at the top" of their field. We all need to make our way through career ladders to approach our dream of success. Some people may need to be educated about the investment needed to reach top level jobs, and then be provided the support, training, and opportunity to begin at a realistic level and then advance.

FOLLOW-UP AND THE EVOLUTION OF PLANNING

Implementing a career plan is the real beginning, not the end, of team planning. Too many people invest time in writing a plan which is never reviewed or thought of again until a year later when it is the perceived time to rewrite the plan. This is then done with no thought or perspective from the previous year's success or disappointments.

Once some direction and strategies have been developed, there should be follow-up to review strategies, efforts, resources, personnel, community changes and life changes. Service providers may need the guidance of family members or professional specialists to help the person meet his or her career dreams, goals and objectives. There should be a lot of communication, discussion and feedback among team members at this time on how services and outcomes are developing.

People's needs evolve unevenly, not in neat annual boxes of time. When change occurs, the guidance of the individual and his or her team members should be sought in revising planned goals and strategies. As careers evolve, career planning needs to evolve as well.

SUMMARY

Selecting a career goal is part of a larger process of working towards a desired personal future and making decisions about what we would like to be and do. The process is a subjective and personal one, requiring both exposure to the world of work and opportunities to reflect.

Starting from the position that anyone who wants to work is ready to work frees us from a counterproductive emphasis on "employability" and allows us to focus on each individual's unique assets. A personal profile, including a career vision and employment goal, can be developed from interviewing a job seeker, spending time in preferred community settings with the person, and interviewing the people who know the person best. A group career planning meeting, a gathering of people selected by the job seeker and held in a comfortable setting of the person's choosing, is an especially effective planning tool. A facilitator guides the meeting, helps the group focus on possibilities and strengths rather than barriers and weaknesses, identifies major themes and possibilities for consensus, and helps develop an action plan.

Not every dream is reached, yet the dreaming itself has enormous value as a way of organizing efforts and mobilizing resouces. Even when a specific goal is unattainable, key elements may be within the realm of possibility. Or the attempt to reach the goal may be merely the beginning of a lifelong process of exploration and growth.

CHAPTER 4

The Job Search

"The real secret of success is enthusiasm."
— Walter Chrysler

Making the right connection between an employer and an employee is a critical task in any employment assistance. A careful career planning process will develop ideas about types of work and worksites desired by the individual, job characteristics, and any special factors to consider. This information then becomes the basis for job development and drives the process of helping the person to become meaningfully employed.

It is important to look at job seeking as a natural extension of career planning. Although ultimately two parties will benefit from job development — the employee and the employer — the job search starts with the individual job seeker. The goal is not just a job but a satisfying career for each person being supported. A job should be part of a logical career development sequence that makes sense to the job seeker and reflects his or her unique aspirations and talents.

Job hunting can be a time-consuming activity. The local business climate, the type of job sought, a given job seeker's qualifications, and how the job search is conducted (how employers are identified, how the individual's qualifications are presented, etc.), all of these influence what strategies work and how much time a job search will take for an individual. But nearly everyone who has ever looked for a job will agree on one thing: There's a lot to be said for being in the right place at the right time.

The trick is to know what that right time and place are. Economists tell us that information is a scarce commodity. We would all make great decisions if we had access to complete information. But there are costs involved in getting the information we need. For the job developer, this includes knowing which employers have a labor need closely matching the dreams and talents of a given job seeker.

We find out about some employers because they advertise job openings, of course, and there are ways of increasing the probability of contacting an employer likely to be interested in hiring. But the fact remains that a large part of job hunting consists of being in lots of different places at lots of different "fortuitous" times.

The vast majority of job openings, by some estimates as many as 85% (Jackson, 1991) are never advertised and represent what can be called the "hidden job market." A review of thirty years of research on job placement of people with disabilities (Vandergoot, 1984) reached essentially this conclusion: *The single most important factor determining whether and how quickly people get jobs is the amount of time spent on job search activity itself.*

Employers, for their part, have only incomplete information about their labor market. Effective job development involves brokering an exchange process, providing usable information to both job seekers and employers. Thus, they can both increase their knowledge about one another and therefore each of their chances of making a good hiring decision.

Job development is an activity, and not necessarily a single job position. In fact, one of the least efficient ways to be in lots of places at lots of times is to relegate the activity to a single individual.

What are some alternatives? The first is to allocate resources of an employment support service in such a way that every member of the organization has job development responsibility. This includes administrators, office and support staff, and even members of the organization's Board of Directors. Everyone means everyone! When the mission of an organization is to create community employment opportunities, every member of that organization needs to participate in carrying out that mission.

The second strategy to open up job search activity is for job hunting to evolve directly from a career planning process that involves a network of family, friends and associates. In this way, a wide circle of people, both paid and unpaid, are able to use their own resources and contacts in the job search process.

This chapter details job search strategies based on these principles. Some of the specific features of the job search strategies described here are:

- Job development is on behalf of specific individuals, never for groups or for an unspecified "one of my clients," and never for the purpose of identifying "job orders" to see which job seeker fits the job.

- Individuals with disabilities are closely involved in job search activities, although not necessarily "independently."

- Instead of using people's characteristics such as skills or aptitudes as data for matching a person to a job, the job search is based on an individual's dreams and aspirations for the future.

- Personal networks and social/professional connections are the basis for most job search activity.

- Agency staff act as brokers or agents, helping negotiate favorable contracts between job seekers and employers.

A MATTER OF STYLE

People obtain jobs in a great many ways; there is not one "best" way. It is important to be familiar with a number of alternatives and the best uses for each. An active and comprehensive employer contact strategy is required to identify employers with a labor need that matches an individual's career vision.

Except in the case of general dissemination of information to the business community, the process of identifying and approaching employers works best when it is driven by the career aspirations of individual job seekers. Other strategies for identifying employers, through a labor market analysis of projected openings, for example, or matching skills and aptitudes with occupational profiles, are likely to result in a relatively narrow band of occupations in which people served by an agency are employed.

The probability that this narrow band of occupations will represent the career visions of the people who have come to an agency for services is small. But more than that, these occupations tend to be those that pay lower salaries, offer fewer benefits, and have weaker support cultures. In the extreme, a small number of occupations can become so saturated with individuals with disabilities that they become stereotyped "disability" occupations. There have been cases reported where non-disabled individuals have turned down offers in what they considered "jobs for people with disabilities." Clearly, these kinds of outcomes defeat the purpose of supported employment.

Employer contacts can be either "warm" or "cold". The first major strategic decision, therefore, is the relative emphasis to be placed on warm contacts versus cold contacts. *Warm contacts* are those based on some existing personal or professional relationship to an employer. *Cold contacts* are impersonal business contacts to employers who (a) have advertised for workers, (b) have a type of work or work setting the individual is interested in, or (c) are likely to be hiring because of turnover or business expansion.

A second major decision is the type of initial contact: Whether and under what circumstances to initiate contacts by mail, over the telephone, or by visiting employers in person.

Every individual has his or her own preferred communication style. For example, some people don't like to use the telephone. Also, different techniques are more applicable to different types of companies and communities. Cold calls in person may suit many smaller communities, whereas initial contacts by mail may be more successful in a large urban area. Individual companies and business managers also differ in their receptivity to different approaches. Each individual should use a style he/she is comfortable with and which fits the particular community type and type of company being contacted.

Any one strategy will "miss" some people. For example, even though one might prefer to use warm contacts, there will be some instances where no personal connection can be found with an employer, and a cold contact is the only alternative. Therefore, a comprehensive job search should not focus solely on any one strategy but use a mix of warm and cold, phone, letter and in person contacts.

Some general information is available on the relative effectiveness of different job search strategies. Zadny and James (1979) conducted one of the most thorough studies of the job search process for people with disabilities. They found that people found their jobs through the following methods:

- Friend or Relative: 25%
- Direct Application: 20%
- Answering Want-Ads: 10%
- Rehabilitation Agency   10%
- Training Programs or Schools   10%
- Former Employers   7%
- State or Private Employment Agencies   5%
- Other   13%

In this study, personal connections were the most frequent method of obtaining a job. If the percentage of jobs obtained through former employers and friends and relatives are added together, and the fact that some rehabilitation agency, training school, and other employment services contacts were based on a personal connection is also kept in mind, it should be obvious that warm contacts are by far the most effective way to obtain a job.

This has been confirmed in subsequent studies of job development. For example, Kregel, Wehman, Seyfarth and Marshall (1986) found that high school graduates from special education who had jobs in the community had obtained their jobs as follows:

- School Guidance Program or Teacher   24%
- Friends or Relatives   12%
- Rehabilitation Service   20%
- Special Job Placement project   20%
- On Students' Own   12%

Again, many school, rehabilitation agency, and independent student contacts may also have been what we are calling warm contacts. Hagner & Daning (1990) interviewed rehabilitation service job developers in depth and found that they had obtained 46% of successful jobs through warm contacts to employers, including (a) contacts to employers a job developer had worked with before, (b) personal connections of the job seeker, (c) personal connections of the job developer, and (d) contacts based on some "inside" knowledge about a company.

Other things being equal, a rule that seems to make sense is to spend a percentage of time on different strategies that roughly corresponds to the relative effectiveness of the strategy. For example, some time might be spent on looking through want-ads, but a far greater amount of time and effort should probably be spent on exploring the possibility of contacts from friends and relatives.

However, we need to consider not just having a job as the outcome, but having a job that is satisfying to the individual and is in line with his or her career vision and career path. For achieving these goals, warm contacts may have significant advantages over cold contacts. Some general considerations in selecting an appropriate mix of employer contact strategies are presented below.

Warm Contacts to Employers

Warm contacts are contacts to employers based on some personal connection, either direct or indirect, between an employer and a job seeker. *Direct connections* are those to employers within a job seeker's personal network of social connections. For example, a job seeker might contact a company department head who attends the same church. *Indirect contacts* are those mediated by a third party with connections to both persons. For instance, when a job seeker contacts his or her neighbor, who then talks to an employer who is a member of their church.

Warm contacts are effective for several reasons.

1. When a network of people is enlisted to think about job ideas and contact people they know, an interpersonal expansion occurs whereby each individual has direct access to a network of other individuals, and indirect access to an exponentially greater number of people to assist in job development. A larger number of people can be in many places at many times.

2. Employers tend to trust and give more weight to information the more they trust its source (Granovetter, 1979). A decision to hire is a big risk, and information an employer has about an applicant is usually limited. It may be only a resume and cover letter, possibly some phone conversations, conversations with references, and one or more interviews.

This is not a lot to go on from the employer's perspective to make a fairly large investment. Lots of people can look good "on paper" or in an interview until they actually show up (or fail to show up) for work. A personal connection adds the employer's social bond and trust in the person or organization making the contact. It helps bridge the gap in information for the employer. Personal connections are probably more important the more out of the ordinary the situation or decision tends to be. In the case of being asked to employ an individual with characteristics or a background the employer is less familiar with, personal connections can make all the difference.

3. A personal connection sets the stage for a more personal discussion about employment. This lends itself well to developing a job or even creating a job that meets an individual's needs rather than merely fills an opening. Also, because initial discussions with employers tend to be removed from the immediate need to fill a job, an employer may be more relaxed when job seekers are not being compared to or directly competing with other applicants.

4. An individual who enters a job based on some personal connection comes with some "social capital" already deposited in his or her "account" and therefore the process of social integration is already underway. Introductions to co-workers may be facilitated and one or two individuals may have a reason to spend a few extra minutes getting to know the new employee. There may even be an individual who can sponsor the newcomer's membership into the culture of the workplace, steer the individual through the informal rites of initiation at the company, or act as an ally in problem situations. The result is a better chance of success and a better

chance that the job will satisfy the employee.

In a career planning process such as that described in Chapter 3, the information collected includes information about an individual's social contacts and interests, and a circle of friends and acquaintances has been brought together to help the individual formulate career plans. This process naturally evolves into support in finding job leads and making warm contacts.

Cold Contacts to Employers

Even though most time and effort may be placed on warm contact strategies, cold call approaches also play a useful role in supported employment. Some jobs (though not most) are obtained through answering want-ads, dropping in on businesses that look interesting, conducting a mail campaign, and through other cold calling techniques. And sometimes no personal connection to the right employer can be found.

Cold calls also serve an important indirect or background function. They can support individualized job development activities by educating the local business community about supported employment and the competencies of workers with disabilities. And they can be useful as an information gathering tool for an employment service about local labor market conditions and trends. Several indirect cold calling approaches can serve this purpose.

Mail surveys. Surveying local businesses on hiring practices, labor market trends, and other areas of interest to employers can be a useful way for an agency to acquire and share information to a business community.

Letters. Direct mail marketing can educate and inform employers about the benefits of supported employment and the competencies of job seekers.

Advertising. A series of ads in the business section of newspapers or in trade or business publications can be effective for building familiarity with hiring individuals with disabilities.

Phone calls. Phone conversations with employers can offer consultation on labor needs and hiring and supporting individuals in ways most effective and targeted to the particular business.

Telemarketing. A specific individual can devote time to making a large number of initial phone calls for the purpose of setting up appointments with employers in a given line of work or in a specified geographical area, depending on the current needs of individuals looking for jobs. Some employment services have contracted with professional telemarketing firms for this service.

In-person visits. Drop-in visits to personally discuss hiring and support needs for a particular business establishes a face-to-face relationship that can develop into a warm contact for the future.

These approaches can be useful in building a relationship with employers and a foundation of trust and credibility. If an individual or a service agency becomes tied to any one approach — even a good one — as "the" way to find jobs, there will be a tendency to become discouraged when that one way ultimately fails for some time. This in turn can cause job development efforts to all be scaled back because "job development doesn't seem to be working." Multiple approaches, and a commitment to sticking with a comprehensive process as long as needed, will eventually position you "in the right place at the right time."

Job Seeker Involvement

Assisting the job seeker to become actively involved in the actual job search is an important aspect of job development. Active job search involvement communicates ability and interest to employers. It increases a job seeker's sense of commitment to employment and keeps job seekers aware that "jobs don't grow on trees." Job seeking is also an excellent form of career exploration, because job seekers become aware of many different work settings, company types, types of managers, and get a chance to envision themselves in those different contexts. Sometimes a career goal will change during the job search. And for people who are currently out of work or employed for too few hours, job seeking is an appropriate way for them to spend their time.

Some job seekers will be able to make phone calls, write letters, visit companies, fill out applications, and go on interviews more or less on their own. Others may benefit from training on job seeking skills or from participation in a job seeking support group such as a job club (Azrin & Besalel, 1981). But other individuals may need significant assistance in every one of these activities. People who find it difficult to learn new tasks or complex social tasks do not need to

Figure 4.1: The Job Hunter

master job seeking skills as some sort of prerequisite work skill. Learning job-oriented tasks is far more important, and other people are available to conduct much of the job search.

But there is a middle option between the two extremes of expecting an individual to look for jobs independently and having other people conduct a job search for the individual. The middle option is participation in the job search with support. Most, if not all, prospective supported employees can and should be at least partially involved in some job search activities. For example:

- Listing the people in their social network or confirming a list developed by others,
- Dialing the phone to call an employer,
- Photocopying resumes,
- Taking tours of workplaces and expressing opinions about job possibilities,
- Obtaining application forms from employers,
- Signing letters to employers, by hand or by means of a signature stamp,

- Answering basic employer questions with a "yes" or "no,"
- Making eye contact, shaking hands, or otherwise communicating interest in working to potential employers.

Many of these activities can be considered as career exploration as well as job development, and in practice, the two processes are often indistinguishable. As many people can attest from their own personal job experiences, looking for work, learning what work is available, and noticing one's reaction and feelings in various settings and contexts, all happen together. In whatever ways appropriate to the individual, job seeker involvement should be a part of every job search.

A Comprehensive Job-Seeking Plan

Anyone responsible for job development will benefit from developing and sticking to a plan. Most plans involve some combination of cold and warm approaches, direct and indirect, mail, phone and in-person contact strategies. Focusing on carrying out a planned sequence of activities helps sustain the effort required to accomplish them over time. Many effective job developers keep to a certain time each day for active job development activities and find ways to reward themselves for completing the process. They are not overly concerned about immediate outcome, but maintain a commitment to the process.

As Jackson (1991) notes, almost every job search looks like this:

NO - NO - NO - NO - NO - NO - NO - NO - NO - NO - YES.

When you develop a plan you are selecting a combination of the best strategies you can think of to shorten the row of NOs and get a YES in the end. Select a point at which your strategy will be evaluated. Then stick to it without worrying about day-to-day results. Think of getting through the row of NOs as your personal challenge. Rejection is simply one part of the challenge.

Below is a sample weekly job search plan for an employment consultant who spends part of the day supporting people in existing jobs, and also works on developing new jobs for some prospective employees:

DAYS	ACTIVITY	HRS/WK
Mon-Fri 9:00-9:30	Personalize and address 10 letters to referred companies from Chamber of Commerce list.	2.5

Mon-Fri 9:30-10:00	Call five employers from network contact leads list.	2.5
Mon-Fri 10:00 -10:30	Call three network members to add new names to leads list.	2.5
Wed 1:00-3:30	One afternoon per week: drive with a job seeker and make four in-person calls to businesses on bus route, then stop in at the coffee shop to discuss job options.	2.5
Thur 1:00-4:00	Meet with prospective employee and his/her friends and family for career exploration, job development planning and networking	3
Other afternoons as scheduled	Appointments with employers for tour or meeting. Target: 5 per week	Average: 7
		TOTAL: 20

In the sample schedule above, some job search responsibilities are carried out by the employment consultant alone and others are carried out by the job seeker and the employment consultant together. The employment consultant also coordinates the efforts of other individuals who have agreed to help or whom the job seeker has identified as possibly able to help. While one individual has the ultimate responsibility for the job search, that individual carries out that responsibility by involving the job seeker and his or her personal support network as much as possible, becoming in effect a job development coordinator in addition to a job developer.

WORKING THE NETWORK

Each of us is embedded in a web of social relationships, with friends, relatives, acquaintances, co-workers, people we do business with, and members of the organizations we belong to. We obtain emotional support from some of these individuals, a feeling of belonging, an affirmation of our worth as people, and sometimes just a chance to forget about our problems.

We also obtain some very practical things from some of the people in our network: help moving furniture, rides to the car repair shop, money we forgot to bring for lunch, information about apartment vacancies, and advice about our family, relationships or our love life.

We can imagine ourselves at the center of a circle, with these other people around the circumference of the circle. This is our support network.

A job seeker's support network is an important tool in warm contact job search strategies. Networking begins with "network analysis," which in its simplest form consists of making a list of all the individuals with some social connection to a job seeker. The following headings can be used to generate such a list:

- Family members (parents, siblings, children) and other relatives (aunts, uncles, cousins, in-laws, etc.),

- Friends, including non-family members who live with an individual and people the individual hasn't seen in a while but likes,

- Others who live in the neighborhood,

- Current and former schoolmates and co-workers,

- People who work in or run businesses patronized by the individual, such as retailers and professionals, and

- Members of any organizations, religious congregations, groups or teams the individual belongs to.

Each individual in a social network can also be placed at the center of his or her own circle of relationships. In a society of any complexity, there will almost always be some people in that new circle that were not in the first person's social network.

A chain can be developed in this way, such that each person "knows someone who knows someone who knows someone" who knows almost anyone! A chain of personal connections can potentially include a very large number of people. For example, a job-seeker might not be a member of any social or civic organizations, but that individual's father may be. A "social snowflake" can be drawn that represents various first order and second order network relationships.

The individuals in a job seeker's support network should be systematically identified and asked to help in identifying and contacting potential employers, and possibly to contact members of their network for the same purpose. A personal connection chain of some finite length can, in theory, connect each person to each employer. This is usually the point at which someone will inevitably mention "what a small world" we live in.

It is possible to assist an individual to weave his way through a complex path of connections provided each connection is made correctly; that is, each person understands what his connection is and what he is being asked to do. A given individual might not be able to comprehend how he could conceivably be con-

Figure 4.2: Social Tie Snowflake

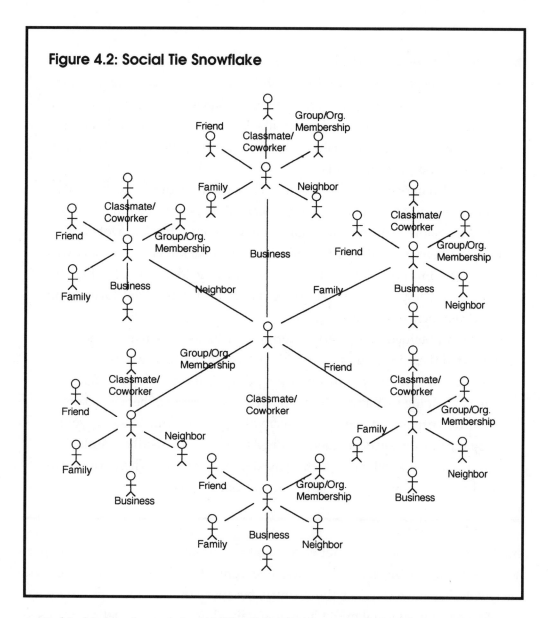

nected to his boss' cousin's neighbor's bridge partner, but each party does know his own connection.

Employers identified through personal connections have a little more reason to trust the job developer, a little more inclination to take up a few minutes of his or her valuable time, and possibly a little more inclination to make a favorable decision.

Social connections will not develop a job by themselves, they simply open the door. An individual does not have to be an employer or, for that matter, an

A FRIEND OF A FRIEND SENT ME

Ellen was responsible for finding a job for Gary. She visited Gary's home to talk with him in familiar surroundings, to find some clues as to what he enjoyed doing, and to meet his parents. Ellen asked Gary and his family about Gary's likes and dislikes, preferences (e.g. he was a "morning person"), and personal goals.

She also informally asked about their social networks. She found that they were strongly associated with a local religious congregation, and was given the name of the pastor as someone with connections to a lot of other people. Ellen visited the pastor and explained what kind of work Gary was interested in and asked if the pastor had any ideas about whom to approach. The pastor gave her three names of different employers who were members of the congregation.

Ellen obtained the pastor's permission to use his name when she contacted these individuals, and called on each one. None of the persons contacted was interested in employing Gary, but one of them was interested in helping further. She remembered that a friend of hers, head of the town department of parks and recreation, usually hired some young people at that time of year. Ellen obtained permission to use that employer's name as a referral when contacting the department head. There was eventually an opening in the department and Gary was hired.

employee to be included as a network member. The goal is to develop a comprehensive picture of the social network. Everyone should be included, even the uncle who has moved across the country, because you can never be sure what connections an individual might have maintained or what information he or she might have until you ask.

Either a job seeker or one or more individuals acting as proxies for the job seeker should be asked to generate a list of social contacts in the six categories described earlier. If a career planning meeting format is used, identification of these contacts should be part of the agenda. If people have trouble remembering names of neighbors, business people, co-workers or fellow organization members, the job seeker can accompany the person coordinating job development to visit key people. Sometimes it is possible to get access to lists of organization members, high school graduating class members, or others.

Four job development strategies that involve social network contacts are discussed below. The first mobilizes a job seeker's personal network, the second draws upon the informal resources of the employment support service, the third expands an individual's connections to groups and organizations in the community, and the fourth builds connections between the service agency and the business community.

Mobilizing Job-Seeker Networks

Each network member should be contacted personally, either by the individual, by the individual with assistance from a job developer or a career planning team member, or by a job developer or planning team member on the individual's behalf. Each planning team member should have copies of the job seeker's resume. The call should be informal and social in nature but include at least the following points:

- Briefly state the kind of job the person is interested in.
- Ask if the person knows any businesses that do that kind of work.
- Ask if there is anybody the person knows at any businesses named.
- Ask if the person would feel comfortable contacting any people named.
- Ask if the individual can think of anybody else who knows about the kind of job the individual is interested in.

Some variations on this contact strategy might be to (a) suggest some sample employers to get the individual thinking about a wide range, and (b) use a two-call strategy, first calling to ask the person to give it some thought, then calling back a few days later to ask if the person had thought of anything, and (c) asking the network member, if they can't think of anything, if they might ask around to find someone who might know something about that line of work.

Some of these ideas, and forms for listing network members, are described in the Job Club Counselor's Manual (Azrin & Besalel, 1981). When using the strategies outlined in this manual, keep in mind that job seekers with disabilities might need significant support with some steps.

Figure 4.3: Networking

The individuals who attend a career planning meeting will be a subset of an individual's full social network. This group, including others who might not want to or be able to come to a meeting, but are willing to devote some time, has an important role to play in mobilizing an individual's full network:

- As part of creating a personal profile, they can assist the individual to identify additional members of their network.

- They can generate a list of potential ties of their own among employers and make contacts.

- They can monitor and track progress in contacting network members.

- They can generate new connections by introducing the individual to other members of their network or help the individual join clubs or organizations they are interested in.

- They can contact other network members on behalf of the individual and ask about job leads.

Network members may play a major role in obtaining a job for an individual or simply pave the way for subsequent contact by a job developer. For example, an individual might say to the manager of her condominium association, "I know a person who is interested in groundskeeping work. He goes to Central High. His name is Phil. A teacher at the school, Jeannie Bush, is helping him find a job for the summer. Would it be OK if Jeannie called you?"

If the individual who has the connection is simply asked to initiate the connection and to mention a name so the employer expects a further contact, then the initiator does not have to worry about making some kind of "presentation."

Finally, some individuals will not have a specific personal connection but may have some general knowledge about a business or about the community that can be of use. For example, one job seeker's neighbor knew that a certain motel manager had a reputation for being especially tolerant and easygoing.

Support Service Brainstorming

Regardless of the size of a job seeker's network, one reliable connection he or she has is to the individual and the agency helping them find employment. If you are one of the people interested in providing assistance to a person, you are in his/her social network. If an agency is sponsoring or coordinating the job search, members of the agency are in the individual's "social snowflake." These include:

- Staff members of the organization and their families, friends, associates and neighbors,

- Board members of the organization and their families, friends, associates and neighbors,

- Former agency employees who left on good terms and now have jobs elsewhere,

- Other organizations which supply goods or services to the agency, such as accounting firms, printing companies, banks, insurance companies, and vending machine companies, and

- Persons who receive services who are now successfully employed, along with their families and social networks.

Some agencies take affirmative steps to ensure that access to rich community contacts is built into the organizational structure. For example, diversity in outside interests and community group memberships may be stated as one of the qualifications for new staff and considered in staff hiring.

The same criteria can apply to members serving on the Board of Directors. Each new Board member may be asked to commit to assisting one individual find a job. Staff leaving the organization may be asked in an exit interview to keep in touch about openings they hear of with their future employers. Persons receiving agency services may be requested to assist other job seekers by sharing job leads or network contacts that might be suitable for someone else.

Most importantly, agency personnel should thoroughly canvass their own personal connections on behalf of every job seeker within the organization. Techniques that agencies have found successful include:

- Devoting part of each staff meeting, or one whole meeting per week or month, to a brainstorming session about one individual. After a lead person presents the individual's career vision and job specifications, the group develops a list of possible jobs that meet those specifications and a list of employer contacts in those job areas. Individual staff members agree to make specific contacts.

- Including a brief written career profile of an individual as an enclosure in agency paychecks, and establishing incentives such as tickets to a sports event or concert to a staff member who provides a job lead that results in the individual obtaining a job.

- Hosting a dinner at a local restaurant with the "price" of admission for friends, relatives, agency staff and community members being the names of two local employers or business people who could be contacted.

- Assigning one staff member to build a relationship with each organization the agency does business with (bank, accounting firm, and so forth) and become familiar with their labor needs.

- Supporting staff in joining organizations and attending social functions in the community that are likely to bring them in contact with business people, including the Chamber of Commerce, Rotary and other community groups.

- Maintaining an active Business Advisory Council comprised of local employers who can help guide the agency and serve as a bridge in job development and marketing activities to the business world.

Staff can also be encouraged to think of job development as part of their daily life in the community. Such naturally occurring situations as attending parties, eating in cafeteria, or standing in line at checkout counters can be occasions for "social marketing." These are informal opportunities to start conversations and make connections. People who take job development seriously become aware of making and using social contacts, and sometimes become a little more socially outgoing than they might otherwise be for the purpose of engaging in social marketing.

When staff are asked for ideas about job leads again and again, the same limited number of contacts can eventually become saturated. The more individualized the career planning process, the less likely this is to happen because each person's job specifications will be different.

Leisure and Other Community Involvement

Leisure or recreational involvements or community groups and organizations ("generic" organizations, not those specifically designed for people with disabilities) are often overlooked as an avenue of entry into the job market. Vocational service personnel may define their work narrowly: "Our business is work, not recreation. That's the case manager's job (or the residence's job or the family's job). We're already overworked just trying to do the vocational part."

This may be true, yet people's lives are not so compartmentalized. The career planning process described in Chapter 3 will have identified interests and talents

---

SOCIAL MARKETING

Tom works as a job developer for a community employment agency. He makes it a point to find out about the work the people do whom he comes into contact with in his daily life, in case it might lead to a job. One Saturday while waiting in line at the local hardware store, Tom started a conversation with the individual behind him in line. The person turned out to be an owner of a small engine repair business.

The following week Tom called the individual and they met to have lunch and talk further about each others' work. They kept in touch periodically, and when an individual Tom was helping look for work expressed a strong interest in working with machines, Tom arranged a visit to the company. The individual was subsequently hired.

---

of the individual that cannot be fully actualized in the work setting. And there are close links between leisure and work:

- Leisure and recreation can help develop new skills, clarify and shape career interests, or develop new pursuits. For example, a photography course at a local adult education program may lead to an interest in and connections to people with an interest in related vocations. These might include, for example, working in a film developing lab or work involving chemical or scientific work, or a job with an artistic side to it, like flower arranging or desktop publishing.

- Leisure and recreation activities can become a meaningful part of the weekly daytime schedule for an individual who works part-time, who is between jobs, or has had his work hours reduced temporarily. Without some other involvement, some of these situations can be stressful for the person, his family or residential support organizations, and for employment support services. As a result, there may be a temptation to "place" people in a segregated program or a work site more for convenience than because it is best for the individual.

- Leisure and recreation contacts add new network members who can then become sources of job leads. People who feel a common bond are more likely to offer support to a fellow member. And when a person is seen as making a positive contribution or as actively participating, it is easier for the individual to be known and described to prospective employers in terms of skills and the potential for productivity.

- Involvement in activities that are fun and rewarding for an individual improve the individual's overall quality of life, and act as reinforcement for working hard and succeeding at his or her job.

For these reasons, connections to community groups and leisure activities should be taken as seriously as involvement in paid work (Liptak, 1991). Any community has practically limitless opportunities for recreation, leisure and community involvement. One survey of a small neighborhood in Chicago (O'Connell, 1990) obtained information on leisure groups from newspapers, interviews with church and community leaders, and a telephone survey of a sample of residents. Over 575 different groups and associations that a resident might potentially join were identified. Here are just a few examples of the kinds of groups and organizations people are a part of in your community:

- Health clubs, aerobics classes, karate clubs,
- Adult education,
- Civic and governmental groups; political parties, environmental protection organizations, advocacy groups for social causes,
- Private classes and studios,
- Interest groups like quilting, antique cars, organic gardening, hiking,
- Food cooperatives,
- Theater groups, and
- Community sports teams sponsored by parks associations, bowling alleys, etc.

Support in joining and participating in classes, clubs, or other activities should be a cooperative process with other service providers and support network members. On an individual basis, staff members of an organization might be willing to assist someone to join and become accepted within one of the organizations they are part of. Or they may have an interest in common with a prospective employee and attend an event together. Assistance may be needed beyond simply signing up, such as for transportation, social acceptance, and learning appropriate skills.

Many of the strategies which will be discussed in Chapter 8 in the context of joining a work culture can be applied to leisure organizations as well.

Cost is always a factor mentioned when discussing how to help people who are unemployed or underemployed afford leisure activities. Many organizations give reduced membership rates or fees to people with low incomes, and more would be willing to do this if asked. Also, it is possible to find community foundations and other organizations which will finance a small amount of money that a town or neighborhood can use to subsidize the costs of organized recreation for an individual. These include such things as membership or admission fees, supplies, transportation, or the need for personal support, all of which can act as barriers to participation by people with disabilities.

Once included in recreation, there are many avenues open to support the inclusion of the person into an employment arena. Individuals can share phone numbers with other participants so that someone can call and let them know of employment possibilities. Or the individual can pass along resumes. Or they can invite one or two people they like to participate in their next career planning meeting.

Becoming a Part of the Business Community

Agencies which assist people with disabilities to identify and achieve their career goals are themselves businesses. They hire staff, rent or buy office space, purchase supplies, balance income against expenses, and produce services to satisfy the needs of their customers. As such, their activities are part of the structure of the local economy. When they do their work well, career support agencies offer an important service to the other businesses in the community. And in order to do their work well, it pays to become knowledgeable about and embedded in the business community.

Consider creating specific business-to-business linkages by using some of the following strategies:

- Do research on local businesses.
- Become familiar with major services and products in the local economy.
- Understand local labor needs and issues.
- Find out who the key business leaders are.
- Participate in business functions.

- Join chambers of commerce and specific industry associations.

- Join local associations of human resource or training and development professionals.

- Start a Business Advisory Council for the organization.

- Tour local companies.

- Survey businesses about their labor needs and growth projections.

Speaking the language of business people establishes credibility and projects an image of seriousness about serving the needs of business. Employers appreciate contacts made on the basis of thought and research as opposed to simply being contacted at random or as part of a mass effort. Whenever possible, the basis for contacting the particular employer should be communicated clearly and immediately. When some specific reason is behind a contact, the stage is set for a specific discussion of employer needs and/or job seeker attributes.

The style and timing of a contact should also reflect an understanding of the business being contacted. Many businesses expect visitors to be dressed conservatively, for example; and many businesses have times of the day or days of the week when they are very busy. Visits to a restaurant, for example, should be after the lunchtime rush but before dinner. Contacts should demonstrate sensitivity to such patterns.

Most communication in the business field, as in any other field, moves through informal channels as people socialize together, have lunch, go to parties or play golf. Employers listen closely to other employers, and new ideas are shared in this way.

Satisfied customers, in this case the businesses benefitting from hiring employees through an employment support service, are the best marketing tool. Employers can be encouraged to communicate with one another through sponsored events, letters of introduction, personal meetings, testimonials or by telephone. Employers can provide reference letters for other employers. Most employers will pay attention to other business persons' hiring opinions.

It is important to be knowledgeable about what supported employment can offer and about issues that employers are concerned about. If you don't know what these might be, ask! It is also important to listen to the ideas of business people about how best to reach other businesses, about economic trends, about local labor market issues, and about the concerns business people face day to day.

TALKING WITH EMPLOYERS

The form and content of an initial contact with an employer will be a significant factor in the chance for success and will lay the foundation for the relationship between the employee and employer. Initial contacts also determine, for better or worse, the role of the employment support service in the employment process.

In some cases, social network members may initiate discussions with employers and set the stage for any involvement by an employment consultant or other job developer. In other cases, job seekers themselves may make initial contacts. Or employers may initiate contacts and already be familiar with supported employment. In these cases, the employment consultant role quickly becomes one of helping negotiate the parameters of the job and any supports or accommodations that may be required.

In other cases, an employment consultant's initial talk with an employer will be a key event, determining the shape of much that follows. So it is important to pay close attention to this point in the process.

The goal of an initial contact is usually to obtain an appointment or interview with an individual in a decision-making role. An initial phone call takes no more than two minutes; an introductory letter is no longer than one page. Drop-in calls to a place of business vary from brief visits to extended tours and or discussions, and sometimes produce even immediate job offers, depending on the situation.

As a general rule, an initial goal is to speak with an owner or manager of a small company; a department head or similar individual in a large company. But this rule, like most others, can be broken often. When a contact is initiated through a personal connection, the individual identified within the company should be contacted first and that individual's advice should be followed regarding whom to speak to next. The person with the connection should be the one to make that initial contact, unless that individual specifies otherwise.

Sometimes upper-echelon managers are receptive to an initial presentation and then direct department heads or the human resource office to follow-up. Sometimes the personnel or human resource office can be an effective initial contact. Most often, however, the appointment with personnel is more a matter of protocol than a decision-making point.

Whether in person, by letter or over the phone, a job developer has a brief time in which to present the essence of his or her message. If the message strikes a responsive chord, further meetings and discussions will follow. If not, the job developer has one more "NO" to add to his or her impressive collection. This does not mean, however, that the relationship is terminated forever. Maintaining a cordial relationship and establishing a connection in which the job developer is seen as a potential resource for the future should be a part of every employer contact. The content of the initial message will shape the conversation and, if successful, set the expectations of the employer for whatever is to follow.

Agency-centered Negotiations

By far the most common initial message provided to employers in supported employment is one we can call the agency-centered message (Hagner & Daning, 1990). Agency-centered messages are about supported employment, the supported employment agency, and the various types of support services it offers to people with disabilities and to businesses. For example, a job developer might say:

> "Hi! I'm Carmen Sandiego from Faraway Employment Services. We're an *agency* in town that helps *people with special needs* to obtain employment through a *service* called *supported employment*. I would like to make an appointment to *discuss our services* with you."

Although it is common and has a certain self-evident appeal, this agency-centered style has a serious pitfall. It establishes a relationship primarily between the employer and the support service rather than primarily between the employer and the prospective employee.

By representing a hiring deal as a programmatic one, agency-centered job developers can broker the relationship too far. The services become the commodity that the employer is enticed to purchase. "We take care of all the training," "We guarantee the production quotas will be met," "We guarantee the position will be filled," and "We can start the individual on a subcontract basis for the first few months so you don't have to worry about insurance" — are promises no other applicants make.

These promises may indeed give a competitive advantage to prospective employees with disabilities, but at great cost. The company is given permission, in effect, to treat the employer-employee relationship more casually than with other employees and to focus attention on the relationship with the support agency. Once the job begins, it will be this relationship that needs to be sustained. If productivity has been promised by the agency to the company, then the company will call the agency when production is unsatisfactory. If training has been promised, the agency can expect to be called in if the person's duties change. It is not an exaggeration to say that most of the difficulties employment specialists encounter in "fading" from job sites or in using more "natural supports" can be traced back to the promises made and relationships established in agency-centered employer negotiations.

It is legitimate to offer incentives and services to a company to accommodate for specialized support needs. For example, one could offer to provide support for the additional training an individual may require beyond what a company usually provides. And when employers will need some extra help or have some reservations, at some point negotiations will cover these topics. But when an initial message is heavily agency-centered, the services promised tend not to be individualized accommodations but general sales pitches about a support agency.

Moreover, what the agency provides is often inferior to what the company provides. For example, we have seen in Chapter 1 that agency trainers are not always in a position to be aware of details of the work culture, whereas an experienced co-worker is likely to be an expert in the culture. Likewise, agency-sponsored benefits to consumers on a subcontract seldom match what companies offer their workers.

Agency information should be presented as a background service that stands behind the individual's capacities and the employer's needs. Building up an agency's reputation and credibility comes not so much with isolated marketing and presentation, but rather with a series of positive experiences and having supporting information accompany them.

Employee-centered Negotiations

While agency-centered job developers start with "Let me tell you about our agency," employee-centered job developers convey the message "Let me tell you about Nancy." In other words, they concentrate heaviest on explaining the qualifications and assets of a job seeker. Representing an individual begins to create a normative relationship between the employer and the prospective employee. What is "marketed" to the employer is not a service but an employee. When the job search is based on a comprehensive career design, the person can be presented to the employer as an individual. Discussions then focus on why the job seeker is interested in that company and/or that work.

Employee-centered contacts establish that the caller represents a certain individual, and — unless the individual has requested otherwise — gives the individual's name. That individual and the attributes that represent benefits to the employer are communicated in the opening statement. The individual's biggest "selling point" — the attribute that will add value to the employer's product or service — is highlighted. Why that employer is being contacted, the personal connection, business research, or other context, should also be communicated.

> "Hi, I'm Carmen Sandiego, a teacher at Central High School, and I'm helping a student named Nancy Miller look into job possibilities here in town. She is a friend of Gloria's in your mortgage department and Gloria suggested that you would be the best person to speak with. Nancy is interested in microfilming and other clerical jobs and she has just completed our clerical training program. Would you have a few minutes to meet with me, perhaps some time next week?"

Later discussions, once an appointment has been obtained, can include further information about the individual, such as career goals, work history, outside interests, personal or character references, etc. While communicating value to the employer is the number one objective, employee-centered contacts also are an opportunity to present the individual as a whole person. Personal information provides the employer with information that he or she does not have or cannot necessarily trust from people who stop in or mail in resumes "off the street."

Personal information is highly useful and includes pertinent data that may well be relevant to selecting an employee. For example, when an employer knows that Nancy wants to work for her bank because Nancy is planning to move into her own apartment downtown, she has some evidence that perhaps Nancy is interested in a stable job, is likely to stay with the bank for a while, and become a solid member of the community. This may be as important as information about Nancy's actual work skills or about the services that an agency might be able to provide to help the bank employ Nancy.

While one wants to place a job seeker in as positive a light as possible, it is important to avoid overstating a person's qualifications. Some job developers portray workers with disabilities as amazing overachievers. To hear this pitch, one would think that all workers who happen to have a disability never miss a day of work, are never late, and are always in a good mood. Brochures and video presentations about supported employment often use this tone. These "super-workers" are as much erroneous stereotypes as the older myths of adults with disabilities as incompetent. Exaggerated claims lead to disappointment and distrust on the part of employers.

Eventually, job seeker attributes that aren't benefits to the employer and might pose difficulties need to be mentioned if they are related to the job and are likely to present themselves once an individual starts working and/or will require accommodations. Talking with employers about these attributes is covered later in this chapter.

Company-centered Negotiations

Neither agency-centered nor employee-centered negotiations are completely effective at directly "getting at" a company's personnel decision making. Both are based on presenting something to a company for a response, which makes the probability of a "NO" response high. A third option is to find out what a company wants to buy before selling them anything. That way, you are not spending any

---

AN EMPLOYEE-CENTERED APPROACH

"The secretary at our agency lives in this condominium and she arranged with the manager to meet with me. The manager said he knew a little about the agency and its work from talking to the secretary about what she does, and he seemed to think it was interesting."

"I thanked him for taking the time to see me and explained that I was helping Wayne look for work in the lawn care or landscaping field. I explained a little about his background, the jobs he's had since leaving high school and how he's zeroed in on lawn work as what he really likes best. Wayne loves being outdoors, loves hiking and loves nature. I told him Wayne is a very hard worker who is pretty quiet but gets along well with people, and asked if the manager would like to meet him."

"He asked me some questions and we talked some about the fact that lawn care is seasonal and what Wayne would do in the winter. He said he's not looking for anyone right now but he met with Wayne that following week. I called every few weeks and I think the secretary kept working on him too. As it turned out, the following spring he did need somebody and he hired Wayne."

time trying to convince people to buy something they don't need. Company-centered negotiations center on finding out about a company and its needs. The individual approaches the company as a listener rather than as a talker.

There are two different variations on company-centered negotiations. The first can be summarized as, "I'd like to talk to you about a particular line of work." The second approach can be paraphrased as, "I'd like to find out more about your company." Sometimes these second types of discussions are known as exploratory or informational interviews. An introductory statement using this approach might sound something like:

"Hi, I'm Carmen Sandiego, from Nearby Employment Services. We are interested in learning more about the labor needs of local businesses here in our community. I would like to meet with you to find out more about your business and some of the hiring trends you are seeing. Could we set up a time?"

The objectives of a company-centered contact are:

- To learn as much about a particular work or company as possible, with an eye towards how a particular person you have in mind would fit in, whom you might approach and what the best approach might be;

- To build rapport and trust with the employer and establish a healthy working relationship, a relationship that will hopefully extend over time and may lead to a job for an individual; and

- To gain greater depth about the particular company and employer so that you can make specific suggestions, find areas to explore further, and engage the employer in looking at personnel issues with you as a partner.

Because the employer is not really being asked to do anything more than help you learn, a company-centered contact is not a high-pressure situation. It is a chance for an employer to help you and the individual you represent for a relatively low investment — a half hour or so of time. This gives you a wealth of information for future contacts and also builds a partnership with that employer that may pay off in a job offer sooner than you expect.

A company-centered discussion can be used as research about a work field, to collect information for use in more targeted discussions with other employers. Depending on the type of business, topics to pursue include:

A COMPANY-CENTERED APPROACH

"I was working with someone who really loved boats and water. I knew there was a commercial fishing company on the coast that I had driven past many times and was always kind of curious about it. I had no idea if anything like this would make sense for the person. I called the owner and told him exactly what I'm telling you. He said the fishing business was almost like a way of life and if I really wanted to know, I should go out on a boat and see for myself. So the next thing I knew I was driving to the coast at 5:00 am and taking seasickness pills and thinking my business is its own way of life too, only stranger. I went out with the fishermen for the day and helped out with the catch, then we went back in to empty the hold and clean the fish at the processing plant."

"They clean one big tub of fish at a time, keeping the rest on ice. Somebody has to hose the tables and floor down in between tubs and they keep getting more ice as it melts. As I watched this I noticed that these pretty skilled cleaners had to keep stopping to hose things down and get ice, which wasted about ten minutes per person per tub. I was unsure if the person I was working with could really do the work on the boats or the cleaning, but I figured for starters, it might work out to do the hosing down and getting the ice. So I calculated how much time this would save and mentioned this to the owner. He was really interested. This was sometimes a pretty marginal business as far as profits are concerned and he really needed one more person. I told him that I thought the person I was working with would love it. He does."

- What are the most significant trends and prospects for this line of work?
- What new technological developments are changing the way work is done?
- What are the major trade periodicals in this field?
- Which trade or professional associations do most businesses in this field belong to?
- Is overtime work common in this business? Are temporary workers used?
- Which job positions do you see as having the potential for growth?

- What advice would the individual give someone entering this field?

Asking for information acknowledges that employers are the experts. It gives them a chance to demonstrate their wisdom and experience, and maybe show off or brag a little. Their needs and perspectives will be the basis for your follow-up contacts and any proposal you might make.

A tour is an excellent way to get information about a company and most employers will agree to have you take a look at a setting or watch how a particular operation is done. You can either follow up a tour with another meeting, if there are things you have questions about or saw something that might turn into a job possibility, or use the information to design your contact with the next employer. For example, a company-centered meeting with one library led to additional meetings at three other libraries with a specific list of questions to ask each one:

- How often are the computer screens and microfilm reader windows cleaned and who does that?

- Who puts the magnetic strips (for the detection system if people try to take books without checking them out) on new books and periodicals? How much time per week is devoted to this?

- Have you had to deal with any deterioration of old books due to acidic dust? (Like rain, "modern" dust is acidic and eventually will dissolve paper.)

- Would you be interested in exploring whether a book preservation program would be an economical way to save your valuable older books?

  A similar list of questions can be generated for any type of company or work of interest.

Agency-centered, employee-centered, and company-centered elements are present in every good negotiating process, but are emphasized to different degrees.

THREE STYLES OF NEGOTIATION WITH EMPLOYERS

Agency-centered	"Let me tell you about our agency and its services"
Employee-centered	"Let me tell you about Nancy and her qualifications'
Company-centered	"Tell me about your company and its needs"

And the emphasis may change as a relationship develops. While an agency-centered approach may be inadvisable to start the process, a presentation about the agency and its services might be an ideal topic for a subsequent meeting with an employer initially approached from a company-centered or employee-centered perspective.

A job will rarely be developed in one or two contacts. Discussions can take a long time, and are a sign that an employer is thorough and careful. Although unusual, one study noted that a single job, for example, took 26 phone calls, 27 letters and 12 meetings over a 13-month period (Training and Research Institute for People with Disabilities, 1991) to finalize. A series of contacts builds relationships and trust.

Many experienced job developers report that one of the skills they master over time is the ability to spot receptivity or the lack thereof to their message fairly early in a discussion. They pay close attention to nonverbal signals such as handshakes, eye contact, the "spirit" in which questions are asked or objections are raised, and other conversational cues. If an employer simply feels obligated to meet and get it over with, then the longer the job developer spends with this employer the more time is wasted that could be spent on another prospect or another "lead' into that company. So it is worth attending to subtle cues regarding receptivity.

Over time, initially "cold" contacts can warm up as people get to know one another more personally and as their discussions begin to include some personal topics. Employers may have pictures, posters, coffee mugs, and other items in their office that give clues as to their outside interests, and sometimes information is disclosed through "small talk" before a meeting officially starts. Discussing commonalities that emerge from attending to these details can help build a personal bond between the job developer and an employer that will not only help you receive a favorable response on what you are proposing, but will lead to an open and honest flow of communication about any issues that will need to be resolved throughout the employment process. A well-established relationship will pay off later because employers will be more apt to tell you what's on their mind instead of being "too nice" until it's too late.

Positive opportunities for repeated contacts with employers need to be created during the development process to keep a relationship growing. Because it is unlikely that an employer will simply hire someone based on one meeting, a job developer should have other interim proposals to keep the employer involved and aware over time of the possibilities you are offering. One can think of these as "fall-back options" when a relationship is worth pursuing but hiring is not realistic at the moment:

- Schedule a time for a visit, tour, and/or fill out an application with a job seeker.
- Schedule an interview for an applicant.
- Schedule a meeting with other department heads or with a specific area supervisor.
- Make an appointment to analyze a specific job or spend a day observing in a setting.
- Make an appointment for another agency individual (e.g. rehabilitation engineer) to look at a job or work area, or
- Agree to a call back at a specified future time.

Other proposals that an employer who may not be able to offer a job in the foreseeable future but can respond "yes" to include:

- Conducting practice or "mock" interviews with job seekers,
- Joining an agency advisory board, and
- Giving the names of other employers or contacting other employers.

Through repeated meetings over time, possibly with a number of different people, a depth of involvement with a company is created. But this involvement is centered on the relationship between employees and employers, with the agency in the background. A career support service can help employers fill real and pressing needs that they cannot fill as well through other channels, and can help employers think about what they need and plan for the future.

THE RESUME

Resumes are a culturally expected and valued aspect of job hunting. Even in pursuit of entry-level jobs which rely primarily on applications, a resume will never hurt an individual's chance of obtaining a job and can usually help. A resume;

- Projects the job seeker as serious and businesslike about job hunting;

- Brings pertinent aspects of the job seeker's background, experiences and skills to the attention of the employer;

- Points out references that can provide follow-up information from a "third-party" source;

- Functions as a "calling card" to remind the employer about the individual;

- Sets part of the agenda for job interviews by providing prompts to potential interviewers. "I see here that you have had some previous experience in a bank. Could you tell me more about that?"

The process of resume preparation also helps the job seeker by providing an occasion for reviewing and analyzing one's skills and accomplishments with reference to how these project a sense of value to potential employers.

It is surprising how few supported employment programs assist job seekers to prepare and maintain resumes. One statewide study found that fewer than 13% of supported employees had presented resumes to their employers (Hagner and Daning,1990). Supported employment professionals may consider resumes unimportant for obtaining entry-level employment, or may be unfamiliar with resume development for individuals with little or no work histories. In addition, we have seen that most employer contacts for supported employment are heavily agency-centered. If any document is left with an employer, it is likely to be an agency brochure.

During the process of career planning, the employment consultant will probably collect most of the information needed to write the resume. Job seekers can be helped to visit a professional resume service for assistance, or a career support service can help with resume preparation. An organization should be careful not to use the same resume format for each person, but individualize formats, paper colors, and type fonts for each job seeker. Organization of the content can be chronological (by time period) or functional (by type of skill or accomplishment) depending on the "best look" of the contents. It is a good idea to keep a resume to one page. Resume writers should use active verbs in describing their skills, and state accomplishments or valued outcomes of their past work whenever possible.

Reference materials are easily available that cover every aspect of resume preparation and give examples of functional and chronological resumes. Below are listed a few tips in resume preparation for individuals with limited community employment experience.

- People who did not drop out of high school, but left on positive terms and did the work that was expected of them while in school, can indicate that they *completed* or *graduated from* high school, unless they have been specifically told otherwise. Many school districts have no policy or an incoherent policy regarding graduation of special education students. The best strategy is not to let the educational system's incoherence reflect poorly upon the person.

- Vocational training sites and community volunteer work should be entered as work experience, in the same way as paid employment. The individual accomplished work tasks at these sites and deserves credit for them.

- Individuals who have worked on a subcontract basis at "enclaves" or "work crews" can list the contracting company as their place of employment, and name the company department manager as the contact person for inquiries, if that individual will agree to serve as a reference. If contacted, the employer or co-worker used as a reference may wish to explain that the employee was subcontracted and not actually an employee, but can also talk about the individual's work at the company.

- People who had sheltered jobs with no actual job title (or where the job title was "client") should create descriptive titles for the kind of work they performed most or are proudest of. "Benchwork Assembler" is commonly used to describe sheltered work; "Electronics Assembler," "Machine Parts Packager" or a similar more specific title is even better. A resume should state jobs and describe tasks in the most positive way possible. After all, the major difference between a "salesman" and an "account executive" are the words used.

- A list of hobbies and special interests can personalize a resume and also supplement a short list of jobs. Some resumes also list personal attributes and characteristics of the job seeker that employers will be particularly interested in (conscientious, dependable, enthusiastic, etc.) for the same purposes.

- The full name, title, address and phone number of two or three references can be included on the resume itself if there is room. These should preferably be people from the business community who know the prospective employee.

PROJECTING JOB SEEKER ASSETS

In every phone call, every letter, every visit, every communication with a potential employer, the primary task is to communicate value (Jackson, 1991). Businesses will purchase labor if and when they are convinced that the labor is likely to produce more than it costs.

Being open and honest about an individual and his or her needs for support and accommodation is also necessary for clarity and career success. Hiding potential concerns or overestimating performance can set up an individual for failure. And full, open communication is essential to the reputation of a career support service with employers.

Along with presenting the value that employees will have for a company, aspects of an individual's need for functional support, and perhaps other worker characteristics may need to be communicated. The skill of job development lies in accomplishing both tasks.

Attributes and Assets

Attributes are neutral facts about something. Refrigerators keeps things cold. They are also heavy and have plastic components. When a buyer is considering a purchase, some attributes may be assets, those attributes the buyer wants and is willing to pay for; other attributes may be neutral, and still others may be deficits — things the buyer doesn't want. Most purchases are of a package of attributes in which the assets outweigh the deficits. People like the fact that refrigerators keep things cold, don't appreciate how heavy they are, and don't really care what they're made out of.

The same principle applies to an employer's purchase of labor. Attributes only become assets (or deficits) in the context of some consumer's needs. Employers are the consumers of labor, and portraying an individual's attributes in such a way as to emphasize the assets and downplay the deficits in the correct context is the essence of employment negotiation.

The same attributes that are deficits in one context may be assets in another. It is for this reason that, in Chapter 3, we rejected the notion that some people are unemployable, as well as the idea that deficits an individual may display in one context will also be deficits in another context. Attributes of people we may label as disabilities follow the same principle as any others: They can be deficits in one context, neutral in a second, and assets in a third.

If we have identified employers based on a solid career planning process, communicating benefit will not be difficult. We target potential employers and work environments that represent an appropriate context. And we identify for the employer the capabilities and interests that will be attractive: *"Ms. West is a hard and reliable worker who is very accurate in her production..."* *"Mr. Owens is a very sociable person who enjoys music and sports ..."* The more difficult task will be talking about perceived deficits and arranging for accommodations. These are discussed below.

What's in a Word?

Under the Americans with Disabilities Act, covered employers are not allowed to ask about an applicant's disability. Applicants can of course mention disability to the employer, and by extension can delegate the authority to talk about disability to a career support service. And employers can ask any questions related to whether, with an accommodation, the employee is able to perform the essential functions of a particular job under consideration.

Disability must sometimes be discussed because it is obvious that the job developer is from an agency that serves people with disabilities, because the person making the initial informal contact mentioned it, because aspects related to disability will need to be accommodated, or because later surprises will hurt the relationship with the employer. But when and how aspects of an individual's disability is discussed should be related to performance on a job. Before an employer is contacted, the issue of how to talk about disability should be discussed with the job seeker and/or members of his or her career planning team.

Describe disability functionally. The same attribute or behavior can often be presented in two ways. *"John is very attentive to detail and careful in his work and enjoys predictable tasks."* Or, *"John is autistic with stereotypical movements, a below average production rate and a tendency towards perseveration."* There is no need to use labels or clinical descriptions. They tend to produce an overly negative reaction and do not specifically relate to job performance.

Mention disability in the related context. In the context of training, the fact that an individual learns slowly needs to be considered. In the context of office arrangement and job design, the fact that an individual uses a wheelchair has to be considered. Mentioning support needs as the proper context arises in negotiations maintains an overall focus on the job and downplays disability as one among many factors to consider.

Describe disability in terms of accommodations. An individual's disability is best described in terms of additional supports or modifications needed to function successfully. Rather than use a label, describe those supports. *"For her to do well on the job, she needs a ..." "In order to move around in the community, he uses a wheelchair..." "It might take her a few weeks to learn the routine here, but after that..."*

Mention the context of previous behavior. The possibility of behavior the employer needs to be prepared for can be stated while placing it in perspective. *"Her last job was confusing, with too many people giving her orders. In that setting, she got angry and would sometimes yell at her co-workers. Here, with one supervisor, we don't expect a similar problem"*. This kind of explanation can be phrased as a compliment to the employer being approached. "We have done a lot of research to find the right job and your company has a reputation for fairness and a management style suited to what she needs."

Pair potential negative traits with assets. Sometimes the same characteristic that has a negative side has a positive or semi-positive side as well. *"He can become upset if things aren't always in the same place, and I think you'll find he'll keep the shelves organized just the way you want them."* If there is no connection of this type, simply repeat one or more of the individual's assets in the same statement as the deficit.

Describe what to expect. Describing for employers exactly what they will observe helps maintain a relationship which is honest and "up front" but avoids extraneous information. *"At first Roger will be a little anxious and might do things like open and close doors or look behind things because the place is new. Then after a while he will adjust and settle into the job."*

Describe agency services. When a potential support need is serious and/or the needed accommodation is significant, this is the time to bring the services of the agency into the negotiating equation. In contrast to an agency-centered initial contact strategy, here the agency's services are being described in a subsequent discussion and in a specific context, because a lesser intervention (i.e. expecting the employer to hire without these services) would not be successful in that individual case. *"We'll be working with you as much as you need, to make sure that..."*.

THE INTERVIEW

Most job applicants have an interview as part of the hiring process. Interviews vary from a simple handshake before starting work to a more formal selection process with questioning by a team. Sometimes interviews are true decision points and other times they are formalities. But except in very unusual situations, every job applicant should meet with the employer prior to starting a job.

Applicants may require preparation for an interview. The job interview is a fairly structured and predictable social situation, and an individual can practice answering probable questions and asking a few questions of an interviewer, to become more familiar with what to expect. Protocol details such as handshakes and eye-contact should also be practiced. Dress and grooming cannot be overestimated, and plenty of time should be allowed prior to the scheduled interview to complete preparations. Employers may be willing to conduct mock interviews and give constructive feedback to help an individual prepare. There have even been cases where a mock interview led to an actual job offer!

Interview situations can be stressful. There is a lot at stake, and the idea of being judged or evaluated can be threatening. For someone with a disability, there may be the added difficulties of reduced or non-traditional communication and little direct interview or job experience. The interviewer(s), for their part, may be just as nervous as the interviewee.

The employment consultant may sometimes judge that a traditional job interview is likely to be a negative experience for both parties. There are alternative formats to a formal sit-down interview that can be considered:

- A brief courtesy meeting in which the individuals are simply introduced,

- A meeting over coffee or lunch,

- A tour of the workplace,

- An employer visit to the employee at a training site or volunteer site,

- A "working interview" in which the employee spends a few hours working at the company to demonstrate that he/she can do it.

Each of these can be useful or harmful depending on the individual situation. In some cases, where it is likely that an individual would be so nervous or inappropriate that it would jeopardize any chance of a positive outcome, a meeting may be skipped altogether. But some employment consultants have found creative ways to deal with even these situations. On one occasion, an employer informally visited a potential employee at his volunteer job site before the possibility of a job offer was mentioned. The individual was relaxed and attentive to his work. Another employment consultant created a "video resume" of an individual working, edited to highlight the individual's most important capabilities, and showed it to the employer.

In a formal job interview, the employment consultant may need to provide assistance and interpret questions and answers for the applicant. Or the interviewer may need assistance to ask questions or understand answers. The employment consultant's role should be that of an aide or "translator" rather than one of dominating the meeting or speaking for the person. Some general guidelines can help make interviews more successful.

- Encourage the interviewee to "be yourself." The interview should not sound overly prepared or "canned." This helps both the applicant and the employer decide whether or not the job is a good match.

- The interviewee should give clear answers and ask straightforward questions. Good communication will help avoid misunderstandings about expectations and support needs. Specific skills an interviewee has or tools and equipment an individual is familiar with should be mentioned early in the interview.

- The interviewee should acknowledge personal strengths and interests and also needs for accommodation. Some interviewers may ignore a discussion of accommodations completely and be uncomfortable talking about disability, while others may focus too heavily on it. Stating in a comfortable and matter-of-fact way what accommodations will be needed to perform the job assists the interviewer to achieve a balanced perspective.

- Don't exaggerate performance capabilities, or undersell capabilities or enthusiasm. Approaching the interview positively and honestly can help make a hiring decision the right one.

SUMMARY

Searching for a job that meets a person's career goals is one of the most important, yet one of the least understood, activities in supported employment. To work in partnership with employers requires understanding employer needs and responding through an approach that links an individual with a need for labor.

Personal career planning estabishes a career vision and direction to guide the job "hunting" process, and helps mobilize an individual's personal network for assistance, including assistance in obtaining job leads. As at least indirect members of consumer social networks, each member of an employment agency should have a role in job development, through both personal and business relationships. "Warm" or network contacts are especially important avenues to jobs tailored to the individual, with possibilities for social connections. Personal networks can be expanded through community and leisure involvement.

A comprehensive job search requires planning, effort, and a variety of both "warm" and "cold" employer contact strategies. The job seeker should play a key role in all aspects of the search.

Organizations assisting individuals with job development increase their efffectiveness by becoming more knowledgeable about and better connected to the business community. Initial discussions with employers which emphasize either the company's needs or a particular job seeker's assets, avoiding a heavy emphasis on "selling the agency," create the best atmosphere for negotiating an employment situation that will benefit both employer and the supported employee. Presentation of a resume and a job interview help establish the employer/ employee relationship and set the expectations of each party toward the other.

CHAPTER 5

Negotiating Job Designs and Salaries

"A job is an opportunity to solve a problem, to create value for others, and satisfaction for yourself. A job isn't the duties which describe it, it is the results which are produced."
— Tom Jackson

Some degree of negotiation between an applicant and employer is a part of most employment arrangements. In an extreme situation, a very talented job seeker may "hold all the cards" and virtually dictate arrangements to an employer. Some individuals in the sports or entertainment industries, for example, are in this position. At the other extreme, employers may adopt a "take it or leave it" stance: a prospective employee either fills the available opening or not. In these situations prospective employees either find that the job happens to be just what they are looking for, they compromise temporarily and accept the job because they need the work, or they turn the job down and keep looking.

Far more common than either extreme is the situation in which employers are willing to discuss at least some of the parameters of a job and both parties compromise. The employer has in mind some ideal notion of what he or she is looking for, and the employee, likewise, has some notion of an ideal job that he or she would like. Negotiating a workable compromise customizes or designs the job to suit both parties. if no common ground is found, negotiations break off.

What are some of the parameters of the job that can be discussed or designed? Any aspect of employment is a potential topic for negotiation:

- Job responsibilities and work tasks,
- The general work environment,
- The specific work station or immediate work space,
- Tools, equipment and furniture used in the job,
- Salary, benefits, and "perks,"
- Type of supervision, standards, expectations, and form of evaluation,

- Work schedule and flexibility of schedule,
- Co-worker or customer interactions and relationships,
- Company policies, worksite rules, and personnel procedures.

In today's labor market, flexibility is the key to a productive work force, and employers make individualized arrangements all the time. If you are an employee, there are probably examples within your own work group:

- the employee who returns from maternity or paternity leave to work only four days per week;

- the employee who is averse to learning word processing and is allowed to continue using a typist for written products;

- the employee who receives permission to leave early on Tuesdays to take a college course, and so on.

The world of so-called "blue collar" employment is different only in the types of examples. Employees often make special work schedule arrangements, rearrange their duties, or alter their work stations to better match their needs.

Why do employers go along with these individualized arrangements? For one reason. Each employee adds value to the company's product or service in excess of what they cost.

An employment consultant assisting an individual with a disability acts as a broker in the job negotiation and design process, helping arrange a satisfactory deal for both parties. If an employer is approached in the right way, employer contacts flow naturally into job design negotiations. They are simply two aspects of the same process.

We have indicated the possible positions of prospective employees and employers in the accompanying figure. Neither party can usually obtain their ideal arrangement, but each party knows *what that ideal would be* and is aware of the *bottom line of acceptability*. In our vocational service system, people with disabilities often compromise their ideal career aspirations and dreams. Since we all make compromises, there may be times when this is appropriate. However, it is inappropriate for vocational service professionals to ask someone to compromise his career dreams completely and permanently without taking the time to find out what the individual's ideal would be and then providing the strongest possible negotiation or "brokerage" on behalf of the individual's position.

Being a broker does not indicate a position of neutrality between an employer and employee. Just as most real estate brokers represent and are paid by the sellers of real estate rather than buyers, employment consultants ultimately represent the sellers of labor (employees), and are paid based on providing services to them, not the buyers (employers). But part of the brokering responsibility in both cases is ensuring that a deal is struck that meets the needs of both parties.

The negotiation process, at its most creative, results in a job that is designed both to meet an employer need and to capitalize on the unique strengths and preferences of the employee. In such cases we can speak, not of job development — finding and filling a job opening — but of *job creation*.

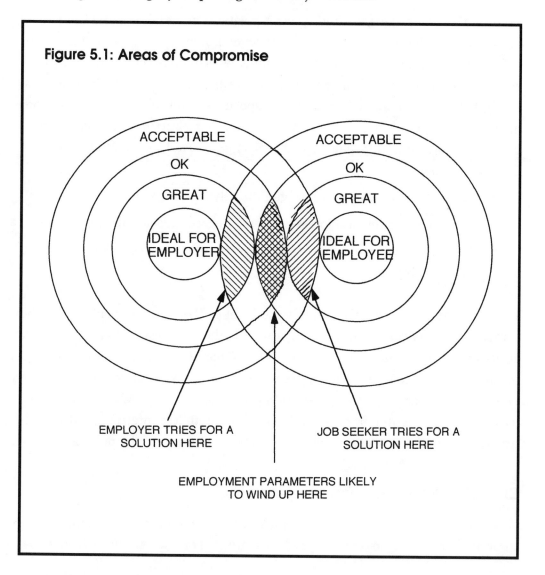

Figure 5.1: Areas of Compromise

How a job is designed will play a large role in determining whether it is successful, and whether the employee will become socially included within a company and work group. This chapter discusses the process of job creation. Job design considerations which foster social inclusion, and considerations that specifically relate to accommodating for a disability, are covered as well. And finally the issues of salary and benefits are addressed as they relate to labor regulations, effects on public benefits, and the role of a broker.

JOB CREATION

When we "develop" jobs, we find open job positions in the labor market and assist individuals to fill these positions. But job development is not the only method of obtaining employment. We can reach a deeper level of involvement with employers in which we adjust and tailor the parameters of a job and in effect "create" jobs. A job that has been created, customized specifically for an individual, is more likely to meet the individual's needs than one that happened to occur; just as tailored clothes fit better than off-the-rack clothes. And job creation has some further advantages:

- The applicant is not being judged directly against other applicants,
- The criteria for evaluation are to some degree individually determined,
- The company is more cognizant of how the employee contributes value to the organization.

The job creation process also reveals the level of flexibility and interest of the company. Just as companies are deciding whether or not to enter into a labor arrangement with the job seeker, job seekers need to decide whether this is a company they want to work for. Companies with less commitment to employee satisfaction and growth, which see employees as just one more "interchangeable part" in the production process, tend to be those with less interest in individualized discussions. These companies screen themselves out of the process.

Changing Jobs in a Changing Market

We can understand job creation best by taking a closer look at the economics of the labor market. Businesses need to produce a product or a service in an economical way and they need labor to do it. But the primary expertise of the business is not in labor efficiency or human resources, it is in producing a product or service. The specific shape of job positions is not critically important. Except in those cases where an external factor like government regulations requires that individuals with certain credentials be on staff — for example, a school must employ certified teachers and administrators — there is considerable flexibility in the decision to define or describe a job in a certain way, or to divide work up into one batch of job positions rather than another.

What are important are the production outcomes of the business and the efficiency of reaching them. Everyone needs to receive the correct mail, but two mail clerks can each sort half the mail, or one mail clerk can sort all of the mail to identify only invoices, and another mail clerk sorts the remaining mail into the other categories. Each "take-out" pizza has to be placed in an assembled box, but there are many options as to who assembles them, when, and how many get assembled at one time. As Jackson (1991) has phrased it, jobs are not lists of tasks but problems to be solved.

Some small family businesses — a dry cleaning store, shrimp boat, a family farm — divide work up literally by sitting down around the kitchen table and reviewing what needs to be done, who is available, and what they can do. (Parenthetically, it is interesting to consider how misleading the term "competitive employment" is as a description of these arrangements.) Larger businesses and those which need to access the public labor market formalize labor into discrete job positions. But lacking specific expertise in matching labor supply to demand, they design and advertise job positions based primarily on:

- Past experience and "common sense,"
- What similar businesses are doing,
- Conventional occupation labels like "waitress" and "secretary," and
- Preconceptions about mythical "normal" people and what they can do.

These can be thought of as "default" methods of designing jobs. The default methods inadvertently "stack the deck" against job seekers with different backgrounds and abilities. Pre-established job positions thus become barriers to employment for people with severe disabilities. Applicants to fill pre-established openings are judged on their ability to carry out the whole set of job functions and are compared with other applicants for the same opening. Applicants with unconventional histories, abilities or appearances are disadvantaged in such a competition.

Every equation has some "constants" and some "variables." Once we have made the decision to help specific individuals achieve satisfying careers, success is our "constant". We do not accept a situation in which some people are successful and some aren't, just like the other businesses we deal with don't accept a situation in which they sometimes produce *their* particular product or service correctly and sometimes they don't. For supported employment professionals, the design of job positions must be looked at as "variables." If it is necessary to change the way jobs are designed to insure success, then that's our job.

This is exactly the way we view our own careers. The teacher who designs his job to allow a certain number of hours each week for employer contacts, the supported employment staff person who inaugurates a person-centered career planning process for an individual; all of these individuals are creating jobs by solving problems rather than carrying out pre-set lists of tasks.

In fact, hardly any jobs in the economy are as "fixed" as they look from a distance. If you observe carefully, over time, you will see gradual changes in the structure of various jobs and the responsibilities attached to various positions. These are precipitated by:

- *Work force changes*, such as when jobs turn over or employees learn new skills. For example, the new waiter is taking a while to build up as much speed as the one who left, so another waiter takes over an extra table.

- *Business changes*, such as fluctuations in volume or product developments. For example, business picks up at the restaurant and neither waiter has the time he used to have to reset the tables and help with stock, so a kitchen helper is hired.

- *Personal advocacy*, such as gravitating towards a more interesting part of a job or jockeying for power within an organization. For example, the new kitchen helper hopes to manage a restaurant some day and spends as much time as possible helping with stock inventory and purchasing.

Because so many factors are continually in flux, if you isolate any one particular point in time in a company, department, or a work group and study it closely, you will find conflicts, inefficiencies, and / or gaps in performance with reference to the work the group is supposed to be doing. Each of these inefficiencies represents some degree of waste, although often in a form that is hard to notice and measure.

- Some tasks may be "tacked on" to someone's job that really don't fit with the rest of the job,
- Some tasks may simply be left undone or done very poorly,
- Some tasks may be done in a haphazard way by whoever can get to them,
- Some people may be frantically trying to keep up while others seem to always be on break, and
- Workers may have ongoing disputes over who is responsible for what and form cliques to complain about one another.

Employment specialists study these processes and use them to broker satisfactory employment situations for the people they represent and the employers looking to hire them.

The Job Creation Process

In order to successfully make a proposal to a company for an individually designed job, or to interest an employer in altering an existing job description, we

---

ACE TRAVEL AGENCY, 1:25 PM

Lisa, the office manager, sorts the afternoon mail. The office doesn't really have a secretary; any agent picks up outside phone calls and receives in-person visitors. Everyone types his or her own forms and correspondence. Fred, a customer, is trying to explain to Betty, an agent, the same information he just finished explaining to Larry, another agent on the phone to someone else. Don, the newest agent, has been in the storeroom for the past 20 minutes looking for brochures he needs. Nobody has had time to organize the storeroom since last year's move and it's piled to the ceiling with who-knows-what. If he finds what he needs, he will stamp the agency's address stamp on the back and mail it out.

Are there any functions in this office that could be made more efficient? Are there any duties being performed by people who appear overqualified for them? Do you think this office is unusual?

need to create a relationship in which the issue of how labor problems get solved — which tasks get assigned to whom — is open for discussion. We need to establish a deeper relationship with a company than simply referring applicants to fill existing job openings.

Once we get in the habit of viewing our role as a brokering or consulting process, and businesses as a type of customer of our services, we can approach employers as any supplier approaches any customer. There are levels of depth in the involvement with a customer, and the approach, negotiating style, and duration of the relationship determine at which level the relationship takes place.

At the topmost level, suppliers merely fill predetermined customer needs. For example, a cosmetics salesperson sells the particular product a customer asks about. Or a computer company sells hardware and software to a business for spreadsheet and word processing . At the second, deeper level, suppliers help

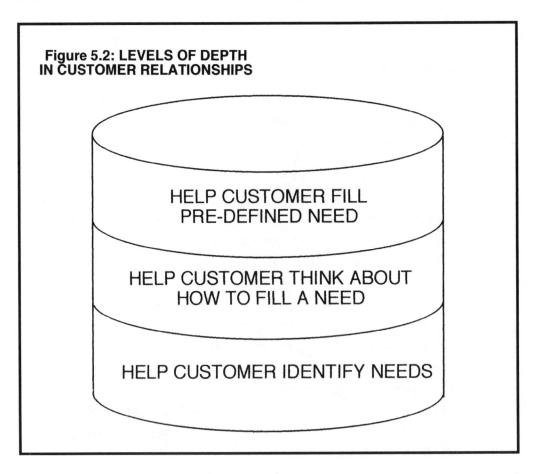

Figure 5.2: LEVELS OF DEPTH IN CUSTOMER RELATIONSHIPS

HELP CUSTOMER FILL
PRE-DEFINED NEED

HELP CUSTOMER THINK ABOUT
HOW TO FILL A NEED

HELP CUSTOMER IDENTIFY NEEDS

customers think about how to fill a need the customer identifies. The cosmetic salesperson suggests a skin softener. The computer company helps the business pick out the right external hard drive to back up records. At the third and deepest level of involvement, a supplier helps the company identify its needs and possibly plan for what it will need in the future. The cosmetics salesperson convinces the customer's spouse to try a new hair-thickening shampoo. The computer company demonstrates the power of an interoffice electronic mail system with connected terminals.

The work of an employment consultant can be viewed in the same way, with job development at the top level of involvement and various degrees of job creation at deeper levels. The groundwork for this type of involvement is established through marketing and job development.

- An employer contact campaign rooted in a career vision and capitalizing on the person's unique assets and interests sets the stage for a personal discussion with employers of what a person has to offer, in a context disconnected from the employer's immediate need to fill openings.

- Employers contacted through personal network ties are more likely to be willing to listen to a proposal and be receptive to multiple meetings, tours, and other approaches.

- Employee-centered and company-centered discussions with employers establish a productive partnership in which company needs and job seeker assets are the focus of discussion. There have been cases where an employer, after meeting an individual and finding out about his assets, offered the individual a job simply because he or she knew there was a place for those skills at the company, without knowing exactly in which job. More commonly, the employer compares the information obtained about an individual's strengths and wishes to current and projected labor needs and comes back with a job offer. Most common is the scenario whereby discussions, tours and observations lead to a job creation proposal which a company considers, modifies, and eventually accepts.

Job creation is not "make work" because it is economically valuable to the company. Unless a company, plant or department is in the initial planning phase

— in which case all of the job positions can be defined from scratch — job creation occurs in one of five ways:

CUT AND PASTE

— One or more tasks are taken from one position and added to another, either in return for a "trade" with some other task(s) or a salary differential. For example, checking invoices is removed from the Stock Clerk's job and given to the Floor Model Assembler, who in return no longer has to sweep up his area. This method is illustrated schematically below.

Before—	JOB 1	JOB 2	After—	JOB 1	JOB 2
	task a	task d		task a	task w
	task b	task w		task b	task x
	task c	task x		task c	task y
	task y	task z		task d	task z
	task e			task e	

FISSION

— One job is divided into two or more jobs, creating a new position. For example, instead of the Machine Tool Specialist being responsible for packaging completed parts for shipping, a Machine Tool Specialist's Helper position is created, who takes each completed part and packs it in its crate.

Before—	JOB 1	After—	JOB 1	JOB 2
	task a		task a	task x
	task x		task b	task y
	task b		task c	task z
	task y			
	task c			
	task z			

FUSION

— Pieces of two or more jobs that are similar are combined from several jobs into one new job. For example, all of the photocopying in the secretarial pool is funnelled to a new Photocopier position.

Before—	JOB 1	JOB 2	JOB 3	JOB 4	
	task a	task f	task l	task q	
	task b	task g	task m	task u	
	task p	task h	task n	task v	
	task c	task i	task o	task w	
	task d	task q	task p	task x	

After —	JOB 1	JOB 2	JOB 3	JOB 4	JOB 5
	task a	task f	task l	task u	task p
	task b	task g	task m	task v	task q
	task c	task h	task n	task w	
	task d	task i	task o	task x	

MARGINAL TASKS

— Tasks that are not being done at all, are done poorly, are not done often enough, or are not clearly anyone's responsibility are identified and collected into a position. Some examples: Careful inspection of incoming parts, removal of obsolete records, rechecking machine-opened envelopes for mistakes, weekly cleaning of municipal busses.

ENLARGING THE PIE

— New market outlets, new suppliers, or new work methods are introduced which increase company sales and justify a new position. For example, capacity to hand-wind electric motors allows a company to expand into experimental and prototype models.

The first three of these techniques are the most frequently used and together they are sometimes known as "job carving." Multiple meetings and workplace visits are usually required, sometimes over a period of many months, to create a job. Very large or bureaucratic firms may have multiple layers of decision-making. Collective bargaining agreements or civil service rules may constrain managers from altering job positions. Any of these situations can be resolved but the process takes longer.

Some cautions should be kept in mind when job creation is being used as an employment strategy for people with disabilities. Many people have the erroneous notion that a person with a disability will enjoy boring, repetitive tasks that no one else likes to do (Olson & Fergusen, 1991) and may, through job creation, relegate people with disabilities to tasks that are less important or that no one else wants.

Second, jobs can be created which are isolated and disconnected from the rest of a workplace and thus make social inclusion difficult. This can be avoided by using the strategies in the following section.

And third, job creators need to be aware that some inefficiencies and some marginal or routine tasks are enjoyable sources of interaction among employees or a welcome break from other tasks. Co-workers may resent a new employee taking away something they used to look forward to. A careful analysis of what people **are currently doing** and **how they view the work** should be conducted before changing the structure of job positions at a workplace.

Background research on a company and presentations to a management group are excellent ways of finding out the needs of a business and obtaining interest in your proposal. Questions asked of a manager or department head in the right way at the right time can assist businesses in thinking differently about their labor needs (Training and Research Institute for People with Disabilities, 1991). For example:

- Do you have any tasks which many employees do that could more efficiently be done as a separate job?

CREATING A JOB OUT OF LEGOS

Have you ever seen the amazing giant sculptures made out of Legos — giraffes, space shuttles, gorillas — on display at malls? These are created by a person named Francie Berger who got her job in an interesting way. She wrote repeatedly to the company explaining about the complex Lego structures she made as a hobby and eventually they gave in and asked her to bring one in to show them. She convinced the Lego company that if they hired her, her sculptures would inspire people to buy more Legos and the position would pay for itself. Francie created her own job out of a leisure interest, and the job later expanded to include supervising a staff of model designers and builders.　　　　— Source: *3-2-1-Contact*, October, 1991

- Do employees have duties which take time away from their main area of expertise?

- Are there tasks which you would like to see done more often or that are not being done at all at the present time?

- Are there busy times of the day or week when you could use extra help?

- Do you routinely pay for overtime work or temporary work services?

- Do you have a problem with any aspect of your production being behind schedule or employees you feel are overburdened?

One job creation idea is to initially negotiate a core set of tasks and identify additional tasks to be either added later or begun but with looser quantity or quality requirements to start. Job creation can also be a post-employment strategy for career advancement. With experience, companies come to be more familiar and comfortable with diversity and job creation to fit people's real talents to what the company needs to get done.

DESIGNS FOR
SOCIAL INCLUSION

Social inclusion is critical to job success and needs to be considered as part of the job design process. How a job is designed will either foster or inhibit opportunities for an employee to be included as a member of a work group and get to know his or her co-workers.

There are some general features of job designs which are more likely than others to lead to social inclusion and these features should be built, whenever possible, into the job structure. They do not guarantee inclusion, but they give inclusion a start in the right direction. When these features are lacking, the outcome of satisfactory inclusion is less probable. It is seldom possible to incorporate all of these elements into each job, but a few can almost always be included.

How much social interaction a job seeker wants or feels comfortable with should also be considered in the job design. Some employees enjoy individual tasks and infrequent interactions with others. But a sense of inclusion in the culture, at whatever level of interaction is appropriate, is an important goal.

WORKERS ADD VALUE IN MANY WAYS

Jim's job helping people with disabilities resolve complaints about their services involved occasional meetings at a local law office. Jim noticed on these visits that the hallways were crowded with file cabinets, so crowded in fact that the office was worried that wheelchair users might have trouble getting through the halls. By asking a few questions, Jim found out that many of the file contents were obsolete and could be discarded, but someone would have to go through each one carefully because there were also some records that did have to be kept.

Jim made an appointment with the Director to explain that he knew a person who would love to work in a law office because he was very interested in protecting the rights of people and also wanted a job involving filing or other clerical work, and asked if it would be possible to establish a position to deactivate the old files. The Director was polite but skeptical, especially about whether any money was available to devote to this purpose, but he did agree to meet with the individual, Paul, and the meeting went well.

Jim made sure to mention on subsequent visits how Paul was doing and that he was still interested. One of the lawyers concerned about how embarrassing it might be for the firm to have problems complying with the Americans with Disabilities Act also helped. Behind the scenes, this lawyer "championed" the need to get the file cabinets out of the halls. After about five months, the Director called Paul and offered him the job. Jim accompanied Paul to a second meeting where the work schedule, salary, supervision, training, and other details were finalized.

Full Work Shifts

Many supported employees work part-time. In some companies, many other positions are also part-time. Four or five hours may be a full work day. But in other companies, supported employees are obtaining part-time jobs in situations where other employees work a longer day or week.

Sometimes an individual is truly unable — physically or emotionally — to sustain seven or eight hours of work per day, and part-time work is therefore a legitimate accommodation to the person's disability. There may be other instances where an individual's unique circumstances make part-time work part of his ideal job specifications. (Fear of losing public benefits is seldom a sufficient justification for working only part-time. Most full-time employees can make use of the work incentives described later in this chapter and retain benefits.) But in most cases, the decision to develop part-time work is made not for any of these reasons but because it is assumed that people with disabilities want or need short work schedules or because it is more convenient for the employment support service organization's staffing patterns or transportation schedules.

Working fewer hours than one's co-workers seriously diminishes opportunities for inclusion. In Chapter 2 we saw that the beginning and end of work shifts are important social times. Greetings and daily planning are common at the beginning, and socializing to "wind down" may occur at the end. A work week may have it's own particular rhythm as well. Participation in these rhythms builds bonds among workers because they share the same experience of the stresses and satisfactions of employment. A person who "comes and goes," who is only partially present, misses these times and may not be perceived as sharing equally in the job.

If for some reason an employee requires a shorter number of work hours, employment consultants should carefully examine the rhythm of the particular work setting and try to capture within a work schedule the most social times of the day in an individual's shift. A fewer number of work days of the same length may be better than a shorter length for each day. This will depend on other people's schedules and job requirements. If possible, any partial shifts should overlap with lunch time at the setting.

Intersecting and Overlapping Tasks

Interactions with other people are built into the design of most jobs. Workers either have to complete jobs together, in pairs or as members of a team, or workers have to communicate with or give things to or get things from one another. **Overlapping tasks** (which two or more people do together) and **intersecting tasks** (where two or more people have to communicate about their tasks or one person's task begins where another person's ends) are important to social inclusion.

Functional, task-oriented relationships at work provide part of the sense of community workers' experience at a job site (Pretty & McCarthy, 1991). Workers usually try to work interactively whenever possible. For example, two housekeepers may clean rooms together, or next to each other rather than starting at opposite ends of a hallway, or two stock clerks may select boxes next to one another from among a roomful of boxes to open. They do this in part because there are economies involved in sharing and helping, and in part so they can enjoy each other's company and "make the time go faster."

Planning for ways in which tasks can intersect or overlap with those of co-workers should be a part of the initial design of a job. When tasks overlap or intersect, a "co-worker" becomes someone who shares the same experiences and confronts the same problems, not merely someone who walks past or works nearby. Task-oriented communications and bonds can then spill over into more social connections and non-work topics because work forms the "bridge" that connects the individuals. It can be more difficult to form a relationship with a co-worker with whom one shares, say, break time or the same bus ride, but no overlapping or intersecting tasks at work itself.

Supported employment personnel are often trained to view positions as isolated, and design jobs with little overlap or intersection. Some supported employment personnel believe that the workers they serve will become confused or distracted if their jobs require a lot of interaction; others simply find it easier to analyze and teach isolated jobs because there are fewer and simpler variables to deal with.

It is true that communication can be unpredictable and complex. But employees are far more likely to become confused from too little communication than from too much communication. And even if social complexities slow training down, the advantages of relationships gained generally far outweigh the disadvantages. Interactions should be built into the design of a job at several points during the course of the work day.

Even if the work is self-contained, checkpoints should be built into job designs when the individual can check in with co-workers and supervisors at various points in the work day. For example, being responsible for a specific assembly operation in a department may seem like a potentially isolated position. Other related work can be explored to facilitate interdependence. Perhaps the materials need to be replenished periodically, or completed work may need to be delivered. These elements become even more important for jobs that are relatively fixed in one physical place.

For employees with speech that is difficult to understand or who use different

---

JOB REDESIGN FOR INTERDEPENDENCE

George was responsible for deburring and other re-work on plastic parts in a manufacturing plant. He placed completed parts in cartons on a pallet in the corner for the shipping clerk but did not interact with the shipping clerk or hardly any other employees at the plant except to say "Hi" as they walked past. George indicated to the employment consultant that he felt isolated and unhappy.

After studying the work procedures in the department more thoroughly, the consultant worked with the employer to redesign the job. George now had to bring each completed carton into the shipping room, place it on a scale, and call the shipping clerk over to verify the weight. When a shipment was ready to go out, the shipping clerk would call George, who had to stop what he was doing and help load the cartons onto the truck.

---

communication systems, job-related communication is easier to achieve than purely informal communication. There are concrete referents in the environment and work schedule that can be pointed to, gestured about, or guessed at. Informal interactions can develop from these communications.

It is a good idea to have a specific person to report to at the beginning of a shift, either for a work assignment, to check for any daily variations in work routine, or just for a greeting. The individual can be the supervisor or a co-worker. But an individual should not simply start work in an isolated way without some social contact with those at the workplace.

Shared Places, Tools and Equipment

Our sense of community and social bond with others is based on the things and places we share, rather than things that are private and individual. The center of many old towns is still called the "commons," the place held in common by the townsfolk (originally, for grazing animals). Workplaces also have their commons: places, tools and equipment shared among workers. Some examples include:

- Supply cabinets and supplies
- Tool cribs and tools

- Photocopy machines
- Vending machines
- Break and lunch rooms
- Rest rooms
- Conference rooms
- Elevators
- Mail slots
- Coffee makers, microwave ovens
- Water fountains
- Coat racks

Common spaces at a worksite, like the proverbial water cooler, tend to be where informal communication takes place. There is even a field of architecture devoted to designing work spaces to increase employee communication (Peponis, 1983). And the use of shared tools or equipment inevitably leads to social interaction. For example, an individual responsible for photocopying will arrive at the machine to find someone else making copies and they will negotiate who has more copies to make or who is in more of a rush.

Jobs that include tasks and points in a day where shared equipment and work spaces are used will tend to have more interaction. Employment consultants should build these opportunities into the design of jobs they are helping negotiate.

Contact for Problems and Reports

When care is taken to specify and organize job tasks, there is a hidden danger that the job analysis appears to be taking care of all of the various contingencies and loose ends of the job. Employment specialists should not give the impression that they are designing a job to be so "airtight" that every contingency is taken care of. That is simply not true.

Part of the design of a job should include whom an employee will contact when he or she is having a problem or notices something out of the ordinary. For example, suppose the employee is responsible for placing plastic liners, obtained from a carton in the storeroom, in trash cans. Whom to contact in case the carton is empty can be part of the job design. Sometimes different people are contacted for different problems. Part of the employee's orientation and training should include which types of problems to bring to whom and how to communicate these.

Employees also need to report production tallies, status reports, and other information to someone. A regular negotiated schedule helps both to insure ongoing social contact and also to avoid a situation where a person is seeking approval too often or from inappropriate people. If these are not taken care of in initial negotiations, there is the danger that the employee or employer, or both, will expect the employment consultant to solve problems.

Chain of Command

Every employee needs a person responsible for checking her work, resolving difficulties, giving assignments and evaluating performance; in short, a supervisor. And it is best if not more than one person has this role. Some supervisory functions can be delegated to a a quasi-supervisor if the particular issues he or she is in charge of are clear. The method and frequency of performance evaluations should also be specified in job negotiations.

Created jobs can be problematic in that they are often not clearly part of the existing job structure. If supervision is not discussed, the job may be imposing on someone a responsibility he or she was not aware of.

Complete clarity in job design is neither possible nor desirable. It is not possible because employment settings are complex environments with too many unanticipated factors and human variables. It is not desirable because it is precisely the unanticipated, the unclear and the human factors which call for communication among workers. Employment consultants shouldn't try to clarify every task for an individual. There should be an allowance for some leeway and a procedure for interruption. Supervisors should not be given the impression that an employee must stick to an uninterruptable routine unless this is indeed absolutely necessary as an accommodation to disability. It is extremely rare that a person cannot adjust to an interruption of a routine or exception to a rule.

Politically Correct Linkages

Some employees have "political" clout in a setting; that is, their opinions and feelings have influence. Sometimes this follows the formal chain of command but sometimes not. The real power structure may be different than the written or stated organizational hierarchy. For example, in some offices a secretary is a key person with a great deal of influence. If this secretary likes something done in a certain way, a wise employee will adjust to it. The question to ask is "Who can actually influence the success of this job?"

Political realities can be considered in the design of a job. For example, dishwashing tasks can be organized so that the cook's favorite food preparation utensils are cleaned first.

JOB ACCOMMODATION AND DISABILITY

Some features of a job design may be related to the need to accommodate for an individual's disability. The negative attitudes and low expectations that have historically limited opportunities for people with disabilities in the workplace are today recognized as a form of unfair discrimination, and the Americans with Disabilities Act (ADA) now requires most employers of over 25 people (15 after July, 1994) to recruit, hire, train, support, and promote qualified persons with disabilities in a nondiscriminatory way. And nondiscrimination may involve providing specific accommodations to the employee.

The ADA only applies to individuals with disabilities who are qualified to perform the job in question. This means the employee must:

- meet the employer's requirements for the job, such as education, employment experience, skills or licenses.

- be able to perform the *essential job functions* or duties, with or without a *reasonable accommodation*. An employer cannot refuse to hire an employee because a disability prevents him or her from performing duties that are not essential to the job. Individuals who are actively abusing drugs or alcohol or whose behavior poses imminent danger to themselves or others are excluded from these provisions.

The scope of potential accommodations is virtually unlimited, and may include:

- Providing or modifying equipment or devices, such as a telephone amplifier to help an employee hear better;

- Changing a job's routine or location;

- Modified work schedules;

- Reassignment to a more suitable, vacant position;

- Training or personal assistance with an aspect of a job;

- Adjusting or modifying examinations, training materials, or policies;

- Providing readers and interpreters, Braille signs, audiotapes, or other communication assistance;

- Widening doorways and aisles, installing railings and ramps, door handles, and modifying desks and equipment for people who use wheelchairs; or

- Adding lighting to a workstation.

An accommodation is considered "reasonable" unless it poses an "undue hardship" on an employer. This is defined as a significant difficulty or expense, taking into account factors such as cost and the business' resources, given the size and scope of the business.

One outcome of the ADA has been the realization that not only are employees with disabilities able to perform a wide array of work tasks, but most of the accommodations individuals need are inexpensive, simple, and a matter of common sense. Employers and employment consultants should be familiar with job accommodation procedures and potential technology solutions for employees with disabilities in the design of jobs, and in response to work and work performance problems on the job.

Job Analysis

The first step in helping someone be more productive is to understand how a job is performed. This includes analyzing the equipment, environment, work procedures used, materials and other aspects of the job.

A quick way of recording information is to use an instant camera. One can take pictures from various angles of a work area and its setup. Also, the consultant might observe and take notes on methods, times and materials; estimate positions of furniture, pathways, tabletops and equipment to be used; note co-workers' movements and how they relate to the job. This information will be helpful in making a good job match for the employer and prospective employee.

All information should be collected in relation to the specific individual for whom the job is being designed. The job creation process described earlier allows a highly individualized approach in which the job is designed with the individual in mind from the start. Everyone has some assets and some areas where support is needed. The focus should depend on the prospective employee's capabilities and limitations and the expectations of the employer. The *first* challenge will be to identify any potential mismatches between the two.

An example: If an individual must work from a sitting position, it would be important to note whether any materials or equipment are out of reach or will be uncomfortable to use. Look for situations in the procedure which may lead to fatigue or inefficiency. If the person has difficulty mastering certain kinds of skills, look at the steps of the tasks, when they occur and how they relate to the completed work.

Adaptive Solutions

The *second* challenge is to develop as many alternative solutions to the identified areas of concern in the job analysis as possible. This requires determining what changes in the setting would enhance the performance of the person doing the job. Researching what others have done can save time and effort, since someone may have already figured out a solution to a problem. There are databases such as the Job Accommodation Network (JAN), and catalogues and books on rehabilitation technology and hardware. Occupational therapists have a great deal to offer, provided they visit the actual work site and have a specific accommodation goal to achieve. The U.S. Rehabilitation Services Administration has established a technical assistance center in each of its ten regions for assistance in implementing the ADA.

Most technology professionals recommend a review of "off the shelf," easily available supplies, such as those obtainable from a hardware store or office supply catalogue, as a starting point. One advantage of this is that the user is portrayed as less different by not requiring unusual technology. Also, the solutions tend to be simple, inexpensive, understandable, and repairable or replaceable without a lot of difficulty. Another source of information on possible adaptations is the employer. A shop supervisor or maintenance personnel, for example, may have an excellent command of the most feasible ways to modify a piece of equipment.

Challenge number *three* is to select and implement the accommodation. Decisions should be made based on availability, safety, price, design and speed of obtaining. In addition, *special care should be taken to be sure the employee, employer and co-workers understand and support the suggested accommodations.*

The primary goal is to achieve safely the necessary performance with a modification that is stable, strong, predictable and as cost effective as possible. The accommodation should accomplish:

COMPLEX TERM; SIMPLE PROCESS

Most job accommodations are a matter of "common sense." Toni worked as a baker's assistant. She was not able to follow the written recipes and job lists posted in the baking area. After several other ideas were unsuccessful, the employment consultant asked the employer if photographs could be used to label supplies and to represent the jobs which needed to be completed.

This meant that to some degree the supply room would need to be reorganized and labeled. The employer was willing to try, but was clearly skeptical. The employment consultant photographed all of the needed items and attached one set of photos to the supply shelves. Another set was provided to the employer, each with velcro on the back so the employer could attach them to an "assignment board" in the order in which he wished each recipe to be completed.

Toni responded immediately to the new system, increasing her output significantly. The employer was delighted with her productivity and quality. Interestingly, the other co-workers quickly adapted to the system as well and the number of mistakes made in the area decreased markedly.

- Improved productivity,
- Reduced fatigue,
- Proper positioning,
- Better potential for socialization and co-worker support, and
- Minimal stigma related to the disability.

The individual for whom the accommodation is developed needs to be actively involved in developing and trying out the accommodation. An accommodation that seems appropriate to others may not feel right or be acceptable to the individual, and the individual will not use or be happy with it. The opposite might also be the case.

Accommodations range in cost from those that cost nothing to costly high technology. Most employees will not require a costly accommodation. According to one study (Harold Russell Associates, 1982), over half of reported accommodations cost nothing; over two-thirds cost less than $100.

Inexpensive. Keep an open, creative mind to equipment and procedures. In one instance, attaching a broomstick to a dustpan allowed a maintenance person to complete a cleaning operation. In another, moving a table eight inches and changing the location of some materials helped an individual increase productivity by 55%. Many changes are simple adjustments and "lo-tech" applications of fixtures, schedules, Velcro, foam, snaps, pictures or key rings.

Mid-priced . A number of accommodations may fall into the $50-250 range, and include electronic timers, digital watches, audio amplifiers, large button phones, buzzers, large print materials, computer switches or "Walkman"-style tape players.

High Technology. More expensive technology should not be eliminated from the menu of options, especially for larger companies where they would not impose an undue hardship. Some individuals may rely on computer systems which respond to eye gaze, interactive visual symbols for communication or simplified input devices such as using head-controlled pointers or enlarged keyboards.

SALARIES AND BENEFITS

One responsibility of an employment consultant might be to represent the job seeker and negotiate fair remuneration for the individual's contribution to the company. How much an individual's work is "worth" can be difficult to assess, especially if one is just entering the workforce. Most employers recognize this difficulty and offer a entry wage that gets reviewed after some trial period, sometimes called "probation."

This trial period is an important one. The employment consultant and employer should agree on a fair probationary period for the employee to demonstrate potential. Most employers understand that they will pay at least the federal minimum wage, and negotiations begin from that point.

People disagree on whether there is ever a justification for paying subminimum wages to employees with severe disabilities. Some argue that if a nation has determined a certain wage as the *minimum* (with no measurements of workers without disabilities to determine whether or not their productivity meets any particular standard), then this should be the minimum compensation for any individual's hour of work. Others routinely "market" supported employees at subminimum wage rates.

A pragmatic position between these two might be that the availability of subminimum wages is a legitimate tool to open a door that might otherwise remain closed because an individual's work output is very low, but that the tool should be used only under very restrictive conditions:

- Every effort should be made to develop jobs and provide accommodation and supports such that each individual is productive enough to be paid the prevailing wage,

- The possibility of subminimum wages should not be used as a general marketing tool to entice employers,

- The job appropriately matches an individual's job specifications,

- But the level of productivity has become a legitimate employer concern, and despite all efforts at accommodation, low speed or an ability to do only a few parts of a job will bar the individual from obtaining the job.

Under these conditions, the mechanisms for payment of less than the federal minimum wage should be available.

Payment Options and Productivity

Many providers of supported employment services are familiar with the productivity measurement procedures prevalent within sheltered workshops. Workshops have developed methods of measuring productivity and paying wages below the usual minimum wage that are acceptable to the Department of Labor. Briefly, these procedures involve:

- Identifying a "prevailing wage" for a given type of work;

- Establishing a "norm," or hourly production quantity supposed to represent the average amount of work a worker receiving the prevailing wage might produce. Usually work is "time-studied" by sampling and averaging the performance of staff members or other nondisabled workers, making allowances for a certain amount of fatigue and delays in an actual production situation;

- Either a rate per piece of work is established and pay is based on a daily count of quantity, or an hourly rate is established by sampling an individual's production periodically and comparing this to the norm. A measure of quality is also entered into the hourly wage equation.

Although this process is legal, it involves a host of assumptions whose accuracy has never been fully explored:

- That occupation types represent the same work across a community and that the scope of a "community" can be identified;
- That the people performing "time studies" might actually be hired to do the tasks being studied;
- That those people would be paid the "prevailing wage" for that amount of work;
- That the amount of time sampled is a true representative sample;
- That the allowance for fatigue and delay is legitimate;
- That knowing they are being tested does not affect the performance of the people performing time studies, and
- That under usual performance conditions, people produce 100% quality work.

Even more questionable is the narrow view of productivity implied by this measurement process. Employers seldom measure work in anything like the way it is measured in sheltered workshops. For most employers, when a job is completed as it should be and when it should be, it is 100% complete. For example, if an employee is responsible for bussing and wiping tables in a restaurant, if there is always a clean table for a customer entering the restaurant, production is full and complete. The employee is doing the whole job. If customers wait too long for a table or complain to the manager, there is a problem.

Also, productivity includes the entire economic contribution of the worker to a company. Employees contribute to companies in all sorts of ways. They may contribute by being dependable, by responsibly following work routines, by being meticulous about noticing any defects in materials or other problems, or by being prompt in tackling assignments and honest about mistakes. They may help maintain team morale, provide emotional support to others, be pleasant to customers, be helpful to co-workers, or instill a spirit of cooperation or accom-

---

PRODUCTIVITY IS IN THE EYE OF THE EMPLOYER

Dottie, who works at a card and gift store, is slow in completing her cleaning and organizing of stock. By traditional time study methods, her productivity is measured at about 16% of the "competitive norm." Her employer, however, is pleased to have her as an employee and does not measure her contribution in this way. Stock is never misplaced or mishandled, and customers often remark on how clean the store is kept.

Dottie is very social, fun-loving, and friendly. Employee morale in the store has improved since she was hired. Dottie has also connected quite well to a large number of customers. Many of these customers make a point of stopping in to see her, and making a purchase while they are there. In recognizing Dottie's value, the employer sees beyond her output in the cleaning task itself and considers her to be doing "100%" of what is expected, and Dottie's wages reflect this.

---

plishment within a work culture. By ignoring these variables, or by placing people in settings where major assets are underused or undervalued, we undervalue the contribution a worker makes to a business. Measured productivity should always be compensated but should only be the "bottom line," not the ceiling in wage negotiations.

A better way to look at salaries is to look comprehensively at the value the employee is adding to the employer's product or service, emphasize that value to the employer, and negotiate a salary that fairly represents that value. If that amount happens to still fall below the minimum wage, two payment mechanisms are available:

- A subminimum wage certificate held by the employer.

- A subcontract relationship to an employment service with a subminimum certificate.

Direct company employment is by far the better option, since subcontracted employment less than a full employment relationship with the company. Appropriate uses of a contract relationship might be:

- Short-term tryouts for people undecided about what direction to take;

- Expandable sites that might accommodate an individual who is between jobs and needs to remain employed (see Chapter 9).

Employer benefits and perks should also be considered in salary negotiations. If an individual is to work full time, he or she should expect the same benefits and same commitment as other employees in similar positions. This might also include unwritten benefits, such as free lunch at a restaurant. If these are informally identified as privileges, they should be available to all employees of the business.

Retaining Public Benefits

As adults with disabilities begin their careers, they and the people supporting them need to deal with issues related to the impact of wages on public benefits they may depend on. Foremost among these are the Social Security programs. Negotiating the maze of the Social Security system requires a basic understanding of terms and programs.

The Social Security Disability Insurance (SSDI) program is for people who have worked and paid social security taxes for one quarter or more each year after age 21 and become disabled and unable to work at a level called Substantial Gainful Activity (SGA, generally $500 in 1992). A person whose disability occurred before age 22 may collect benefits if his/her parent is eligible for Social Security. People receiving SSDI are called "beneficiaries." The benefit amount is determined by how much an individual paid into the system. A person can have unearned income and resources of any magnitude and still collect SSDI. SSDI beneficiaries are eligible for Medicare.

There are three work incentive provisions for people on SSDI:

Trial Work Period. Designed to allow a beneficiary to "test" work ability, the trial work period provides the usual SSDI cash benefits for nine months (not necessarily consecutive) in which the beneficiary has gross earnings of more than $200.00. To be eligible, an individual must meet the initial SSA definition of disability with at least five years between "disability periods."

Extended Period of Eligibility. SSDI beneficiaries who have used their nine trial work months begin an extended period of eligibility for the next 36 consecutive months. Any month during this time that the beneficiary earns over a certain amount in gross income, he/she will not get a disability check.

Reducing Countable Earned Income. A beneficiary's counted income may be reduced below the SGA limit so that the individual may continue to get checks in addition to wages. These reductions cannot be used during the nine-month trial SSDI work period. If the beneficiary can show that he/she was paid an amount higher than he or she would have earned without special supervision and support, the additional amount is considered a *subsidy* and is discounted from earnings. Subsidies include on-the-job training reimbursements and situations where supervisors or co-workers provide significant support to the employee, whether or not the employee pays for them.

Another technique is to average earnings for several months when wages fluctuate. If the average is less than the minimum, this can maintain benefits. Expenses an employee pays related to the disability and necessary in order to work, called Impairment Related Work Expenses (IRWEs, discussed below) can also be subtracted from gross earnings to help retain SSDI.

Supplemental Security Income (SSI) is designed for people who meet disability requirements and who are in financial need. The applicant must show financial need by having countable income (gross income minus applicable exclusions) below SGA and limited resources.

People who receive SSI are called "recipients" and the monthly SSI check varies as income varies. Estimates of income from the previous two months are used to calculate the payment amount. The SSI program includes Medicaid coverage, including extended medical benefits despite increased earnings once a recipient has been on the rolls for one month. Two important work incentive provisions are available to recipients.

Impairment-Related Work Expenses. As for SSDI, expenses related to a disability and necessary for the individual to work can be disregarded from earned income in payment calculations. The recipient usually retains about $1 for every $2 spent.

Plan to Achieve Self-Support. This provision, called a PASS Plan, allows workers to recoup expenses they incur to achieve a career goal, up to the SSI maximum benefit. PASS is available to SSI recipients and has also been used by SSDI beneficiaries to lower their counted income enough to become SSI-eligible. The

PASS must include a specific occupational objective, a budget of expenses and income, timeframes, how the money will be spent and why these expenses are needed to achieve the goal. Funds can be used for purchasing services, equipment, supplies, training, transportation, or anything needed to assist a person to find and keep a job. It is often useful to enlist the help of a state vocational rehabilitation counselor to write a PASS Plan, but any recipient can submit his or her own plan with or without assistance. The local Social Security Office will review the plan and must provide written approval or denial. If the plan is denied, the Social Security Office is required to state what is wrong with the plan. It can then be resubmitted with the required changes.

SUMMARY

A job offer is usually finalized through some form of negotiation in which an employer and employee agree on the details of the job. Individuals and organizations assisting job seekers with disabilities act as "brokers" to help design satisfactory arrangements. Attention to such job design features as full work shifts, points of task intersection or overlap with co-workers, sharing the use of places, tools and equipment, clear lines of supervision, and attention to workplace "politics" sets the stage for inclusion and support for a new employee.

Job creation can be a natural outcome of an individualized career planning and employer negotiation process, and is an especially important tool for job seekers who are less able to compete for established job openings. Job creation results in a position that reflects the unique assets of a job seeker and meets a specific company's labor need.

Every employer provides "job accommodations" for employees with and without disabilities. Such accommodations pay off in incresed productivity and improved morale. Job accommodations to a disability are also required by law of many employers. Most cost little and are easily developed using existing employer and employee resources. In some cases employers need help from an agency to design, implement, or pay for a particular accommodation.

In negotiating salaries and benefits, the impact of working on public benefits must be carefully weighed and work incentive provisions of programs used when needed. Alternative wage mechanisms can make community employment available to individuals whose rate of productivity is low, but these should be used with extreme care and only under very specific circumstances.

CHAPTER 6

Employee Training

"Although life may turn out to be a messy affair, it's still life and not a series of extractions of square roots."
—Fyodor Dostoyevsky

It's your first day of work. You're excited but a little nervous. The job has been explained to you and you think you understand what you're supposed to do, but there's a lot of things you are not sure about. Everyone else looks like they know exactly what to do. How do you learn what is expected and how to do well at the job? How did *they*?

General information will only take you so far. You might know how to run a photocopying machine, but the machine in this office has some "quirks" to it. And how do you know when it's expected to let someone else go ahead of you and when it's OK to make them wait? Where do they keep the toner for this machine? And who is responsible for calling when it doesn't work?

Every company has it's own "ways of doing things around here" (Deal and Kennedy, 1982) and procedures for passing on information and skills related to the job to new employees: specific information, specific work methods and specific social customs. The day a supported employee shows up for work will not be the first time an employer confronts the issue of training new employees. Employees "pick up" some information by watching and copying those around them. Other information is specifically taught to new employees by more experienced employees. This guiding and tutoring of less experienced employees is called *mentoring*, after a character in Greek mythology named Mentor, to whom Odysseus entrusted the care and education of his son, Telemachus.

Mentors are a valuable resource for providing support for new employees, both with and without disabilities. Yet the development of a mentor relationship is often overlooked by supported employment agencies. Understanding the various roles of someone on the inside who can provide information and support, and developing a closer partnership with businesses will help achieve a satisfactory mix of internal company resources and outside agency expertise.

Agencies take over the training function not because companies demand it or because employees require it but because agencies are following a rote "job coach model" of services and are unsure of the proper strategies for working with co-worker trainers. One study (McConaugh, Curl & Salzberg, 1987) reported that about 40% of companies prefer to conduct their own training, with assistance and consultation, than have an outside person do the training. Supported employees also may have strong opinions about whom they wish to have as a trainer. Many agencies have reported instances where supported employees have deliberately worked less well in the presence of an agency job coach, or have asked the individual to leave. There can also be the reverse problem. When a job coach takes over the training and support function on the job, that person then has a hard time leaving the job site so that the supported employee can work as part of the work culture. This difficulty in "fading" from the job site is generally due to the intense interdependent relationship that develops between job coach and supported employee, effectively screening out the potential for more natural mentor and co-worker relationships.

Companies like to have control over their human resources and training is a critical component. But companies do appreciate having access to new ideas, new management tools, and new skills. These can be provided in a way that does not circumvent company control over training. Programs which work with trainers who come from the ranks of the employer are able to make better use of agency personnel and provide better quality employment services.

Identifying a mentor, arranging a training schedule and other details, and working as a consultant to a co-worker mentor are covered in this chapter. Issues involved in helping individuals to learn their jobs, obtain help with job problems, and learn self-instruction strategies are discussed.

THE MENTOR ROLE

Some larger companies have developed structured mentorship programs (Lawrie, 1989) and some have even established internal job coaching projects specifically for their employees with disabilities (Fabian & Leucking, 1991). Other companies may benefit from instituting such formal programs. If a company is interested in the mentoring process, you might suggest the possibility of your consulting with them on a wider project that includes all new employees.

But accessing company supports does not require a formal program. In fact, most mentoring is informal. The supervisor tells Joe, "Go around with Fred. He'll show you what to do." Fred then "shows the ropes" to Joe, introducing him to other employees, explaining the work and the social aspects of the job, and answering questions. There is some evidence that less formal, more spontaneous mentoring arrangements are more effective than formal mentor programs (Noe, 1988). Whether formal or informal, mentors are extraordinarily important. One study (Greenhaus, 1987) found that employees who had experienced a mentor relationship earned more money and were more likely to stick to a consistent career path.

Mentors serve a number of functions. The most obvious is that of teaching the job to a new employee. But the role of mentor can be more expansive than job training and include other important functions as well.

Information about personalities and politics. Succeeding in a company requires working with individual personalities and dealing with the realities of various workplace relationships. How to figure out the boss' moods, how much real power the secretaries have, who the troublemakers are — all may be essential to survival on the job. As survivors, mentors have abundant information of this nature. One mentor, seeing that a new employee was upset over being reprimanded by the supervisor, told the employee "You don't have to worry when the boss yells at you. The time to worry is when he doesn't say anything."

Tricks of the trade. Experienced workers build up a vast storehouse of important information and technical skill through experience at their jobs. They are able to point out the best tool to use, what to bring with you to save a trip back down the stairs, how to perform a task most efficiently, which day of the week is the busiest, and many other key tips. A lot of this expertise is local and situational. Rarely is it written down, and people may not even be conscious of how much they know until they begin explaining it. Experienced workers may be justly proud of their expertise and glad to have a chance to share it and even "show off" a little as they do.

Passing along tricks of the trade is a way of demonstrating self-worth and status. Some employees consider showing the ropes to a new employee one of the more enjoyable aspects of their job.

Not all tricks of the trade are known to or authorized by the managers of a company. For example, a mentor may instruct an employee to work slower than necessary. In extreme cases, a mentor's instructions may even violate company policy or the law. This difficult issue is discussed in Chapter 7.

Initiation. Various initiation practices and rituals may be developed by a work group for new recruits. In part, employees, especially in what are called "blue collar" jobs, develop initiation rites as a way of asserting a small or even symbolic control over their work environment. Some initiation rites function as a kind of unauthorized "job interview" to screen new recruits, who may be driven to quit if the group feels they do not fit in. The message is something like this: "The boss isn't the only one you have to deal with here. You also have to play the game our way." Initiation rites also create a sense of cohesion for a group. One aspect of belonging comes from sharing the same experience of the initiation. Workplace initiations usually involve a small prank or other humorous event.

Introductions. People need to be introduced into social situations; "sponsored" is perhaps the best word to describe this process. A work group is like a club with its own admission policies. The best person to "get you in" is the person with good connections. Mentors are able to invite the new person to sit with a group at lunch. They may include the individual in conversations or physically position the individual to be included.

Mentors help interpret behavior or characteristics that might be the subject of stereotypes or misinformation. A statement like "he isn't mad at you when he does that" helps interpret a situation that might otherwise be uncomfortable or frustrating. Explanations are easier to understand when they come from someone a co-worker has learned to trust. Members of groups who have been the victims of stereotyping and prejudice find this type of support especially helpful (Raggins, 1989).

Social customs and jargon. Mentors pass on the social customs and the specialized language or jargon of a workplace to newcomers. They tell a new employee how much to contribute each week to the coffee fund, which meetings it's OK to miss and which are absolutely critical, which comments are meant as jokes and which are serious.

Much co-worker communication is in the form of shorthand expressions, jargon or acronyms particular to the workplace. During employee training, co-worker trainers begin by giving full descriptions of tasks to be performed and supplies and equipment to be used, but gradually shift to using

---

ENTRANCE EXAMS AT BEVERAGE BOTTLING

The Beverage Bottling Company issues a uniform to each new employee and stresses an employee's responsibility for the uniform. Then, at the end of the first day, co-workers take the uniform and hide it.

For Albert, the supported employee, wearing a uniform was an important part of his new job and losing his uniform was extremely upsetting. Mike, Albert's co-worker trainer, saw Albert's reaction. He went over to Albert, explained to him that the same thing had happened to him on his first day, and told him where to find his uniform. This probably saved Albert from losing his job. It also helped Albert to handle the stress of the situation and to develop his social skills at the job.

---

shorthand expressions and jargon (Curl, Lignugaris/Kraft, Pawley, & Salzberg, 1990).

Mediation of disputes. Interpersonal disputes are a fact of life in any social situation. Newcomers are bound to make mistakes, misinterpret intentions, and have more trouble getting along with some people than others. Mentors act as allies, mediators or defenders in problem social situations.

Supported employees might find it particularly difficult to negotiate the complexities of some social situations. In one company, most workers listened to a radio station that played country music. The new supported employee preferred rock music and thought nothing of going over to the radio and changing the station. This created a difficult situation for everyone involved. A respected co-worker took charge of this situation and negotiated a treaty that all parties accepted.

Support beyond initial training. Mentors have a kind of continuing investment in the success of an employee with whom they have worked. After all, failure would partly reflect on their mentorship. There is a natural incentive, therefore, for mentors to remain involved and interested beyond the initial training period. A mentor may even keep in contact with an employee after the mentor has moved on to a new job or company, remaining available for advice and support (Kram & Isabella, 1985).

POLITICS AT WORK

Bob, a janitor in a medical transportation company, was told that there were complaints about the quality of his work. The offices weren't being cleaned well. The supported employment agency sent an employment consultant to assist in solving the problem. This job coach had seen enough work settings to know that work problems are often personality problems in disguise, and she took an unusual approach.

Instead of focusing on task analyses and intervention techniques, she found an employee who liked Bob. She asked this employee to help her look over Bob's job. This employee explained that if he had that job, he would clean rooms in "political" order: the Dispatcher's office first because he was the owner's best friend, the Office Manager's area next because she was a complainer, and so on. The consultant reordered Bob's tasks and posted the new list inside his locker. There were no further problems.

ESTABLISHING A MENTOR RELATIONSHIP

The issue of training will usually arise as the agency representative discusses an applicant with the employer. A question like "How do your new employees learn this job?" or "Who will be helping Sally learn the job here?" will lead into a discussion that establishes a training partnership between the agency and the company. This partnership can take innumerable forms. Some companies have orientation sessions or training videotapes for new employees; some even have employee training departments. Whenever possible, training arrangements should include some type of mentorship arrangement with one or more co-workers.

Selecting a Mentor

It is usually best if a mentor is assigned as the trainer for a supported employee as part of the initial employment arrangements by the supervisor or department head. Supervisors may use assignment of mentors as a management tool. The worker chosen to teach the new employee is the one who can best represent the way the job should be done.

An alternative strategy is to start a job without assignment of a mentor and either enlist the help of co-workers as needed later or watch to see which co-worker emerges most receptive to taking on a mentoring role. This procedure can risk some confusion on the part of an employee and resentment on the part of co-workers. If an employee is expected to need specific skill training procedures, or a significantly longer training time than the company has experienced before, then training should be part of the discussions with an employer and not left to chance. The best way to look at it is that the agency will be providing not the training, but the assistance the company needs to adapt its training.

There is seldom a need to specifically mention to a company that a job coach will not be training the supported employee. Companies do not generally expect the training function to be taken over by someone outside the company *unless they have been educated to think that way by the rehabilitition community*. A statement like "I will be available as much as you need to work with your staff on training" communicates the appropriate message. Agency staff should offer to teach, support, and supplement company training as much as is needed but stop short of offering to take care of all of the training.

Workers who are good at their jobs, are respected within the organization, and enjoy guiding new employees make the best mentors. People who have benefitted from a positive mentor relationship themselves are sometimes excellent mentors. The following guidelines are useful in targeting an appropriate mentor for a supported employee:

- Does the individual know his or her job well? Has the individual been doing the job for at least several months?

- Is the individual well liked by other employees?

- Is the person included in the social culture of the workplace? Does he or she have interpersonal skills and perceptions to help in negotiating social relationships?

- Is the individual expected to remain on the job for at least six more months?

- Can the employee be scheduled to work, at least for the next several weeks, on the same work schedule as the supported employee?

- Will the employee agree to accept responsibility for training and to receive the necessary assistance from the consultant?

- If more than one individual fits the above description, one who is newer at the company may remember better what a new person needs to know.

Figure 6.1: Targeting your Co-worker

A supervisor rather than a co-worker may serve as a mentor for a supported employee. The advantages of this are that (a) the supervisor has the authority to make decisions about task reassignment and notifications that may be necessary, and (b) the supervisor is the individual that someone functioning as an employment consultant is likely to be in more contact with. But the disadvantages should also be considered:

- Close association with supervisors can actually hinder social acceptance by line employees in some settings;

- Co-workers may have specific task information that supervisors do not have because supervisors don't actually do the job; and

- In general, supervisors have more demands on their time and are available less consistently than co-workers.

The best arrangement is for a supported employee to have both a supportive supervisor and a co-worker trainer, and to obtain different types of support from each.

Training Schedules and Arrangements

A mentor or co-worker training arrangement may either be "closed-ended" — for a specified number of days or weeks — or "open-ended", for as long as it takes. This should be discussed along with the new employee's schedule and duties. One option for an individual who will require extensive training is to begin with the individual assuming only a few duties. The co-worker teaches these duties for an hour or two each day until they are mastered, then adds new responsibilities. Created jobs lend themselves to this type of arrangement.

Probably the next most common approach is for agency staff to teach a central task which can be assigned to the employee during periods when the co-worker trainer is not available. Other tasks are introduced by the co-worker trainer as time permits.

More than one co-worker can also be assigned, each to teach a part of a job. Direct training of supported employees by the employment consultant can be in the context of demonstrating training techniques or filling in when the co-worker trainer is not available.

Trainer Compensation

Most of the time, activities the mentor performs during his or her normal work hours, including teaching a new employee, are simply a part of the job for which the employee receives his usual salary. If the arrangements include learning about training in an after-work session, or coming in extra early to set things up for the supported employee, then a stipend can be considered. Also, if a company has to reassign employees or lose productivity beyond what can be considered a reasonable accommodation, a training fee can be negotiated with the company.

Local funding agencies such as the state vocational rehabilitation agency or the Job Training Partnership Act (JTPA) agency have established mechanisms for contracting directly with companies for on-the-job training. Or, a supported employment agency can use funds it receives to enter into subcontracts with participating businesses or individual co-workers rather than exclusively employing its own personnel. An employee can also pay a co-worker directly to provide a service they provide on their own time, through a Plan for Achieving Self-Support or as an Impairment-Related Work Expense as discussed in Chapter 5.

A stipend can be a useful and fair means of compensating for some types of support. However, the introduction of a payment risks changing the nature of the relationship from one of equality and mutual support to one of service provider and service recipient. It can position the supported employee as someone in need of care rather than as a peer. These potential disadvantages need to be weighed against the benefits in individual situations.

Some supported employment service providers are skeptical about co-worker training. They feel that many supported employees require specialized training that companies cannot be expected to provide without a promise of agency training. For them, not offering a training package removes a key selling point to supported employment. There are several responses to this position.

Keep in mind that businesses are not in general being asked to do more than they are already accustomed to doing. Orienting and training new employees is a customary procedure. It is sound business management. When that person requires specialized training to succeed, employers should be fully supported, but not supplanted, in their training efforts.

Obtaining jobs in situations where employers are unwilling to make an investment in new employees reaps a short-term gain at the expense of potential long-term difficulties. By promising that agencies will "take care of everything" and by giving the misleading impression that only rehabilitation professionals are qualified to teach employees with disabilities, psychological walls are built around supported employees in the workplace.

Providing extensive or specialized training for an employee with a disability can be a "reasonable accommodation" that a large employer is required to provide under the Americans with Disabilities Act. The appropriate role of the supporting agency should be to keep the employer's accommodation costs and efforts reasonable, but not eliminate them or even eliminate the need for the employer to put more resources into training an employee with a disability than other employees.

Supported employees do offer real and tangible benefits to employers that are more than adequate "selling points."

Businesses which have been previously "sold" on an agency-trainer model of supported employment may now feel cheated when supported employment does not include a trainer. Situations such as these require re-education efforts that often are far more challenging than negotiating new sites. We need to remember, though, that a history of workshop marketing, enclave marketing, and job coach marketing all involved educating employers to disregard the previous message!

Every effort should be made to select a mentor who will commit to giving appropriate notice if he or she changes jobs or elects to discontinue training before it is complete. As a precaution, and to cover for mentor days off due to illness or vacation, sometimes a second back-up co-worker learns to support the teaching strategy. The employment consultant or other employer resources can take over as the back-up to this back-up.

TRAINING THE TRAINER

There is an old saying that goes something like this:

> feed a person bread, and you feed that person once; teach him how to
> bake, and the person can be fed for a lifetime.

Many, though not all, supported employees require specific and detailed training to learn their jobs correctly. One of the most important features of supported employment is its emphasis on systematic instruction to teach job tasks.

These teaching techniques have remained central features of supported employment. But agencies actually have two basic options by which to implement them:

- to directly train each supported employee on each job

- or to impart teaching techniques to employers, giving them the tools with which to teach employees.

Some co-workers are already excellent trainers, through natural talent or through experience being a mentor. Other co-workers are potentially good trainers who need to be shown basic strategies and helped with some of the finer points. Still others may require extensive assistance and back-up efforts but can be successful.

A co-worker or supervisor can begin to learn most of the skills needed to be a competent trainer in a session of no more than a few hours prior to starting the training, or through on-the-job pointers and modeling of the technique by someone with training experience. Specialized training problems can be handled through consultation provided to the company by an employment consultant from a supported employment agency. Arrangements should be established individually with each employer, and countless variations are possible. Three general strategies cover a wide range of training needs: pre-employment co-worker training, on-the-job-training, and a training partnership approach.

Pre-employment Co-worker Training

Some supported employment organizations develop an orientation package for use in training co-worker mentors to provide systematic instruction and use of basic behavioral principles. Any of the numerous job coach training manuals can be used or adapted for co-workers. One method specifically developed for teaching co-workers to be trainers is the "show-tell-teach-watch" approach (Curl & Hall, 1990). Using a videotape and workbook, co-workers learn a specific teaching sequence: the co-worker demonstrates a task, describes how to perform the task, requests that the employee try the task, and then observes whether the employee does it correctly. Co-workers also are shown an approach to common training problems. The strategy takes about two hours to learn. Another manual for explaining training to co-workers has been developed by an organization in Australia (York, 1991).

Pre-employment training of co-workers should be individualized as much as possible and specifically focused on the learning style and training needs of a particular individual. Talking about how to train "people with severe disabilities" rather than about how to teach John or Barbara may convey the false message that "they" are more like other people with severe disabilities in their needs and learning styles than like other non-disabled people — a message contrary to the intent.

Pre-employment training sessions should be small and informal. The "mechanics" of skill training, such as completing data sheets or using stopwatches or counters and making charts, should be introduced only when needed and focused on how to use these procedures with the specific individual the co-worker will train. This avoids projecting an overly "clinical" or impersonal orientation. When supported employment agencies "deputize" a co-worker with too much emphasis on technical skills, they turn co-workers into human service paraprofessionals.

On-the-Job Co-worker Training

Co-workers can learn about training on-the-job by having an employment consultant teach training techniques as the employee begins the job and the co-worker begins training. The employment consultant may provide some initial information in a meeting prior to the start of employment. For example, Gerry learns best when he can watch a task done a few times, then has opportunities to practice it

---

PRE-EMPLOYMENT TRAINING

Ted was scheduled to begin his job as an advertising layout assistant. The advertising company needed someone to review ads carefully and correct minor errors, using a pagemaker computer program. Ted had lost a previous job as a dishwasher because he worked very slowly, but the agency felt that the friendly company atmosphere and the pace of the job, emphasizing quality over speed, might suit Ted's needs.

In developing the job, the employment consultant learned that the advertising manager had had some previous experience teaching people labeled autistic and was willing to teach Ted the job. She spent about two hours on the Thursday before his first day, reviewing some general tips about skill training and also some of Ted's history and learning characteristics. For example, Ted tends to take several minutes to respond to a question, but eventually he will reply.

On the first day, the employment consultant made sure Ted got to work on time, met the manager, and then left the building, leaving a phone number where she could be reached. She returned at the end of Ted's shift to make sure he caught his ride home and then met with the manager for about fifteen minutes to review the day. She continued this practice each day for the first few weeks. At the beginning of the second week, in response to some concerns the manager expressed, she spent the entire day at the site as an observer, then discussed what she had seen with the manager at the end of the day. Using this strategy, Ted learned his job successfully and also became socially connected into the workplace. The employment consultant continued to visit but on a reduced schedule. Even though the consultant and Ted were hardly ever at the job site at the same time, the company felt adequately supported.

with someone guiding him along. The employment consultant explains this to Gerry's co-worker Bill, and gives an example.

Second, the employment consultant accompanies Bill and Gerry, demonstrates and explains a few training ideas to Bill, and observes Bill's instructional procedure with Gerry. The consultant meets with Bill for a short debriefing session once or twice each day to answer questions and give pointers. In this example, Bill has been varying his verbal cues in a way that confuses Gerry. One time he will say "wipe the whole thing" and another time he will say "get the corners too." The employment consultant suggests that Bill stick to one consistent prompt, "Remember the corners," and Gerry learns fairly quickly to do a thorough job.

Third, the employment consultant no longer visits every day but calls Gerry's co-worker trainer once a day for a brief description of training progress, and visits when something comes up that needs attention. This continues until everyone is satisfied that initial training is complete.

The same principle governs the amount of initial information, the length of observation, and the frequency of contacts as governs all supported employment:

As little as possible, as unobtrusive, short-term and culturally normative as possible, but as much as is necessary to get the job done.

An option that may occasionally present itself is to first observe how the mentor teaches another (non-disabled) employee and base consultation on that "baseline" information.

Co-worker/Consultant Partnerships

A third general option is for the external support person and company personnel to divide up responsibility for training by time or by task. For example, the employment consultant may take responsibility for teaching steps of a task that will probably take a great many trials or occur at a point in the day when a co-worker cannot be available. The co-worker is assigned to teach the remaining tasks. The more responsibility the external trainer has, the more this option resembles traditional job coaching, but the company is in charge and the co-worker trainer has an important role.

Even small amounts of co-worker training give a sense of confidence to the company. For example, if a co-worker has responsibility to spot-check at 2:00

ON-THE-JOB TRAINING

Barbara, the head housekeeper, was assigned to teach Rose her new house-keeping job. Sarah, the employment consultant, observed Barbara and Rose most of Rose's first day and met with Barbara at the end of her shift.

"Rose is OK," Barbara said, "But one thing that bothers me is you have to tell her everything. She was finished mopping to the top of the stairs and I asked her to wait there until the floor dried. About a half hour later the floor was dry but Rose just kept standing there until I specifically told her to go and dump the water out of the bucket. Do I have to keep telling her everything?"

The fact that progress in decreasing dependence on training cues may be slow is something co-workers may need to be prepared for. But on this occasion Sarah, reviewing her notes for the day, was able to show Barbara that Rose had followed her instructions exactly. What Barbara had actually said to Rose at the top of the stairs was "Don't move."

Sarah explained to Barbara that Rose pays attention very carefully to what she is told to do. With this information, Barbara's subsequent training proceeded smoothly.

every afternoon to see that photocopying orders for the day were completed correctly, and asking the employee to do any incorrect copies over, success on this one activity may be enough to build internal confidence and also provide a means to "jump-start" co-worker interactions and relationships.

Keeping it Going

In practice, pre-employment training, on-the-job training, and training partner-ships are often combined to support a job. Training needs, availability of co-workers, and other variables may change, requiring flexibility within each option. What remains consistent is the commitment to the supported employee receiving the benefit of the experiences and skills of his or her co-workers in learning the job.

When training is provided with internal company resources, supported employment agencies relinquish some control over the quality of the effort.

Giving up control doesn't necessarily mean letting whatever happens, happen. Employment consultants need to remain available and advise and supplement resources as needed to keep things heading in a successful direction.

Monitor progress. Sometimes co-worker training may proceed inefficiently because some aspect of a training strategy is implemented incorrectly, and both the employee and co-worker can become frustrated. Employment consultants need to be familiar with systematic training principles and practices, spend time observing the training, verify repeatedly that training is successful, and step in promptly when they have a suggestion. Serious or persistent problems call for a retraining session or replacement of the mentor.

Don't hover. Hovering over the trainer and trainee can make people uncomfortable and interfere with a naturally evolving co-worker relationship. Employment consultants have to develop a feel for how their presence is affecting other people, when it's OK to be present, and when to stay further in the background and possibly miss noticing something.

Provide reinforcement. Mentors are bound to be less than perfect in their training. There may be setbacks or areas in which it is hard for them to see a lot of progress. Some encouragement and "seat-of-the-pants" counseling comes with the territory in this work. Co-workers should be given frequent feedback about what they are doing right and be assisted to notice signs of progress. And rewards like being taken out to lunch or a birthday gift are more important than many people realize.

Keep learning. Employment consultants need to ask the right questions to monitor how things are going and what kinds of support mentors need. Simply asking how things are going is inadequate; asking specific questions and follow-up questions is essential. And relationships and task demands evolve over time. Employment consultants need to keep up with the changing nature of the workplace.

CO-WORKER TRAINING ISSUES

Although a co-worker may not have the level of training expertise that human service staff develop, there are advantages of co-worker training that far outweigh these imperfections. Most co-workers can, with help, teach well enough to get the job done. They often have such major advantages as knowing the tasks to be performed on the job and the ways in which they are done at the site. Hence, in specific situations their training may be superior to training provided by human service staff. New trainers, whether from human services or business, seem to experience the same training problems and need to deal with a set of common training situations, depending on their background and personal style.

Training Tips

Employment consultants with experience teaching tasks to people with disabilities will remember making mistakes along the way and will be able to help other trainers correct these same mistakes. Here are a few of the most common training tips they give.

Maintain prompt consistency. Trainers should usually stick to the same way of showing or explaining something until the person "gets it". Once the task is being done correctly, the prompt can be varied or decreased. A trainer needs to attend carefully to the prompts being provided and look for signs that too much variety (e.g. saying "turn it over" one time, then "no, the other way" the next time) is confusing a trainee.

Reduce "auctioneering." Directions should be simple and concise, with pauses for an individual to absorb the prompt and react. Some training is too conversational. A constant stream of directions and comments can begin to sound like a foreign language or like an auction.

Fade prompts. If a trainee has performed a step correctly when given a particular prompt, the trainer should try delaying the prompt or decreasing it in some way. There are many techniques to do this, such as reducing volume,. giving two instructions together, or giving an indirect prompt like "what comes next?"

Some beginning trainers get stuck in the "if it ain't broke, don't fix it" mode and keep giving prompts that work without checking to see if they're still necessary. The employment consultant may have to suggest and encourage or even model prompt reductions for co-worker trainers.

Recheck performance. Trainers need to check that an employee has carried out a task correctly, and verify correct performance several times. Co-workers, especially if they have other duties and can give only occasional attention to training, may give instructions or a demonstration and then leave, failing to check actual performance. Or they may assume that once something is done correctly, it is learned. The best way to explain the need for rechecking is that it saves training time in the long run.

Reference or develop natural cues. It is tiring and overly restrictive for a trainee to depend on continual prompts from a trainer to govern performance. Other cues, pictures, lists, timer buzzers, and so forth, can substitute for trainer prompts.

Provide sufficient practice. Some tasks may occur so infrequently that there are never enough natural trials available to teach them. For example, spray bottles may only need to be filled once every two weeks or so. While a person is learning, these tasks may have to be made artificially frequent. Perhaps extra spray bottles can be filled until that task is learned.

Responses to emergencies and safety procedures — such as the quickest exit route — are one type of infrequent task that is extremely important to teach. If co-workers are not able to teach these procedures with enough frequency, the agency employment consultant should do so.

Give positive feedback. Many trainers fall into the habit of reprimanding trainees for errors but not praising trainees for what they do right. A related problem is to become too emotional in pointing out errors. Co-workers may need to be reminded of the effectiveness of positive feedback, and of the need to correct errors in a matter-of-fact way; or to learn to praise progress as enthusiastically as they express frustration with lack of progress.

Stress safe work methods. Employment consultants need to verify that all of the work methods taught to supported employees include all required safety procedures. Some co-workers may have developed a habit of cutting corners on safety — not bothering to wear safety glasses or removing a guard mechanism from equipment. The agency should insist that the required safety procedures are taught to the supported employee. Sometimes taking on the role of trainer helps co-workers reaquaint themselves with how tasks should be done.

TRAINING ASSISTANCE WITH NATURAL CUES

One of Richard's jobs in the hospital food service department was to peel vegetables. The peelings went in a garbage container lined with a plastic bag. Each afternoon Earl on the maintenance staff came by to pick up and dispose of the bag of peelings.

Richard became good at peeling. By the end of a day he sometimes filled the container to the brim. Unfortunately, it is impossible to lift a plastic bag completely full of vegetable peelings. The first time this happened Earl explained to Richard that he shouldn't fill it so much. Richard agreed, but the next day the container was too full again.

Earl repeated his request, this time a little annoyed. The employment consultant observed what happened but did not directly take over and solve the problem. Instead, the consultant approached the co-worker. First she acknowledged the problem, and empathized with the co-worker over the situation. Then she made some suggestions: to get Richard a smaller-sized bag and container or to stick a piece of masking tape at two-thirds full on the container. She let Earl decide which strategy to use and explain the new procedure to Richard.

How Do You Teach That?

Besides teaching and monitoring training, agency employment consultants will be expected to have particular expertise in areas of training difficulty. When co-worker trainers are having a problem it is particularly important to establish a partnership style of consultation. Co-workers should not be left to solve a specialized problem unassisted, but neither should they simply drop the problem into the hands of the consultant.

When possible, the best role for the consultant to assume is as the facilitator of a "brainstorming" session to generate approaches and suggestions in such a way that strategies are jointly developed. Careful monitoring will avoid a situation where co-worker trainers only contact the consultant when they are so frustrated that they can no longer approach a problem positively. Consultants should follow a schedule of observing co-worker training and notice a problem long before this. The techniques involved in facilitating brainstorming and other strategies for consulting with co-workers are presented in Chapter 8. Below are some examples of ideas that have developed from brainstorming sessions with co-worker trainers in response to three typical training roadblocks.

Increasing work speed. Work tasks need to be done not only correctly but fast enough or in enough quantity. Some trainers find it difficult to figure out how to help people develop speed.

- In initial training, quality (correct performance) usually takes priority over quantity and speed. It seldom makes sense to do something fast but wrong. The initial lower quantity can be considered an accommodation issue. Most employers will allow a smaller production quota for a beginner. If quantity of production has to be reached quickly, perhaps one or more less important tasks can be put on hold to allow more time, the employee's work day can be extended, or another employee can be assigned to help complete the required quantity. Speed usually develops over time.

- To help an employee maintain a consistent work pace, break the work time into smaller segments — start time to morning break; morning break to lunch, and so forth — with a production quota for each segment.

- Work methods can be made more efficient and equipment can be adapted. For example, entering information by pushing a self-inking stamp is quicker than writing it. Instead of washing items in the order they are brought over to the dishwashing area, an employee can wash items that are used frequently before items that are used infrequently.

- Create a strategy for marking time segments. Employees who tell time can have a list of what should be done by various times. Other employees can use timers to indicate some point in the production schedule or use natural divisions of the work day like bells or delivery times for the same purpose. An employee can listen to an audiotape through headphones with her favorite music and messages recorded between cuts like "You should be on the third row by now."

- Employees can record production amounts by checking boxes, making tally marks or filling in sections of a bar graph on a record sheet, next to a picture of the product or task if necessary, as they complete steps or batches or work up to an agreed-upon quota.

- Employees can receive a "bonus" for reaching or exceeding a quota, either a monetary bonus beyond their usual salary or something enjoyable like going out to lunch or tickets to a sports event.

Interfering behavior. Some employees may engage in behaviors that bother others, violate rules, or get in the way of completing their work. Always make sure it is the standards of the company and/or co-worker culture that govern decisions about what is acceptable, not the agency's preconceptions about "appropriate behavior."

- Systematically reward behavior that is incompatible with the interfering behavior. Set small goals and a realistic timetable and reward progress towards it. Don't wait for perfection. One way to reward something is to follow it with assignment to a very enjoyable part of the job.

- Be specific about what is and is not allowed. Compromise by identifying the circumstances in which the behavior is permitted. For example, it may be acceptable to speak very loudly in the stockroom but not in the customer sales area. Decide on one most important behavior to work on at a time if there are more than one.

- Assign tasks to the employee in which less of the interfering behavior occurs. An individual who consistently prefers engaging in interfering behavior over most of his work tasks may be interested in further career planning to clarify his career vision more fully.

- Some employees need assistance to be able to use their paychecks to purchase goods and services that increase their quality of life. Most people will put effort into changing behavior if the corresponding rewards are substantial enough. If an individual is not working as assigned, "docking" pay by informing the individual that she is off duty and will not be paid until she begins working again can help the individual learn the connection between work and pay, and is also a type of workplace accommodation akin to allowing a flexible work schedule.

- We all use behavior to communicate messages to those around us, sometimes especially when we can't or don't want to talk openly about something. There may be a message behind negative behavior that needs to be attended to. Or the individual can be shown an alternative way of communicating a message. One individual, for example, disliked having dirty hands and became disruptive when assigned to pot plants at a nursery.

Managing time and keeping on schedule. Time is an abstract notion, and precision in measuring and noticing time is difficult for some people. Time management is a common form of support co-workers provide to supported employees (Hagner, Cotton, Goodall & Nisbet, 1992).

- A tape or other mark on a wall clock or wrist watch, or a timer at a work station, can indicate when to start or stop a task. An individual does not have to know how to tell time to match the display to some predetermined time (pictured on a piece of paper, for example). Analog clock or watch displays may be easier to use than digital displays for this purpose.

- There may be a naturally occurring cue in the workplace that corresponds to a certain point in an individual's routine. One school janitor knew he should be finished mopping up to a certain pole by the time music class was over.

- Personal assistance can be provided in the form of a co-worker willing to keep track of time for an individual. Such assistance seldom takes more than a few seconds. One factory worker, for example, checked on a supported employee as she walked past his work station on her way to lunch.

HELP!

Regardless of who conducts training or how thoroughly an employee learns a job, training will never prepare an individual for every situation. For one thing, no finite list of tasks can ever cover every possibility. Imagine that you have written a task analysis of a cleaning job. It might begin with the following large segment steps:

1. Open door and enter building.

2. Go to closet and hang up coat (if applicable).

3. Greet supervisor.

4. Go to supply cabinet and open door.

5. Get clean rag from bin.

6. Get spray can of polish (red mark) from shelf.

7. Point spray nozzle at rag and spray small amount of polish on rag.

8. Go to dining room.

Note that this task analysis has been crafted to include a social interaction (greet supervisor) and an adaptation (cans of polish have a red mark because other spray cans on the shelf look similar). Vanessa, the supported employee, has completed training on this job and is about to complete step 7, but the spray can is empty or the nozzle is defective and nothing comes out.

What should she do? A complete task analysis must cover such possibilities, so we might add a Step 7a: If *no polish sprays out, obtain new can from storage room.* But what if there are no cans in the storage room, or there are several kinds, none with red marks? Steps 7b - 7e might be developed to deal with these situations but the list is becoming complicated. And what about the day that the light is out in the storage closet? Or the day a dog wanders into the building?

A complete analysis of a job is impossible. Unpredictable circumstances like those above are far from rare in work settings. In fact, workers will tell you that "no two days are alike" at most workplaces. Workers call in sick or quit on short notice, equipment breaks, supplies don't come in on time, special occasions or rush orders change production schedules, and so forth. No rote routine can accurately deal with the realities of community work.

How can training accommodate the reality that a complete and accurate task analysis of a job in the "real world" is virtually impossible? One unfortunate response has sometimes been to artificially isolate a supported employee's job and "sanitize" it against disruption and change. This strategy usually requires a great deal of specialized intervention by other people, who must continually "set the stage" for the supported employee to perform her unvarying routine in the face of constantly changing circumstances. Or other people take over when anything is out of the ordinary. This strategy reduces an employee's value to the company and inhibits opportunities for social interaction and teamwork.

A second response is to hope that either the supported employee or others in the environment will figure out on their own what to do when reality doesn't quite match the task analysis. This "place and pray" attitude or "supernatural support model" is inadequate for some employees.

More adaptive alternatives include teaching employees techniques for solving work problems and learning new responses, and insuring that supported employees are part of a network of mutual assistance in the workplace. Techniques for self-instruction are covered in a succeeding section. Participating in mutual support networks involves several elements:

- Identifying an individual or individuals the employee is supposed to ask or report to,

- Insuring that both parties can communicate effectively and are comfortable communicating with one another,

- Insuring that one or more co-workers can identify and watch for signs of frustration or trouble, and

- Helping the supported employee to give as well receive help.

Asking for Help and Reporting Problems

At the beginning of training, trainers do most of the talking, but a shift in interactions usually occurs at some point. Trainees begin taking responsibility for asking questions when they don't know something or need help (Curl, Lignugaris/Kraft, Pawley, & Salzberg, 1990). Asking for help is not a sign of weakness, incompetence or inadequate training but a critical and valued skill in the workplace (Salzberg, McConaughy, Lignugaris/Kraft, Agran, & Stowischek, 1987). Employees need to know how to report a problem, ask a question, or get assistance.

Part of designing a job should include identifying the appropriate co-worker(s) to ask for help or to notify when something is wrong. This may be the mentor or co-worker trainer, the nearest co-worker, the supervisor, or another employee, depending on the setting and the issue. The mentor or employment consultant should include such notification as one of the tasks to be taught to the employee. Asking for help can also be rehearsed or problem situations artificially created. For example, in a dishroom an employee was asked to notify the food service manager when a particular buzzer sounded, indicating that the water had drained out of the machine. In order to practice responding to this rare type of event, with the approval of the manager, the co-worker trainer opened the drain and let the water out. When the buzzer sounded, the co-worker trainer coached the employee to notify the manager.

A variety of communication systems can be devised so supported employees and people who need to be notified can understand one another. In the above example, the manager was notified that the employee would be approaching in a while to say "The water drained out." When this happened, the manager knew what the employee said, even though it was something the manager may not have understood out of context. In a future situation of this kind, the manager would know what the employee was saying if he spoke that same sentence again.

Other communication systems include written messages in a book that an employee can point to, signing, and verbal messages programmed into a touch talker machine. Co-workers can also become comfortable with making and testing hypotheses about what an employee is trying to communicate in a specific context. One supported employee went up to his co-worker and pointed to his wrist watch. The co-worker said "Yes, you better take it off so it doesn't get wet." The employee scowled and shook his head "No." The co-worker made another guess: "Do you mean is it time to turn the machine on?" The employee nodded "Yes." The co-worker responded "In a few minutes. I'll let you know."

Giving Help

We have seen how providing support is an integral part of being on a job. The reverse should also be a part of workplace culture — asking supported employees for help. Support is based on mutuality and reciprocity. An interdependent job design will result in numerous situations in which supported employees can support their co-workers. Co-workers should feel comfortable approaching the supported employee for a hand. Employment consultants can show supported employees situations in which they might notice that someone needs help and offer it.

Disability and Stigma Issues

People with severe disabilities may be less able to improvise a creative solution to a problem or may be confused about or simply not understand what to do. Every employee can identify with these feelings, but employees with disabilities may be embarrassed that an admission that something is not well understood in effect reveals her disability. It is natural that this should happen but may have unfortunate consequences.

Asking for help is valued on the job. Trying to "fake" understanding almost always backfires. For example, one supported employee plugged a vacuum cleaner in and turned the switch on but the motor did not go on for some reason. Not knowing what to do or whom to notify, the individual "vacuumed" the rug with the motor not working.

Sometimes employment consultants and supported employees can talk straightforwardly about these issues. Employment consultants should emphasize to supported employees that reporting problems is necessary and desirable. Through unobtrusive observation of situations in which problems are likely to arise, without intervening, consultants can verify whether or not the employee is able to ask for help.

If necessary, problem situations can be artificially "staged," with permission, as a form of practice. For example, a spray bottle that is empty or doesn't work can be substituted for a good one as a test.

Recognizing Confusion and Frustration

It is also sometimes helpful to explain to co-workers the situations in which an employee is likely to experience a problem and that the employee might need encouragement to ask for help. Supportive co-workers can then spot signs of trouble.

Employment consultants need to be sure that one or more co-workers can recognize signs of confusion or frustration on the part of the employee. For example, Brenda becomes tense and anxious when she feels pressured. Her supervisor has learned to "read" this cue and respond to it. "Other workers will come up to me and say they don't like something," the co-worker explains. "Brenda is telling me that too, only she communicates it in her own way."

SUPPORT SELF-INSTRUCTION FOR ON-THE-JOB LEARNING

Many supported employees have become dependent on verbal instructions and reminders they need to complete tasks and solve problems. A fairly new strategy called *self-instruction* allows individuals to serve as their own agent of learning. That is, employees guide their own behavior after training assistance is withdrawn. The technique has been used to help people to solve work problems (Hughes & Rusch, 1989) and seek out assistance (Rusch, McKee, Chadsey-Rusch

& Renzaglia, 1988).

Self-instruction and asking for help can complement each other. Depending on the particular workplace culture, each may be appropriate for different sorts of work problems. There may be situations in which no appropriate support person is available to help with a problem, or an expectation that for certain issues a worker should "figure that out yourself." And assistance can be provided in such a way that it builds the individual's capacity to solve other related problems in the future.

Through self-instruction, a person learns to model someone who is competent and who successfully completes a task while speaking the instructions out loud. The sequence used is simple:

- First, the trainer models a task while giving the instructions out loud.

- Then, the employee performs the same task while the trainer continues to speak the instructions.

- Finally, the employee performs the task while speaking the instructions.

By verbally rehearsing the steps to a task, an individual is able to "take over" the role of the instructor. When a step is left out, a review of the instructions can help find the missing piece.

This same instructional sequence can also be used for teaching someone to solve problems with work tasks. An employee who does not know what to do when something goes wrong (for example, the equipment doesn't operate when the start switch is flipped) may stop work and wait for someone else to fix the problem, or simply continue going through the task operation even though something is wrong. Either strategy is likely to be ineffective. Most workplaces expect an employee to take the initiative to fix a problem or seek assistance quickly.

Employees can learn to develop coping strategies for problems through following a self-instructional sequence. For example, when the spray bottle an individual tries to use is empty, the employee may use the following problem solving sequence:

- State the problem   "Out of spray."

- State the general solution to the problem   "Gotta fix it."

- State the specific response to solve the problem   "Need more"

- Report the result   "Fixed it."
- Self-praise   "Good."

Some problems are not so straightforward. If potential solutions need to be tested, a more involved strategy might be needed. For example, if turning on a switch to a piece of equipment produced no result, then several hypotheses might need to be checked:

- State problem   "It's not turning on."
- State general solution to the problem   "Gotta fix it."
- Seek source of the problem   "Is it plugged in?"

                                                  "Is that outlet broken?"

                                                  "Is it the right switch?"

                                                  "Is the equipment broken?"

- Identify the problem source if found   "It's not plugged in."
- State the specific response
  to solve the problem   "Got to plug it in."
- Report the results   "It's working now"
- Self-praise   "Good, I fixed it."

If the problem source cannot be found, or if the problem cannot be resolved by the individual, then he can learn to seek help within the setting ("Better get Mary to help me").

During training, the person teaching the strategy should provide feedback if the individual does not verbalize an approximation of each statement. Feedback consists of stopping, saying the correct statement and having the employee practice the statement. In addition, the employee can learn to identify errors and return to the self instruction sequence.

To use self instruction as a general strategy, employees need to learn several different problem situations and the potential solutions to each. Over time, with increased confidence and experience, many employees may be able to transfer the general skill of solving problems to new situations.

The specific statements used for self instruction should fit with an individual's own style. Either co-workers or employment consultants can provide the instruction, though it may be a bit more complex than most co-workers feel comfortable with. Attention should be paid to the possible social perception of an individual talking out loud while using a self-instruction strategy. Employees may learn to speak the statements silently after training, or can employ the strategy on more isolated aspects of a job. In some settings talking out loud would not be noticed. In others, the advantages of more independent problem solving might outweigh the possible disadvantages and/or co-workers can learn to regard the strategy as a necessary accommodation and disregard its unusual nature.

SUMMARY

Learning the tasks that make up a new job, as well as learning the informal cultural norms of the setting, can be challenging for anyone. Before setting up a separate training system, supported employment professionals should first make use of existing worksite training resources, especially co-worker mentorship possibilities. It is easier to give a mentor access to training and support techniques than it is to give an external trainer access to all the social connections, information about customs and personalities, and "tricks of the trade" that an experienced worker possesses.

An employment consultant can take on more of a "train-the-trainer" role, providing consultation on the supported employee's learning style and pointers on effective systematic instruction. Partnerships between mentors and employment consultants can be tailored to each situation, with arrangements including pre-employment training sessions, on-the-job teaching and consulting, and sharing of responbsibilities.

Strategies for employees to ask for and receive needed assistance, and to direct their own self-instruction, help reduce dependency on external training professionals and develop a level of independence that is expected within each worksite.

CHAPTER 7

Building Bridges and Joining the Culture

"Next to family, it is work and the relationships established at work that are the true foundations of society."
— E.F. Schumacher

Becoming a member of a work culture — achieving a true sense of belonging — is not a simple matter of showing up or expressing one's intent to join. The membership of a culture will vary with the expectations of its members on what makes up "belonging." Some cultures have initiation rites, waiting periods, or required participation in activities before a member is considered "one of the gang." Each workplace has its own culture with a wide range of defining characteristics. For instance, there may be an informal dress code, an expectation to take turns buying the coffee, or a work requirement that a specific task always gets done first (see Chapter 2).

When a supported employee first approaches a work setting, he or she is unsure of the rules and expectations and may have difficulties in assessing and joining the culture. One role of an individual providing support is to assist the employee in this activity.

The preliminary step is understanding the culture of a workplace. Some aspects of culture are not readily apparent, and the employment consultant may be required to become a sort of anthropologist or social detective. Once we begin to understand the norms, rules and expectations, we can support the individual to participate in the culture of the workplace. A wide variety of strategies are available to facilitate inclusion. Most of them require a support person to adopt a different role than that of "job trainer." Negotiating complex social situations is not something that can always be accomplished with a task analysis and shaping technology.

Whatever strategies are chosen, they should fit the setting and the learning style and history of the supported employee. Some employees have less interest in forming close social bonds with co-workers than others.

In learning about a workplace culture, consideration must be given to minimize stigmatizing the individual with a disability or being intrusive. Other difficult issues may arise. Co-workers may ask questions about disability as they to get to know a supported employee, or they may begin to include the individual in customs that are very complicated, unauthorized, or otherwise undesirable. Each of these issues is discussed below.

UNDERSTANDING THE CULTURE

Some key features of workplace cultures were listed in Chapter 2:

Social Customs	Tone of Interactions
Stories and Roles	Gathering places
Language and Symbolism	Celebrations
Social Activities	Power and Influence
Work Space	Company Image
Style of Leadership	

These aspects of a culture are specific to each setting. The norms you may learn at one job probably will not apply to the next one. In the traditional hierarchical sense, some aspects of a culture are produced from the "top down" by company management. Other aspects are produced from the "bottom up", as workers interact with each other and with the physical surroundings. Some cultural features may be immediately obvious; others may be subtle or hidden. To understand a culture requires some of the skills of a detective. One of the roles of the employment consultant may be that of anthropologist, uncovering the day-to-day interactions of the members of a social group.

Collecting information about the culture can begin even before initial contacts to a company, by investigating a company's image and reputation in the community. If a personal contact job development strategy is used, the contact person can be a rich source of information about the company's culture. Additional information can be collected from written material produced by the company, including memos to staff, annual reports, brochures, notices on bulletin boards, and other documents. By far the richest source of information will be obtained through observation and informal interviews by employment consultants as they spend time on site at a company.

Observing a Work Culture

Although we may not think about it, we are all fairly accomplished free-lance anthropologists. All of us know how to pick up cultural information. We pay close attention to the social meaning of events around us. In a new setting, we don't know at first what is governed by social rules, what is a matter of individual choice or expression, and what happens if a rule is violated. The style of dress, for example, may be a part of company image, and/or may denote power and influence. Over time, the meanings become clear to us. We find out how to fit in because fitting in is important to us. We have been doing this all our lives and are good at it. In a workplace, some of the things we pay attention to are:

Dress and grooming. What are the norms of dress and appearance (these might incorporate hair style, jewelry, and fashion of clothing) for the setting, job, time of day or other considerations?

Ownership and territory. What are the customs related to use of space, such as knocking-upon-entering rules; using a particular booth or seating arrangement in the lunchroom; where to hang one's coat; gathering places for social conversation; sharing items, like borrowing pens, using the copy machine? Who has keys to what, and how are they obtained?

Eating and drinking. When and where do people have breaks and lunch? What customs exist for coffee break or the water cooler. Do people bring lunch or buy lunch? Do people take turns "treating" each other to meals or drinks?

Pace of work. How important is it to appear busy? Are there peaks and valleys in the work pace? What times are more social? How much informal socializing is acceptable? What cues do workers attend to in pacing their work?

Cliques. Are there particular subgroups that stay together? What are their primary ties? What dominates their relationship — sports, family, a shared hobby?

Initiations and terminations. How are new employees oriented and initiated, and what expectations are there to become an accepted member of the work group? Are there formal or informal rituals?

Ceremonies. What transitions and events at the workplace are marked by formal ceremonies? Who gets rewarded and for what accomplishments? Who attends ceremonies, where are they held and who plans them?

Celebrations. How are birthdays, showers, or promotions noted? What else is celebrated? What are the traditions related to each?

Power relationships. What are the interpersonal patterns of power and influence? Who initiates discussions, work, items covered first at a meeting? What is the "pecking order" of decision-making?

Humor. What are the expectations and norms around teasing, joking and "horsing around?"

Interviewing Members of a Work Culture

The members of a culture are the experts on the culture. But their knowledge is local and situational, and sometimes they don't even realize what they know. A question like "what are the important customs here?" is probably too big. You are likely to get a blank stare. But if you ask specific questions as you begin to see what goes on — "Do people do this every week? How did you know it was your turn?" — you will obtain important and practical information.

Most people enjoy talking about their work, the job setting, and the people with whom they work, and casual conversations (don't call them interviews) are a relatively non-intrusive means of gathering information. Invite a worker for coffee, or sit down with an employee during a break and explore "what it's like to work here."

Ask naive questions as you see and hear things. For example, "Did you ask Fred because he is the one who knows how the equipment works?" You may have to stick around a while and become a familiar face before people will trust you. If people ask you why you want to know, be perfectly honest: "I'm here to help Sally be able to fit in with everyone."

Interview a number of different people in this way, making sure to include representatives of any different roles or work groups that impact the individual's employment. Try to determine as quickly as you can who has a good reputation.

You wouldn't want to use someone as your main "informant" who does not fit in well or is about to lose his/her job. In your conversations, some things to ask about might be:

How widespread a practice is...

"Do most of the workers usually sit here?"

How to interpret events...

"When Tom said that was he joking?"

How much personal information is discussed...

"Do you ever bring in pictures of your vacation to show around?"

Terms, language...

"What do you mean by the 'bar towels'?"

Clique and group identity...

"Do the doctors ever have lunch with the technicians?"

Style of supervision...

"How often do these get checked?"

There may be a rule not to discuss some customs because they may not be officially allowed. Part of learning about the culture is learning *how to learn about* these customs. As you talk with employees, avoid a "soap opera" curiosity about people's personal lives. The employment consultant's role should be simple and direct.

Recording and Analyzing Information

There are two different kinds of cultural data. Quantitative data are the aspects of a culture you can measure and count—for example, the number, type, and duration of social interactions. Qualitative data are the more narrative and anecdotal aspects: stories, initiations, expectations, traditions, and the like.

Quantitative data can provide fairly reliable but very basic information on who talks to whom during the course of the work day. Collecting this kind of information can be intrusive, as it may require observers to carry around timers, counters or forms, or use cameras or tape recorders. If this is perceived as unusual within the culture, the assessment itself can become a new obstacle to inclusion.

Qualitative information can handle complex and subtle aspects of a culture, and can be collected less obtrusively. But its subjectivity can be a weakness. An observer risks hearing only one version of a story or distorting what is observed with his or her personal biases and experiences, thus obtaining a slanted understanding of the culture. Sometimes some careful counting can be used to test a hunch or as a reality check on something that seems to be occurring. But most information that is easily accessible will be qualitative. Some consultants have an intuitive knack for getting the feel of a work culture. Others employ more organized strategies to help them in this effort.

- Keep a small notebook handy and jot down what you see and hear. People usually don't mind having you take notes if they are explaining something. If this is a problem, then record notes off-site as soon as possible. Notes can also be completed in an area of the workplace where similar behavior fits in — an office, the library — or on trips to the bathroom, in the consultant's car, or in a nearby area outsite the worksite.

- Write down your interpretations, guesses, and "editorial comments" on what you see in the notebook, but keep these separate from the descriptions of what is actually done or said by putting brackets around them or some similar convention.

- Pay attention to how you are perceived. For example, being seen as a tool of management or as a scientist studying some unusual phenomenon may harm your efforts to connect people to a work culture. On the other hand, you might adopt the explicit role of job analyst and writing things down might be viewed as natural and valuable.

- Read your notes and look for themes that emerge. See if what people say is borne out by what you see them do, and vice versa. Test out ideas. For example, if you observe a prank being played on a new employee, you might hypothesize that it is an initiation custom new employees go through. But of course you may be wrong. Find the next newest employee and ask that person to tell you about when they started work there.

- Test out your ideas in conversations with co-workers to verify that you are on the right track.

- If there is more than one support person who visits the site, discuss the culture together after few days. Or, ask another individual who does similar work at another job site to listen to your description of the culture and ask you questions.

Hanging Around, Looking Cool

It is easy to feel out of place or in the way when one's role is to observe or ask questions at a work setting. The same social pressures shaping the behavior of the other participants is exerting a pressure on your behavior. Being uninvolved with company production may be considered "just standing around" and frowned upon. People don't need anthropologists or detectives checking them out; they have work to do. The wrong kind of agency presence can send the wrong message to the workplace about the supported employee and hinder her acceptance.

But there may be a need for on-site agency presence at a company. Some reasons are:

- To understand the culture on behalf of the employee,
- To verify that training and performance are proceeding as planned,
- To consult with co-workers or a supervisor,
- To help with training or talk with the employee,
- To meet funding or administrative requirements,
- To act as a resource for problem solving.

Strategies for being available on-site while not interfering with the culture are possible. The key in these efforts is to avoid the "Bobsey Twin Syndrome," the close association between employment consultant and the supported employee. Not every strategy will make sense for every circumstance. Sometimes the risks involved with a particular approach will outweigh the benefits. Good judgment and sensitivity must always be used when approaching a culture from the outside to help someone become part of the inside.

Stay inconspicuous. You can become a "fly on the wall" by taking advantage of the fact that a constant presence recedes into the background of people's awareness. There may be natural locations in a setting where observations can be made and where it is more or less acceptable to be around. Some settings have a designated breakroom; restaurants may have a table or booth where you can sit and drink coffee. At some settings it may be appropriate to complete reports or paperwork while keeping aware of what is going on.

Consult with or learn about other areas. Becoming a consultant is discussed in Chapter 8. This type of activity can allow opportunities for observation of the work and social interactions of a supported employee in a different capacity. For example, developing job descriptions for a department provides a rationale for repeated on-site observations and discussions.

Help with tangential work. Many work sites have no location for observation convenient to the supported employee's work station. And from any one location, only a fraction of a work setting can be observed. An observer may find ways to be useful by noticing something that needs straightening out or attending to. Careful observation will almost always uncover a set of tasks that are useful but not critical and are not perceived as helping complete the supported employee's work. Making things neater or cleaner or helping with any form of material handling (stocking shelves, unloading or restacking boxes), for example, is appreciated almost anywhere.

Fill in. When a co-worker is absent (sick, on vacation, on a delivery) it may be sometimes acceptable to volunteer to fill in and do some of the individual's job for a few hours. Some companies won't allow this; others will. Of course, you should be sure that you can do the work before offering. You can even use these occasions as a sort of "test" to see whether you correctly understand the work area and its social customs.

Beware of "Going Native"

A consultant will find that his presence at a company begins to take on a particular meaning or interpretation within the setting, and will come to occupy a particular role:

- An observer,
- Someone who helps out,
- A teacher,
- A person who is part of the work force but "on loan," or
- Someone who arranges the work so it is more efficient.

Becoming at least a partial participant in a setting is an ideal way to find out about it. But in most cases it is really not feasible for an employment consultant to become a true insider. Your time at a company is circumscribed and has a different purpose. Pressure to be a part of the setting and to do more than you really should will be real, and it is easy to fall into behaviors such as:

- Taking responsibility for what the supported employee does because "if they don't look good, you don't look good,"

- Becoming tied into the production aspect of the business,

- Wearing the same uniform, dressing and acting like an employee,

- Making friends at the site (including the supported employee) so you don't want to leave, and

- Making friends at the site (including the supported employee) who don't want you to leave.

There are no easy ways of dealing with these issues. Each consultant has to find a role that feels comfortable. Wearing a uniform and pitching in with work can help you understand the culture but can also make you ineffective as a management consultant. Involvement may bias you towards one particular work clique or work area. Even worse, one can get caught up in group feuds or politics. An effective consultant will recognize potential problems and make needed corrections in her role.

BUILDING BRIDGES: SOCIAL INCLUSION

Developing co-worker relationships is one of the main functions of supported employment. We saw in Chapter 2 that several different levels of rewarding relationship are possible with co-workers:

- *Social friends*, with whom an employee spends some non-work time;

- *Work friends*, with whom an employee interacts informally and during free time at work; and

- *Workmates*, with whom an employee interacts regularly at work but usually regarding work topics.

A fourth type of relationship, *conflict relationships*, may also develop, and strategies for dealing with these are covered in Chapter 8.

The groundwork for developing positive relationships should be taken care of as a job is developed and designed. Basing a job search on individual preferences

---

THE SOCIAL WORKER IS "IN"

The workers at Dynamatic knew that Mary had left the company a year or so ago to work for some sort of human service agency, so when she returned as an employment consultant to help Dynamatic employ James as a machinist's helper, that's how they perceived her. They talked to her about anything on their minds that had some connection with human or social problems. As it turned out, there were plenty of these. One woman's unmarried daughter was pregnant, a secretary's husband seemed to have a drinking problem, and an office manager was concerned about his child's special education services.

Mary saw this as an opportunity to define an interesting social niche at the company. She talked with each person who approached her. Through a combination of counseling skills and knowledge of community agencies, and expertise from others in the agency, Mary assisted these workers to deal with their concerns. During her weekly visits, she made sure that James was doing OK. When any problem arose, such as James getting into arguments with one co-worker, she asked one of the employees if they would keep an eye on the situation.

---

and dreams, using personal connections in the job search, and following company training procedures, are critical prerequisites to facilitating co-worker relationships. Several additional strategies can help "build bridges" to co-workers and broker the process of social inclusion.

Build Familiarity

People are more comfortable interacting with a person who is familiar, recognized and predictable. Predictability occurs with establishing some basic routines. Getting coffee at the same time or going to the same spot for break are examples of routines.

The consultant should help a new employee learn co-workers' names and participate in greetings and good-byes customary at the site. For example, Robert had a difficult time remembering his co-workers' names at the restaurant where he worked. The consultant suggested to the head chef who worked with him to rehearse co-workers' names with Robert at the start of each shift. Robert eventually learned everyone's name and also formed a work friendship with the chef.

Another familiarity-building strategy is to ensure that the supported employee reports to work to the appropriate people. Still another is to encourage casual conversation through a variety of informal measures: letting a co-worker know how excited Tom was about getting to a sports event, or suggesting that Susan ask a co-worker about a television show they both watch regularly.

Some work settings may have particular customs that signify social legitimacy. Having your name up on the sign-out board, for example, symbolizes that you are a full-fledged member.

Add Personal Touches

Relationship development is partly a matter of being seen as more than just an employee. We can foster social connectedness by helping people to express their personality to others in the work group. Examples would be to assist the supported employee to bring a home-baked snack to offer others at break or sharing a small selection of photographs of family, vacation, or the individual involved in a favorite activity.

At some worksite employees adorn their personal work spaces with "artifacts" of their personal lives: pictures of their families, a coffee mug or wall poster that tells a story, or something similar. Employment consultants can assist supported employees to identify something that expresses their interests or tells of their travels and bring it to work to add a personal touch.

Explore Common Interests

People like to identify connections with others: "We both used to live in Ohio," or "We all like Roy Orbison music." Commonalities are often established through casual conversation, observation, or by people making reference to something they have done.

If the employment consultant has come to know the supported employee through a career planning process and personal involvement, he has the advantage of knowing about the person's interests and experiences. The consultant can then assist the supported employee to discover co-workers who share these interests and experiences.

PICTURE THIS

Ron had always been interested in learning about people's families and would often ask to look at people's family photographs. This interest led to Ron learning photography. Through informal conversations at the work site, the employment consultant learned that photography happened to be a hobby of one of Ron's co-workers, Larry, and encouraged Ron to bring in some of his photographs to show Larry. Larry responded by bringing in some of his favorites. They sometimes take a few minutes to talk about photography at work. When an interesting photography exhibit opened in town, Larry and Ron went together to the opening.

If a lot of people at a setting have an interest in common, it might pay to explore if the supported employee would also have an interest in it, even if he or she never explored it before. Another idea is to encourage an employee to contribute to a charity or belong to an organization or volunteer cause favored by the employer or which co-workers are interested in.

One workplace helped maintain the library grounds in town after work hours. By volunteering to participate in raking leaves or planting flowers, the supported employee was able to connect and share time with co-workers in a different setting. This provided fodder for conversations at work. Volunteering can also provide a new valued social role for someone traditionally seen as on the receiving end of assistance.

As relationships grow, supported employees might need assistance to nurture and maintain relationships. For example, an employment consultant can assist the employee to purchase an address book and obtain the names, addresses and phone numbers of people she likes or who like them; or to ask when their birthday is, or about their families.

Follow Social Customs

When important social customs are identified, their nature and importance for fitting in should be communicated to the employee. For example, if employees take turns making a "coffee run" to the shop across the street, the employee should learn to do this as if it were a central job task, and take the appropriate turn making the coffee run. An employment consultant can either teach such customs directly, or guide someone at the worksite in teaching them.

As cultures evolve within a particular environment, there are places where people naturally tend to congregate and socialize. In the workplace, gathering places may be breakrooms, reception areas, or a centrally located office. Gathering spots tend to have their own set of norms, forming a subculture within the workplace. The gathering place often acts as a key site in connecting to other individuals. A supported employee should be assisted, if necessary, to identify and make use of gathering places.

Translate Rules of Teasing and Humor

Humor is integral to most work cultures. Unfortunately, the norms that surround humor, teasing and joking can require complex judgments of appropriateness and timing. Helping people to come to learn how to be the good-natured recipient of humor is often a good place to start. This requires understanding how teasing works and being able to pick up cues that signal well-intentioned teasing.

Being able to joke and tease someone in turn also requires knowing the right

---

WHO DEALS?

Breaktime at Global Plastics was the scene of two spirited card games. The rules of participation were different for each. For one group, serious card-playing and strict observance of card rules was discouraged. The game served primarily as a source of conversation. Someone who entered the game and actually tried to keep score would not fit in.

The second group, on the other hand, was serious about their game. They kept score, argued hands, and competed. Joining the right card group was an important consideration to successful belonging on the job.

Coming to understand the rules of the card game was not easy for Jose, who had a learning difficulty. The employment consultant wanted to link Jose with the looser card game, but the co-workers with whom Jose mostly worked were serious card players. She decided to meet Jose after work each day and help work with him on the rules of the game until he became familiar enough with the rules that he could participate.

time and place, along with the boundaries for acceptable topics and taboo topics. There is a rule of reciprocity involved with humor; as one co-worker put it, "If you dish it out you'd better be ready to take it." It is also important to know when to stop joking.

Reciprocate Support

Support is a key aspect of working relationships. A sure way to receive support from co-workers is to provide assistance to those same people. The level of support given and received does not have to be equal as long as there is some degree of reciprocity (Morey & Luthaus, 1991). The consultant might look for and mention occasions when a supported employee could help someone out. A supported employee might not be able to solve complex life problems for a co-worker, but may possess other qualities or behaviors that are supportive, such as the ability to empathize with a co-worker who is having a bad day, or boost her spirits. And most employees can learn to attend to common situations at a setting in which someone might use help.

Showing appreciation is another way of reciprocating. Supported employees may need assistance in sending thank-you cards, taking a co-worker out to lunch to say "thanks", and similar gestures of appreciation.

Identify Allies

Most people have one or two key work friends (Henderson & Argyle, 1985). One role of these individuals is that of an "ally," helping facilitate new social connections, "sticking up" for the individual in conflict situations, interpreting the culture, and so forth. This type of support is invaluable, especially when one first enters a new culture. The importance of a "champion" or "benefactor" (Edgerton, 1967) in the successful adjustment of people with disabilities to community settings is well documented.

Identify The Social Co-ordinator

An ongoing task of an employment consultant is to identify and nurture one or more individuals who can reliably serve as allies. Workers who are central to workplace social networks make ideal allies. Every workplace tends to have one or two individuals who seem to "know everyone" and act as social coordinators. These are important people. They may plan events, suggest celebrations, and provide introductions. They understand nuances of work and non-work relationships. Their focal position and depth of understanding can provide access to social gatherings and help cement the supported employee to other individuals. But an ally does not have to be the most socially connected individual at a workplace. Other possibilities include:

- The co-worker trainer or mentor;
- The original contact person at the site;
- The supervisor;
- Someone of similar age and gender;
- A person who smiles and says "hi"; and
- A co-worker who gives work to or receives work from the employee.

Two allies are even better than one. If reliance is placed on one individual for providing significant support, it can be experienced as a burden. And there is always the chance that that individual might leave the individual without someone to turn to. Assisting allies to offer support is covered in Chapter 8.

Play a Role in Celebrations and Gatherings

When the members of a work culture recognize the significance of an event, they may hold some sort of celebration. The event may be personal, such as a birthday, or work-related, such as a promotion.

Celebrations provide important opportunities to become a part of things. The work culture should make sure everyone, including the supported employee, receives invitations to participate in planned social or recreational events and support if needed to participate or attend.

An individual may require assistance to learn the behavioral norms at a celebration, since these are typically different from the norms during work itself. At one work setting, complaining about the cafeteria food was a common topic of conversation. But at the annual company picnic, with the boss tending the barbeque grill, a co-worker explained to the supported employee that it would be wise not to complain about the food.

Playing an active role in celebrations is an excellent vehicle for social inclusion. When appropriate, the supported employee can be the one who takes the birthday card around to collect signatures or calls the balloon-o-gram company. Assisting the supported employee to participate — e.g., explaining how not to give the secret card to the person whose birthday it is until the end, or suggesting that the employee ask a co-worker to help with that — stimulates participation in a positive and socially meaningful aspect of the culture.

Increase Interactions

Chapter 5 explored several strategies for increasing the level of social interaction on a job. Work tasks should intersect or overlap with other jobs and require communication between employees. A job design should allow for exceptions and changes to a routine.

Perhaps most importantly for building relationships, the employee's job should include the use of shared spaces and things at the workplace. Being responsible for obtaining supplies from the supply closet or for distribution of memos in mailboxes are two examples. A feeling of community and interdependence centers around the things people share in common.

Assure Effective Communication

Effective communication is essential for participation as a member of a social group. For some supported employees, communicating effectively will require planning or accommodations. This might include:

- Allowing more time for the individual to put his thoughts into words;
- Being patient in asking an individual to repeat a message;
- Putting aside distractions to attend fully to a communication, and, if a person reads lips, looking at the person when speaking to him;
- Using the context and a process of elimination through "yes/no" questions to establish meaning;
- Learning sign language;
- Providing audiotaped or large-print versions of written material;

- Developing a series of pictures or cards an individual can use to communicate messages;

- Assisting an individual to use a communication board, or facilitating typed communication (Biklen et al., 1991).

Sometimes one individual at a setting takes primary responsibility for helping an individual communicate effectively with other members of a group. Or all members of a work group might learn how to use a communication strategy because the company values and accommodates diversity, because the whole business benefits, or just because they want to.

Employment consultants should observe co-worker reactions in situations that require communication and head off potential problems. For example, noting that a co-worker is irritated by an exchange could lead to some helpful advice to the supported employee and a suggestion, if appropriate, to the co-worker.

ALTERNATIVE COMMUNICATION SYSTEMS CAN BENEFIT A BUSINESS

Jerry was an excellent worker whose main concern in seeking a job was that he might be isolated from his co-workers because of his deafness. Indeed, the catering company approached about hiring Jerry had the same opinion of his ability and the same concern. The employment consultant explained that part of his role would be to teach sign language to some of the employees.

Two co-workers were selected to learn sign language. As the consultant began teaching these workers the signs for key terms used in their business and they began signing with Jerry, they began to realize what an advantage it was to have a mechanism for communicating across large, noisy dining halls. If table 19 was short two desserts, or everybody asked for decaffeinated coffee, the kitchen was notified in an instant. The entire catering business increased its efficiency, and ultimately, everybody learned to sign.

Most communication in dining areas is now done via sign language, even on Jerry's days off. The company pays the consultant to teach new employees to sign as part of regular orientation training.

Strengthen the Culture

We have been talking about fitting in and interfering as little as possible with existing cultures, but workplace cultures are evolving, creative enterprises. The inclusion of a new employee may be an opportunity to start new customs or strengthen aspects of a culture. Supported employees can sometimes be a positive force in a work culture. Comments such as "He helped our morale," or "The workers here have a soft side, and she can bring it out" are not unusual to hear.

For example, a supported employee might initiate social gatherings. This should focus on a work event or a co-worker celebration rather than centering on the supported employee. Or a new custom may evolve from efforts to build workplace ties. One supported employee initiated a practice of going out to lunch at a restaurant on Fridays at a company where people usually pretended they were too busy to take a full hour for lunch, but were secretly wishing someone would take a leadership role and organize a lunch expedition.

Some employment consultants define their role as helping to create more effective work teams. This role, known as organizational development (Lippitt & Lippitt, 1984), expands the focus of employment consulting beyond disability and beyond one employee. As an organization works through issues of effective communication, conflict resolution, or workforce diversity, the consultant can provide guidance on ways to strengthen the culture.

Interactive jobs, occasions for celebration, convenient gathering places, strong traditions — in short, *exactly* the same things that are conducive to good social integration for supported employees — promote cohesive work teams and job satisfaction more generally in any work group. But when involved in efforts to build a stronger team, a consultant should be aware that a culture can be radically dysfunctional and a bottomless pit of problems. One should avoid trying to reshape these cultures.

Give it Time

Working relationships develop over time, and the amount of time can be considerable when people's backgrounds are dissimilar (Gabarro, 1987). The work itself serves as a common bond drawing people together, and commonalities forge additional connections. But trust and social bonds are built over time. If an employee enjoys a job, and there is no serious problem of isolation or conflict relationships, and several of the above strategies are being followed to a reasonable degree, relationships may evolve gradually, in their own way. There is no productive way to hurry them up.

DISCLOSURE AND DISABILITY

As they get to know supported employees, co-workers and employers may be curious about and ask questions that include questions about disability, or they may want to ask a question and not know how to do it. Even though the questions may be unsophisticated, ("What's wrong with James? Was he in an accident?"), the intent is often innocent. The development of relationships usually involves the gradual disclosure of personal information.

In general, people know very little about disability and ignorance often breeds anxiety. Mistaken stereotypical images of people with disabilities as children, as dangerous and unpredictable, or as having a lower level of awareness or feelings, are still widespread. They need to be confronted and dispelled, one person at a time. Most people, and people with disabilities are no different, don't generally mind respectful curiosity about themselves. It is part of learning about who a person is. It provides an occasion to explain disability accurately and dispel myths (Royse & Edwards, 1989).

But like any exchange of personal information, the degree of disclosure should be controlled by the supported employee. By law, an employer or co-worker has no right to specific information about disability, only the nature of the accommodations required for the employee to perform the job.

Some support programs include group sessions for the members of a workplace to help sensitize people to working with an individual with a disability (e.g. Laabs, 1991). The authors are familiar with programs which hand out written material about disability or about interacting with an individual with a disability to employers. A more personal orientation of co-workers to an individual or tips about how to communicate with a specific person are usually more helpful than general information. A personal introduction to the individual's background, current situation and plans is sometimes a good way to reduce social distance. It highlights similarities between the individual and her co-workers.

A prepared meeting format might be useful in a situation where the appearance or behavior of an employee is likely to stand out dramatically for those who are just meeting the individual. If a person's reputation and social image would be aided initially if his co-workers had an understanding of how the person walks or talks or breathes, then explaining that first might be useful. Again, the employee or guardian should be the final decision-maker.

Recognizing and working with a diverse workforce is recognized as an important aspect of contemporary business management (e.g. Thomas, 1991). Rather than an informational session geared towards introduction of a supported employee, a support service might offer a diversity workshop for employees encompassing a range of issues (gender bias, cultural and ethnic diversity, age) in addition to disability. Valuing employees with diverse backgrounds and experiences is a positive, team-building message. Some larger companies may already sponsor a workshop of this kind and can broaden the scope of an existing program to include disability issues.

Combatting Stereotypes

All of us employ strategies to construct and maintain a positive social image. Some politicians employ "image managers" or "spin doctors" who pay attention to minute details of how various statements, appearances, and behaviors are perceived and interpreted. Employment consultants have a role to play in attending to the social image of a supported employee.

- Emphasize commonalties between supported employees and their co-workers. This can include common likes and dislikes, common experiences, and common reactions to situations.

- Look for occasions and contexts where an employee's positive characteristics or positive side of a characteristic can be emphasized.

- Look for ways to sensitively "advertise" positive accomplishments and aspects of an individual that are valued within the setting.

If people at a worksite express stereotypical assumptions ("She couldn't handle that job;" "He'll be out sick a lot," etc.), the employment consultant should provide information that conflicts with the stereotype. This should not be done in a confrontational way, but in a matter-of-fact exchange.

Atypical or problematic behavior can be particularly damaging to an individual's image and reputation. Efforts to support this issue are required on

---

DO YOU KNOW WHERE YOUR DRIVERS ARE?

Rick works as a janitor at a transportation company. He is very interested in the whereabouts of the drivers and other employees, and he keeps track of knowing where everybody is. At a previous job people considered this trait as being "nosy" or a "busybody." But at the transportation company a lot of time and effort used to be wasted trying to track people down. People are always coming and going. "Is Frank on a run or at lunch?" "I don't know, he was here a while ago."

The support consultant suggested to a couple of people that they ask Rick. When they did, he always had the correct answer. His job is now structured in such a way that he is a consistent source of information. Rick has taken on a central role in the social system of the company and is considered a resource rather than a bother.

---

two fronts. Chapter 6 outlined strategies for assisting the individual to change behavior. Equally important are those "impression management" strategies we all use to maintain a positive social image despite our flaws and imperfections. Consultants should be aware of how behavior that breaks cultural norms is being interpreted and assist co-workers to see instances of negative behavior as:

- A reaction to the same frustrations all employees experience. "Marty dislikes it when the supervisor is on his back" is a much better explanation than "Marty has difficulties with authority figures and antisocial tendencies."

- An ordinary personality trait, such as "Tim has a lot of energy" or "Brenda is afraid of falling down so she walks slowly."

- A response to a situation rather than the expression of some underlying trait. "Ella gets nervous when there are this many people around."

- A logical result of an individual's personal history. "George was never allowed to have any of his own possessions when he lived in the institution..." "The school treated her like a child until she was 22..."

- A form of communication. "That's his way of saying he's having a bad day." Everyone knows people who express their likes and dislikes dramatically, and we all identify with the need to communicate our feelings — verbally if we can, but in other ways if we have to.

People can deal with all kinds of events and behaviors if they feel confident and comfortable that they know how to respond, and if they in turn receive the support they need. Therefore, consultants should take care to explain to people at the worksite what, if anything, they need to do to deal successfully with a particular situation.

Co-workers may need to feel that it's OK for them to talk about and examine their feelings and stereotypes about disability. They may need opportunities to process and interpret what they are experiencing, as they are exposed, perhaps for the first time, to an individual with a severe disability. People can be respectful and yet still be struggling with their feelings. They should not feel that they may be criticized unless everything they say is "politically correct."

When an employee has a positive relationship with one or two co-workers who are able to serve as "allies," these individuals can help interpret events for and maintain the social image of the employee in the eyes of other employees. The employment consultant can work with these individuals who can in turn share information with others.

Minimizing Human Service Trappings

One of the things that can make people with disabilities appear "different" is the service supports around them. Service providers with experience serving people with disabilities in group or segregated contexts may find it difficult to unlearn the negative messages and habits they have picked up. Their language, techniques, and approaches at a worksite may reflect older habits and can stigmatize a supported employee.

As in every field, supported employment staff mentors pass their attitudes and approaches on to new recruits — the good ones and the bad ones. Particular trouble spots to look for include:

Disability jargon. There are terms and concepts that people use to communicate with other individuals interested in supporting people with disabilities when they get together at conferences or meetings. But at the worksite, this "disability language" is out of place. Anything worth communicating can be stated in ordinary language. If you tell a supervisor "I'm picking up Joe after work for his ISP meeting" the supervisor could think Joe is being abducted by aliens from outer space. Why not say "Joe and I are getting together after work to talk about some of his plans?"

Service techniques. Behavior change procedures (including the use of artificial and sometimes childish reinforcers) and data collection paraphernalia such as counters, stopwatches, clipboards, and graphs, can be intrusive and stigmatizing. Most employees' experience with "behavioral technology" is along the lines of making a New Year's resolution or counting calories, and whenever possible behavioral strategies should be — or at least appear — that simple. One exception is those manufacturing settings where the collection of sophisticated production data is routine.

Agency connections. Agency-related contacts such as tours or photograph sessions can link the supported employee too strongly to being a recipient of special services. Ordinary analogs of these practices are available. An employee can have someone take pictures of her birthday celebration at work, or can invite someone to see his work station who happens to be a prospective supported employee thinking about a job in the community.

An external consultant needs to keep in mind that he or she acts as a model for how to deal with situations others are unfamiliar with. Co-workers will observe

HUMAN SERVICE JARGON	REAL LIFE MEANING
• Gross motor	• Dirty engine
• Fine motor	• Mercedes Benz
• Case manager	• Beer distributor
• Eight-bed residence	• A small hotel
• Acting out	• An outdoor theater production
• Severe outburst	• Heavy downpour
• Down time	• Time to be depressed
• Dually diagnosed	• Very sick; confirmed by second opinion
• Fading program	• Poor TV reception; should get cable
• Reasonable accommodation	• Decent motel
• Natural support	• Comfortable underwear

body posture, tone of voice, and reactions to situations for clues on how they should act. Even subtle nuances of behavior like voice tone or physical positioning can communicate a message. Messages such as "be very strict" or "she can't think for herself" are not very effective for working as a partner for the employee with a disability. In working directly with the supported employee, model a stance of equality, inclusion and respect.

UNAUTHORIZED AND COMPLICATED CUSTOMS

We have emphasized the critical importance of fitting in with workplace social customs for an employee's social acceptance and inclusion. But occasionally customs at a workplace may be so complicated that it is very difficult for an employee with a disability to learn them correctly. How far to go in teasing a co-worker, how to play an initiation prank on a new employee, when to swear and when not to swear; all of these are governed by complex social rules. Humor, for example, is complicated because it often involves a subtle twist of a usual rule (Dwyer, 1991). It may be hard enough to learn the usual rule, never mind the subtle twist.

Difficulties with complex social situations of these kinds are one of the most frequent reasons for job loss among employees with disabilities. The skills themselves are complicated, and the identification of appropriate contexts for using those skills can be even more difficult to grasp (Morrison & Bellack, 1981).

Not all co-worker customs are known to or authorized by the managers of a company. Some may conflict with management ideals. For example, avoiding notice by supervisors and appearing very busy when supervisors are present are complicated skills many employees learn (Molstad, 1988). Working more slowly than necessary is another rule sometimes practiced informally. Criticizing management and working conditions in conversation with co-workers is still another common unauthorized custom.

Other workplace customs may be officially prohibited. Eating food in the storeroom or extending a break time by several minutes are two examples. In extreme cases, customs can even be crimes. The fact that people avoid discussing unauthorized customs (or lie about them) and hide them from view makes them particularly difficult for an employment consultant to grapple with.

Covert workplace practices can be quite extensive. In one interview study of American life (Patterson & Kim, 1991), workers reported spending more than seven hours of each work week, on average, drinking, using drugs, calling in sick, or loafing.

Efforts at inclusion and involvement of co-workers in employee training lead to a situation in which the employment consultant does not directly control what goes on. A mentor may teach or attempt to teach unauthorized customs. An employee may learn a custom on his or her own. Not following the custom, or following it wrong, may have significant repercussions. A decision about how to respond in these situations should be made carefully. Usually several considerations have to be balanced against one another and there is not often an easy answer.

Will the employee be able to follow the rule or an adapted version of the rule after training? In one dishroom, employees threw wet rags across the room at each other when the supervisor was in another area. An individual who had a rag thrown at her waited a few minutes (so it would be a surprise), made sure the supervisor wasn't around, picked an individual who wasn't looking, and threw the rag at him. A worker who kept the rag ruined the game. If the rule is complex, there is a chance that a co-worker will need assistance to teach it. In this case, the consultant determined that the employee could probably learn an adapted version of the custom. Whether teaching the rule is possible depends to some extent on how accessible the custom is to an employment consultant.

How does management view the custom? What are the risks and consequences of practicing the custom or in getting caught? Some practices displease managers but they "look the other way" and accept them. Other customs are serious violations and possibly grounds for dismissal.

Is the practice safe? Some customs are unauthorized because they are dangerous. For example, some machine operators remove safety guards from equipment, work without safety glasses, or leave machines running unattended. These individuals may be imagining that they are following a "higher" rule — "I always put them back on if it's *really* unsafe" — but most likely they are just being imprudent.

Can one individual follow a different rule without exposing the custom? Working faster than one's co-workers, for example, may give away the fact that they have been working at a set speed by design, claiming they can go no faster. One person's decision not to go along may affect everyone.

How do co-workers view the custom? In some cultures, an employee who doesn't participate in an unauthorized custom may be perceived as being too closely connected to management, as too serious, or as a child. Other cultures respect an individual's decision to participate or not.

What is the role of the agency? For an individual co-worker to encourage an employee to break a rule is one thing; for an agency to officially sanction and even teach it is another.

Is there a trustworthy individual at the site willing to act as the individual's ally? If someone on the "inside" can be counted on to help negotiate the ethics and norms of the setting, problems will be easier to work out.

Do the unauthorized customs and worker/management conflicts indicate an inappropriate work site? Unethical customs may serve as early warning signs that the job or the setting will not be a positive experience.

Before choosing a course of action, an employment consultant should first understand the custom in as much detail as possible and evaluate it in the context of the setting and culture. Several options are available:

- Take the time required to teach the custom to the supported employee, or support the co-workers in teaching the custom. Part of the complexity in following some unauthorized customs involves knowing when not to mention them. Supported employees may need very specific and direct information about when it is acceptable to talk about what.

- Adapt or simplify the custom so that the supported employee can partially participate. For example, at the dishwashing setting Tim learned to throw the wet rag at someone when the supervisor was out of the room, but he always threw it at the same person (his mentor, John) and it wasn't a surprise. But following the adapted version kept Tim from being per-ceived as someone who ruined the game.

- Ask a co-worker to provide the necessary prompts to the employee to indicate what to do. For example, the supported employee can learn to

---

AN ETHICAL DILEMMA

The housekeepers in one motel seldom followed the officially sanctioned cleaning procedure. They quickly inspected a room and did only a cursory cleaning job if they could get away with it. For example, in the bathroom they folded the end of the toilet paper under, and slipped the "Sanitized for Your Protection" banner on the toilet seat but didn't actually clean it.

Beverly, the new housekeeper, would have trouble making the discriminations necessary to get away with this procedure, and the employment consultant could not help support the job without being aware of the discrepancy. Doing the job correctly, Beverly would finish far slower than her co-workers and appear to be a poor worker. Discussing the problem with the supervisor might jeopardize the jobs of the other housekeepers.

Ultimately, the supported employee left for another housekeeping position with higher levels of control on cleanliness and more flexibility in reaching standards.

---

return from break not when the bell rings (nobody does that) but when George says "let's go." George knows how many extra minutes is about right, depending on what kind of day it is.

- Ask the employee not to follow the custom and ask co-workers not to teach it or encourage it. For example, Lisa was the only employee with a key to the stockroom who strictly followed the official rule about not taking any food. Her friendship with co-workers did not seem to suffer because of this; they simply viewed her as admirably ethical.

- Reassess the appropriateness of the job. Cultures that support illegal or morally distasteful customs may not be very high in other standards of job quality for an individual. The presence of these customs may signal the need to consider alternative vocational options. Counseling and support will help the employee and/or his or her guardians and advocates understand the choices available.

- Intervene to alter or stop the custom. This option is the least likely to succeed. Customs are deeply ingrained practices and people like them. An employment consultant decision to side with management, for example, and make the supervisor aware that the housekeepers have been cutting corners, would have serious repercussions. Organizations that adopt a company-centered approach and enter a setting as consultants on work methods and job structuring might have no choice but to intervene in a situation such as this.

Some social customs may be personally distasteful or violate the personal ethical standards of the employment consultant, yet be accepted and legitimate within the context of the culture. For example, some teasing might seem too harsh to an outsider (Dwyer, 1991). Such matters should always be viewed from the perspective of the setting rather than someone's external biases. Social customs that distress the employee are another matter. Such customs are likely to be a source of job dissatisfaction.

SUMMARY

Joining the culture of a worksite and forming relationships with others is as important as learning the tasks required by a job. The people who know the culture best are those who are successfully participating in it. Outsiders can come to understand a work culture to some degree through inconspicuous observation and informal and talks with these insiders. In doing so, the outside observer needs to pay careful attention to his or her role and social image within the work site.

@#$%&!

At Ideal Baking Company the bakers and bakers' assistants never complete a sentence without swearing. David, the supported employee, fits right in with the social culture and has become as good at decorating language as he is at decorating cakes.

Once in a while, though, the owner's wife visits and she is offended by swearing. So everyone "cools it" on days when she is around. David has trouble adjusting to these occasions. Al, his supervisor, makes it a point to go over to David as soon as he sees the owner's wife to remind him not to swear, and in that way prevents problems.

As employees begin to follow important social customs, become more familiar as individuals, share common interests, and participate in the give-and-take of workplace support — with assistance from an insider mentor or other "ally" and/or from an external employment consultant — working relationships begin to take shape. Interactive work tasks and effective communication between the supported employee and his or her co-workers are especially important ingredients of an overall social inclusion strategy.

Disclosure of disability information should be controlled by the wishes of the employee and can be part of a natural process of coming to know about a person. Employment consultants can play a role in dispelling stereotypes that hinder inclusion.

Sometimes complicated social customs at a worksite or customs that violate a company's official policies require careful attention. A co-worker ally may be willing to give the assistance needed by the individual to deal with such situations successfully. In other cases customs may be adapted for an individual or the social cost of not fitting in may have to be accepted. Where discrepancies between official and unofficial behavior are extreme, job change may be the preferred solution.

CHAPTER 8

Ongoing Job Support

"In business, be competent. In action, watch the timing."
— Lao Tsu

A department manager relies on the executive secretary to coordinate a daily schedule of appointments.

The executive secretary's car is in the shop for repairs and she is getting a ride to work from one of the salesmen. The salesman, recently divorced, is staying at the business manager's home temporarily.

The business manager has been so overly critical of the billing clerk's work that the clerk asks to meet with the department supervisor about it. The department supervisor cancels his scheduled meeting to meet with the billing clerk, explains to him that the business manager is always on edge just before the annual audit, and reassures him not to take it too personally.

These employees have something in common. They all receive ongoing support to succeed at their jobs. In fact, this is something they have in common with every other employee in the work force — past, present and future. Employees do not imagine for a second that they are completely "independent" at their jobs. Nor do businesses expect employees to succeed without support. Support is essential to maintaining productivity for the employer (Schermerhorn, Gardner & Martin, 1990), and is a key component of job satisfaction for employees. Support helps us manage the demands placed upon us and reach our goals.

In addition to initial training and adjustment to the job, employees with severe disabilities, like all employees, require ongoing support. But the intensity, scope, and nature of some of these supports may be new and challenging to employers.

The variety of types and sources of support available to a supported employee are covered in this chapter. Strategies for providing services that enhance the support that is naturally available and specialized services that involve not just the employee but the employee-employer *relationship* are outlined. Issues involved in adopting a consultant role, and in dealing with co-workers who may be unsupportive, are also addressed.

SUPPORT COMES IN ALL SHAPES AND SIZES

Employees receive different types of support and assistance from different sources. Support is an expansive concept, and is important at work at different times for different reasons. In a particular situation, support may or may not be related to an individual's disability, and may or may not be perceived as above and beyond the support that other employees receive.

Types of Support

An important distinction can be made between *instrumental support* and *affective support*. Instrumental support is aimed at solving a specific problem or achieving a specific result. A baker may need the assistance of a co-worker to pour a large container of batter because it "takes more than two hands." Or an office clerk may go to a supervisor for clarification of a new procedure. Instrumental support may extend beyond work itself to other areas as well. Employees help each other get back and forth to work, find apartments, get by until payday with a loan, and in countless other ways.

But instrumental support is not where job support ends. Because workplaces have people, and people have ups and downs, evolving relationships, emotions, personal crises, illnesses, and the like, affective support is also needed. When someone is depressed, worried, or anxious, co-workers may express comfort, concern, tell a joke, or offer advice. Affective support may simply express solidarity, caring or group cohesion. Not only does this help productivity, it strengthens the human aspect of a workplace.

Another important distinction can be made between *routine* and *episodic* support. Routine support needs occur predictably and relatively often, such as help in stacking heavy boxes at the end of each shift. Episodic support is needed less regularly or relatively infrequently, such as help loading boxes onto a truck for a special shipment.

Sources of Support

Still another way of viewing support is to understand the source. Support can be personal or organizational, and can come from within the setting or from an external source.

Internal support. Individual co-workers and supervisors with a work setting, as they go about the business of being together through each work day, provide personal support. Some companies, and especially many larger organizations, also sponsor their own programs of employee support. With adequate support, companies can increase the work performance of employees (Schermerhorn, Gardner & Martin, 1990). Some of the more common organizational supports are:

- Employee assistance programs
- Skill development workshops
- Wellness programs
- Employee recognition programs
- Mentorship programs
- Company parties and picnics
- Sponsorship of bowling and other sports leagues
- Retirement and outplacement counseling

External support. Families and friends support employees from outside the workplace by helping with getting ready for work, with transportation, and by listening to an employee about the events of the day. Vocational rehabilitation and supported employment programs also fall into the external-organizational category, as do a number of types of consulting firms, especially human resource development consultants, and labor unions.

Employees with disabilities, like others, need and receive both instrumental and affective support from co-workers and supervisors, from companies, and from outside organizations. Some workers with disabilities need intensive or specialized support some of the time, including external support services from a human service agency.

In any satisfactory employment situation, most support will be internal. It only appears that people with disabilities need a lot of external support if we are used to the support coming from an external agency source. If someone is sad, we may think he/she needs to talk to a counselor. If someone forgets what to do, we may think he/she needs a retraining program, a more structured environment, or some other special procedure. In our own lives, we handle most sadness or forgetting without professionals, and we know how to handle a situation where

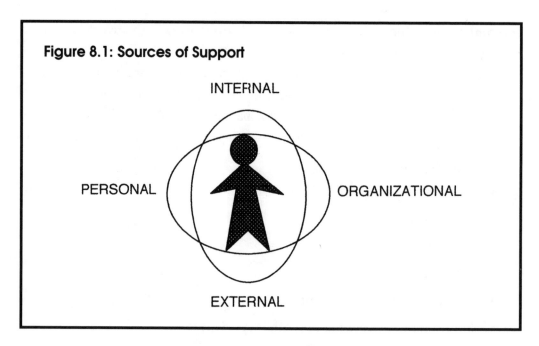

Figure 8.1: Sources of Support

INTERNAL

PERSONAL   ORGANIZATIONAL

EXTERNAL

a co-worker of ours is sad or forgets what to do.

When people with disabilities receive on-the-job support we may think that something special is going on. To the participants in the setting, giving and receiving support is something they may not even be very conscious of providing. As one co-worker put it, "We don't do anything special — we just give whatever help is needed."

If the employer has been involved in employee training, and working relationships have developed on the job, ongoing support will not be a separate issue. People who know each other and depend on each other will support each other. One study of supportive co-workers (Hagner, Cotton, Goodall & Nisbet, 1992) found that support provided to employees with severe disabilities by their co-workers included:

- Help managing time, including pacing one's work and knowing when it's time to finish one task and start another;

- Feedback on performance and reassurance that the employee is doing a good job;

- Attending to the impact of personal problems or life crises on work performance and helping the employee work through a "bad day;"

- Explanations and assistance dealing with personnel, workplace layout, or other changes at the site;

- Modifying or shifting work tasks to find the best match with the employee's interests and abilities.

Co-workers do not view support of this nature as burdensome or especially different from the support they give to anyone else. And they do not view support as a one-way street. Supported employees are in turn a source of support for their co-workers.

When effective supports are available at a worksite, the best "service" an employment consultant can provide is to let them happen and not get in the way. At times, when support systems within the worksite do not develop spontaneously, they will need to be partly "engineered" or facilitated by a support consultant. Other support resources may need to be adapted or supplemented. And some individuals do present emotional, physical, intellectual, or behavioral challenges that call for specialized expertise or skill which must either be taught to internal support persons or be provided externally, by agency staff. When support is provided externally we speak of providing *support services*. When support is simply available at the worksite with no particular assistance from outside we speak of it as *natural support*. When some effort has to be put into developing or accommodating internal support resources to suit someone's needs, we sometimes refer to *facilitating natural supports* (Nisbet & Hagner, 1988).

Both companies and employment support agencies can make a range of support options available as needed by the employee and the setting. Current federal supported employment regulations require that a source of ongoing, or extended, support for a prospective supported employee be identified. Extended support usually involves agency staff contacts at the job site with supported employees related to maintaining the job at least twice per month. Allowances for exceptions regarding location and numbers of contacts may depend on individual circumstances.

But the source of support does not necessarily have to be a traditional disability organization. And ongoing support partnerships can be maintained without a formal arrangement or official designation as "supported employment." Support may be provided from a variety of different sources,—agency staff "as well as other qualified individuals, including co-workers, through natural supports" (Federal Register, 1992). The frequency and type of support beyond the minimum twice monthly contact should be dictated solely by the needs of the individual and the setting.

Keeping in Touch

It is possible for an employment consultant to remain aware of a supported employee's progress and be alert to problems when they arise in an informal, unobtrusive way by simply maintaining contact with the employee and/or contact with a supervisor or one or more co-workers. In this role, the consultant is not the provider of support but acts in a background or back-up capacity. We might say that in these situations the consultant supports not the employee but the relationship between the employee and employer. If the support system at the worksite were to falter or confront an especially difficult situation, the employment consultant would be available to intervene.

Contacts do not have to be restricted to the business location. One employment consultant met a supported employee's co-worker after work once a week at a local tavern. A report on how things were going at work, and an occasional word of advice or encouragement to this co-worker was all that was needed to maintain the employee's job.

It is important to be assured of the overall trustworthiness of information provided. It may be necessary for an employment consultant to spot-check the accuracy of information by on-site observations. Employees may not tell the full story about support needs because they have only their personal perspective, because they are trying to "be nice" and not say negative things, or because they want to "cover" for negative behavior and protect their colleague.

Issues may arise that require more intervention. For instance, one supported employee was having a disagreement with a co-worker over lunch clean-up that had the potential to develop into a serious situation. The employment consultant asked questions of both parties to fully explore the issue, visited the work site on two occasions to see what was going on, then offered several suggestions.

The following sections describe strategies for consulting with co-workers and supervisors.

CONSULTING WITH CO-WORKERS

When sustained external support services are needed to support a job, it is helpful to use the concept of a "culturally valued analog" (Wolfensberger & Thomas, 1983). That is, to identify some existing service or practice which is positively valued and closely resembles or can be adapted to provide the needed services.

The role of "job coach" is foreign to the business world and refers to a specialized disability service unusual in a business setting. In fact, as we have seen, "coaching" refers to an important supervisory role, not an external service. A function more closely related to the kind of intervention provided by human service professionals in the business world is that of a consultant. The role of a consultant is familiar and valued. Businesses regularly call upon outside consultants to help solve problems and to provide special expertise which the organization does not have the time or resources to develop internally. Supported employment personnel *are* a type of business consultant, and we use the term "employment consultant" to emphasize this role.

Co-workers and supervisors have different roles in an organization. The consultation provided to each will be different. While supervisors have more authority to make decisions and modifications, they are usually available less often and less reliably than co-workers. Thus, supervisors may be better suited to providing episodic support, while co-workers are more likely to offer routine support.

Consultation with co-workers may take different forms at different times throughout the duration of a job. When co-workers are providing ongoing support and agency assistance is required to maintain or facilitate their efforts, several strategies are useful.

Ask for involvement. Co-workers may not be spontaneously aware of the ways in which support would be helpful to an employee and they need to be asked. An important role in marshalling support is to "go a'calling" (Schwartz, 1992); explaining what an individual needs and asking for help with it. People can either say "no;" they can say "yes" and not mean it and not follow through; or they can say "yes" and offer the needed support. But nobody can say "yes" when they aren't asked.

The best source of regular assistance with something is often a person who can easily fit the assistance into his or her usual routine.

"Would you mind noticing, when you are on your way over to Building B, whether Lisa has started her mopping yet? And if she hasn't, could you tell her she should hurry up?"

"Could you just look over once in a while and see if Jeff seems to be getting frustrated? Sometimes he doesn't realize that a part is defective and he tries to fit them together."

"Could you be behind Ellie in line in the cafeteria and help her carry her tray to the table? Sometimes by the time she gets her lunch to the table, lunch period is almost over."

The support most employees with severe disabilities need can be broken down into a string of small interventions of this nature. Spreading out different types of support involvement over a few different co-workers reduces the demand on any single individual.

Offer ideas. Simple, non-jargon explanations of work station set-up and work methods ideas can solve what may appear at first to be a significant problem. Knowing the supported employee allows the consultant to give specific ideas about training or motivation strategies likely to succeed. Advice about ongoing support is an extension of the training consultation discussed in Chapter 6.

Whenever possible, try to give indirect "hints" to co-workers rather than complete solutions. For example, a co-worker may need help learning to praise productive behavior instead of attending to and criticizing negative behavior. If you present a general principle, such as one of the behavioral strategies discussed in Chapter 6, and then ask "How can we figure out a way to do that kind of thing to help John here?," the co-worker may come up with a feasible plan for a particular situation. Then, knowing the general principle, the co-worker may generalize it to new situations and develop confidence in her problem-solving ability. Worksites may eventually get so good at solving problems that they call on the consultant only to report what action they took.

Observe performance. Accurate information is needed for a consultant to be able to effectively provide a perspective on how an employee is doing. How do co-workers react? What strategies do they use? Observing in detail can provide clues as to what kind of suggestions to make. The first response to most problems, complaints or support-related issues should be to spend time at the site and observe.

Some problems mysteriously disappear when an agency staff person is on site. Others mysteriously *appear*. For this reason, even direct observations may need to be validated. Asking other workers to keep a log and note what is happening at certain times or in certain situations will allow the consultant to develop a variety of perspectives that can shed light on a problem.

After a consultant has validated that internal company resources are dealing effectively with problems and communicating relevant information, a point may be reached where the company prefers to call when assistance is needed, and the consultant seldom initiates follow-up contacts.

Model supportive behavior. If as an employment consultant you solve a problem or intervene directly, make sure to work as openly as possible, while always respecting the privacy needs and reputation of the individual. Informing someone at the site as to what you are doing and why you think it will work will make the situation one of *modeling* the strategy.

Others can also be involved in monitoring progress. If others are aware and paying attention to what you do, they are in a better position to replicate it the next time a support need arises.

Assess complaints. Employment consultants encourage co-workers to bring any difficulties to their attention as soon as possible. But consultants should not run to a worksite to solve every problem. Asking good questions over the phone, helping generate alternative strategies, and scheduling a visit to follow up may be sufficient assistance in many cases.

It is important to ascertain the scope and the source of problems from the company's perspective. The interpretation of events does not always follow the direction one might anticipate. Some problems that seem minor to a consultant may be a big problem to the setting. For example, one employee was assigned a co-worker to check her work periodically. The supported employee began to ask this co-worker to review her work at frequent intervals throughout the shift. This particular co-worker found the steady questioning irritating. The reverse can happen as well: What seems a big problem to an outsider is viewed as minor at the site. This illustrates how behaviors and attributes are only positive or negative in a given context.

If a consultant maintains open communication, co-workers will be less likely to cover up problems in an attempt to be "nice." But it is not necessary to respond to every tiny complaint either. All of us become annoyed with something a co-worker does over the course of a working relationship, and a consultant should not communicate a sense that some technique can make a relationship perfect.

Facilitate brainstorming sessions. Rather than fixing the problem, better response to a problem in the long run is to teach the worksite how to approach fixing it. A strategy that works well in some cases is a brainstorming session in which everyone takes "ownership" of whatever problem has arisen and helps develop a solution.

Because this strategy has the effect of making a "big deal" out of a problem, it

---

SOMETIMES IT AIN'T BROKE

Robert, a newly hired supported employee, politely but firmly ordered some co-workers out of the cafeteria on their break in order to clean the floor. To the job coach on site, this was a terrible infraction and he began to develop a program to extinguish the behavior. But in the eyes of the supervisor, this was not a problem at all, but in fact was a sign of dedication and conscientious job performance. To the co-workers, it was nothing more than someone doing what had to be done to get the job finished, although they humorously expressed a desire for a little more flexibility.

Glen, a co-worker who gave Robert a ride back and forth to work, explained the importance of respecting people's breaks to Robert. The behavioral program was discarded.

---

should be reserved for situations in which the problem really is big, or situations in which something similar would be done for other employees.

There is usually some way to convene a meeting of a work group. If no meeting time can be made available as part of the work day, a few minutes before the start of a shift or during break or lunch is all that may be needed. The more key people involved, knowledgeable, and invested in solving a problem, the better. We might go so far as to say that having people invested in brainstorming is even more important than the actual solution to the problem. The employment consultant should play the role of moderator (unless there is a more appropriate internal person) and advisor to the brainstorming group.

Give permission. Through feedback, teasing, and criticism, co-workers shape the behavior of a new employee to conform to the workplace culture. They may be hesitant to act the same way when that employee has a disability, unsure how to act or how "natural" to be. Employment consultants often need to give co-workers permission, in effect, to use their typical behavior:

> "What would you do if someone else walked across the floor when you had just waxed it? Well that's exactly what you should say to Sam."

On occasion, co-workers may need to be more socially blunt with a supported

---

TEAMWORK

After lunch, Tim liked to walk throughout the building where he worked and visit with people in their offices instead of reporting back to his work station in the stock room. Everyone agreed that this behavior was annoying, unproductive, and potentially dangerous. The employment consultant brought all of the workers supportive of Tim's employment (including Tim) together for a meeting in the cafeteria.

Numerous ideas were generated at the meeting and a general approach was agreed on. Several of the workers Tim enjoyed visiting with would eat lunch with him. At the end of the lunch period they would walk with him back to the stock room and politely refuse to talk with him if he entered their offices instead. Tim's supervisor agreed to check on Tim five minutes past the end of lunch and if he was not at work, Tim would have to work right up to the time his bus arrived, missing the chance to purchase a snack for the ride home.

---

employee than people usually are. For example, a co-worker may say directly "You're standing too close." Many people feel uncertain or awkward being directive and blunt. Although they wouldn't tolerate the same behavior with anyone else, they may permit it from someone labeled as disabled, because they are worried about hurting the individual's feelings or because they are used to having people catch subtle hints.

The support consultant might help. He or she might say to the co-worker, for example, "Tom doesn't seem to notice that everyone keeps their shirt tucked in and he should try to keep the same standards as everyone else. It might be more effective if you mention it to him as his co-worker." This shows the co-worker how to help with inclusion and gives permission to be a little more socially direct than usual.

Respond immediately to serious incidents. Maximizing workplace supports does not mean letting whatever happens, happen. If a major incident or disruption is likely or has happened, employment consultants need to respond immediately and facilitate an action plan that ensures the safety and well-being of all involved.

As this may be a stressful time, a period of intensive follow-up communication with everyone involved is usually a good idea. The consultant may need the expertise of outside consultation as well if the situation indicates.

Critical incidents often become teaching opportunities. But this usually happens only after some safe time and distance allows for consideration and perspective on what happened, why it happened, what were the consequences, and what are people's feelings about the event. The most immediate response should always be to protect the emotional and physical health and safety of the individual and others involved.

Reinforce co-workers. Unfortunately, inadequate reinforcement is a common problem for employees and managers alike. This translates for many of us as a feeling of being unappreciated or uncertain about how we did in a given situation or over time.

Support efforts should be recognized and appreciated. A consultant can provide feedback to workers, not as a supervisor but as someone skilled in working with the supported employee. A simple "You handled that well. Raymond seems to really listen to you," and possibly an invitation to lunch, can be all that is needed. Reinforcement may also involve monetary compensation, as discussed below.

CONSULTING WITH SUPERVISORS

Some employment situations do not make a clear distinction between the role of co-worker and supervisor but, in general, supervisors have responsibility for evaluating employee performance. Supervisors also have more authority to make workplace decisions than co-workers, and are also usually less regularly available on an hour-by-hour basis. The support supervisors offer includes:

- Modifying or adapting job assignments and requirements;
- Approving schedule changes and time off;
- Giving feedback on job performance, including recognition for good performance and reprimands for mistakes;
- Responding to special problems or concerns; and
- Projecting a feeling that an employee is valued and the job is secure.

An employee's supervisor should provide these supervisory functions, never the employment consultant. Correspondingly, supported employees should directly notify their supervisor when they have a problem. In far too many workplaces, agency staff take over supervisory functions. This turns the supervisory relationship inside-out and creates a situation in which the real supervisor may ask the agency staff person "How's Claire doing?" or hesitate to make a decision without checking with the agency.

One of the authors visited a worksite where the supervisor kept an employee phone number list for her work team which listed an agency job coach's name and number instead of the supported employee's. An inside-out arrangement of this kind creates a barrier to a normative relationship and builds dependency on human services. Respecting lines of organizational structure helps keep "walls of disability service" from building around a supported employee.

Most supervisors are fairly well matched to their jobs and know how to supervise people. They know how to evaluate performance, how to deal with personnel issues, and how to help people develop. Good supervisors are "job coaches" for their subordinates (Orth, Wilkinson & Benfari, 1987). Not only are they good at it, but supervisors often obtain a great deal of job satisfaction from this side of their work. To some extent, supervisors even enjoy dealing with personnel problems; especially helping an individual overcome difficulty or develop a new side of their personality. If supervisors need assistance, employment consultants should act in the capacity of advisors.

If a company has an established format and schedule for employee performance reviews, the same procedure should be followed for a supported employee. If an employment consultant helps establish or revise a review procedure, it should be for the benefit of the entire company or department, not just one employee.

Supervisors generally are less interested in employees achieving a specified level of performance than they are in seeing progress. The meaning of job performance — whether it is improving — not its actual level, determines the feedback given by supervisors (Sandelands, Glynn, & Larson, 1991). Supervisors need to be able to interpret events and respond effectively. Employment consultants can help supervisors figure out how to evaluate performance: What to look for, and how to see progress.

A personal relationship and mutual interests with one's supervisor can be important. Such nonperformance factors as liking, perceived similarity of values,

---

SUPPORTING THE SUPERVISOR

Eva's supervisor learned that Eva was taking pens and folders home from work. The supervisor notified the employment consultant and they met to discuss what to do. The employment specialist avoided solving the problem directly. Instead, she suggested to the supervisor the parameters of the discussion that the supervisor should have with Eva, and helped her think through each step.

The supervisor would need to define exactly what Eva could take from work and what she couldn't. And she would have to establish a hierarchy of consequences. The supervisor was unsure about this idea as she had never approached discipline in this way before. But the employment consultant educated the supervisor about the benefits of this approach and encouraged her to develop a policy. The policy developed was a one-day suspension for the first stealing episode, three days for the second, one week for the third, and dismissal for the fourth.

The supervisor discussed the policy with Eva and implemented it. Outside of work, the employment consultant helped Eva to purchase office supplies for her home with her paycheck. After one further incident, the stealing stopped.

---

and "fit" with the organization play a large role in a supervisor's performance evaluation. Supervisors reward employees who offer extra help and show an interest in the supervisor's personal life with higher performance ratings (Ferris & King, 1992).

If a supervisor does not feel confident in approaching someone with a disability, it is a good idea to actively encourage the supervisor by building familiarity, providing tips for communication, and suggesting how and when to approach the person. Employers also pay attention to and learn from one another. There may be occasions when an employment consultant can assist supervisors to develop networks for information sharing. One agency sponsored a monthly employer breakfast for informal sharing of ideas and experiences.

Remember to assess any problems from the perspective of the company. And not every problem has to be "solved." Supervisors can make allowances for variations in job performance. For example, one employee was adamant about not taking orders from a substitute supervisor. He refused to work and became very angry when his usual supervisor was not on duty. While behavioral change interventions were certainly available to help this employee change, the supervisor devised a quick and effective accommodation of her own. She gave the employee every day off that she was off. While it might be better for our personal growth to learn how to deal effectively with certain situations, the reality is that avoidance works fine too.

In cases where an employee has very extensive support needs, it may be necessary to rethink the job design or switch to a job sharing or personal care support strategy. Both are discussed below. If even this level of ongoing support is inadequate, a poor job match may be the problem and the career planning process should be reestablished.

EXPANDING THE SCOPE OF SERVICES

Kram (1988) has noted that many work performance problems that appear at first to be individual skill or training problems turn out on closer inspection to be problems with the design of a job or with a production system. Reversing the typical procedure, she advocates that managers look first for problems at the system level, second for problems at the job design level, and only last at the individual employee level to resolve a job problem. In the same spirit, employment consultants need not confine their attention to the work behavior of one or two employees, but can expand the scope of their consultation to the job design or the production system level.

Supported employment and other rehabilitation professionals have a great deal to offer to a company. Flexible job descriptions, specific evaluation criteria, and efficient job designs benefit employers as much as they do supported employees. An employment consultant should put all of his or her expertise to work in the service of the company.

Thomas (1990) has encouraged businesses to evaluate every business practice to determine if it truly constitutes "affirming diversity." The test should be "Is this practice something everyone can use or benefit from?" Only if the practice applies to everyone does it truly meet the test. The practice of accommodating for individual differences is the ultimate affirmation of diversity.

We have already expanded the scope of consulting services to a company if we have consulted with employers on creating a job or redesigning job positions,

---

SOMETIMES TOO MANY ARE BROKEN

Juan was throwing away too many dishes. His job in the dishroom included separating trash (including plastic dishware) from the ceramic dishware and silverware as it came by on a conveyor belt and placing the latter into the dishwasher. The agency was called in to help with retraining Juan. The employment consultant conducted detailed observations over two shifts.

A detailed analysis of the work revealed that the white plastic dishware looked so much like the white ceramic dishes that when quick decisions had to be made based on visual cues it was too easy to make a mistake. Every dishroom worker was throwing away about the same percentage of "good dishes." The consultant recommended not a behavioral intervention but the purchase of another type of plastic dishware, and one with a floral design was chosen. Everyone could tell them apart and the problem was resolved. This employer calls in the consultant for advice on similar production problems.

---

helped inaugurate a mentorship program, assisted with compliance with the Americans with Disabilities Act, modified equipment or work procedures in some way, or helped in establishing a performance evaluation procedure. What is now required is a more thorough approach to this side of the employer relationship.

What specific assistance a consultant or an agency can offer to a company depends on the mix of skills and resources available. A partial list would include:

- Workplace communication and team-building,
- Accommodating and affirming workforce diversity,
- Job design and work methods,
- Job analysis,
- Employee training,
- Personnel management,
- Safety and disability prevention,
- Performance evaluation,
- Government regulations and incentives, and

- Employee assistance, counseling and referral.

A consultant who expands the scope of services and generalizes her work breaks the close association between her presence at the company and the supported employee. This accomplishes two interrelated goals. It avoids stigmatizing the supported employee as the one different employee who needs a consultant. And it provides a different opportunity for the consultant to be present at the company and keep aware of how the supported employee is doing.

Getting Started in Consulting

Individuals and organizations can expand their consulting role in any of several ways.

- By advertising expanded services in marketing literature;
- By mentioning services during job negotiations with the employer;
- By mentioning possibilities as observations are made at the worksite during support visits; and
- By manager inquiries in response to what they see the consultant doing.

This fourth method is probably the most common. For example:

Bakery manager: "Bob tells me that Betsy is making a lot of progress. She is following the different muffin recipes with no problem."

Employment consultant: "Yes, she is doing well, and I think part of it is that she really likes it here. She is comfortable with Bob and the other workers. She follows recipes from a strip of pictures that Bob posts each day showing the ingredients of each type of muffin. Since we did that she hasn't made any mistakes."

Manager: "No mistakes? That's amazing. I wish I could say that about my other workers."

Employment consultant: "Actually, I wondered if you wanted to see these recipes. A couple of other workers said they thought they might be helpful."

Manager: "Sure, let's see them. Maybe we can incorporate this idea so everyone can benefit from it."

Acting openly and transparently, and in an inclusive style that draws work teams together to solve problems, maximizes the chance that a consultant's role will expand and generalize.

About Consulting and Indirect Services

A consultant role is difficult to manage. One must avoid doing too much or too little. One must intervene at the correct level. One must take care to bolster rather than threaten internal support resources. Some people find an indirect or consultative role difficult to achieve for several reasons.

- They may want to "fix things" and be uncomfortable holding back when something is not immediately take care of, or taken care of less well.

- They may receive satisfaction from direct "caring for people" or from providing assistance or protection to people who need help.

- They might experience invisibility or a great deal of ambiguity when not in control of anything directly.

- If a job doesn't work out, it may mean a great deal more work, and consequently they may want to do the most they can to make it successful.

Overcoming these feelings is important if we are to promote social belonging and not limit a supported employee to one caretaker. This is not a release of responsibility, nor is it a denial of some people's vulnerabilities.

French and Bell (1984) have recommended that organizational consultants resist the temptation to act as experts. Instead, they encourage consultants to assist companies to develop their own expertise. Lippitt and Lippitt (1984) have cautioned that "external consultants are a threat to natural helpers" (p. 510) and recommend that consultants look for ways to coordinate their efforts with internal support systems.

Effective consultation is an active process that requires judgment, sensitivity and technical skill. The best consultants are:

- "People people," that is, personable and able to put others at ease;

- Careful observers and good listeners;

- Expert at one or more specific skill areas.

ALTERNATIVE SUPPORT ARRANGEMENTS

A common arrangement for extended support involves some combination of

(a) company flexibility and supervisory or management time,

(b) informal "natural" co-worker assistance, and

(c) visits by staff of a vocational support service for individuals with disabilities, to maintain the support system and intervene in specific areas.

Funding for agency support services beyond initial training is typically provided through the various state departments of mental health and developmental disabilities. But employees vary widely in their support needs and companies vary widely in their support resources. This arrangement is ideal in many cases but not in others. For example, some supported employees have disabilities for which no state agency is designated to provide ongoing vocational services. Alternative strategies for sources of support and methods of paying for support are important to providing a range of options that match the needs of individual employees and employers. A number of alternative arrangements for ongoing support are possible.

Stipends to Companies or Co-workers

An agency can make some or all of the funds it receives for ongoing support available to a company or to individual co-workers. Instead of agency staff visiting the company and providing support services, the company takes responsibility for support services. Or, one or more individual co-workers become subcontractors of the agency and deliver support services to the supported employee. Agency visits in this arrangement are for the purposes of contract monitoring, although this could take the form of technical assistance on support procedures which might resemble closely in some cases the role of an employment consultant.

This arrangement is useful when an employee has significant support needs, beyond what a company can provide without compensation or a special arrangement, but the company is willing and able to provide them if a fair arrangement can be negotiated.

Providing support for pay involves two important issues. First, it can interfere with the formation of natural relationships and friendships. Paid co-workers may take on a quasi-staff role, with many of the same disadvantages noted in Chapter 2 in connection with job coaching. Second, an agency undertakes some degree of liability for services provided by its subcontractors, and therefore must take care that the quality of support services provided by the company is adequate. The following suggestions may assist in dealing with these issues.

- Co-worker support responsibilities should fall clearly outside the ordinary scope of the individual's job. Driving someone back and forth from work or staying late to check the quality of work at the end of a shift are two clear examples.

- Specific company or co-worker responsibilities should be spelled out clearly in a contract between the two parties.

Formal Company Resources

Some larger companies have well-run human resource departments, employee assistance programs or other internal resources with the capacity to serve as sources of ongoing job support for supported employees. Some employee assistance programs or training and development offices may be ideal for this purpose. Mid-sized companies may purchase the same services from a free-standing human resource or employee assistance firm. It is likely that the services provided by these organizations would have to be significantly adapted to meet the needs of employees with severe disabilities (Kiernan & McGauhey, 1992).

Company-funded Supports

Under the Americans with Disabilities Act, larger companies are required to make accommodations that would allow an employee with a disability to perform the essential functions of a job, unless this would pose an "undue hardship." Accommodations can include assigning one or more co-workers to provide various kinds of ongoing support that an employee might need. This arrangement can even resemble the reverse of the previous option, whereby a company enters into a contract with an outside agency or individual and pays for the services provided. Companies and agencies can also split the cost of ongoing support.

Employee-funded Supports

Two work incentive provisions of the Social Security programs discussed in Chapter 5, Impairment Related Work Expenses (IRWE) and Plans to Achieve Self Support (PASS), can be used by individuals receiving these benefits to purchase ongoing supports.

In some cases, families can also directly purchase portions of services either through personal funds or vouchered payment mechanisms arranged from public funds. A caution here is for families not to displace fundable supports that they should receive by law, but to supplement them or be empowered to directly purchase needed services through direct-to-the-family grants.

Other Funding Sources

Some local revenue may be available from municipal or town funds or county funding. A variety of state and federal options may also be available, including unemployment resources, workers compensation, personnel preparation grants, assistive technology projects, Job Training Partnership Acts funds, Small Business Administration loans, social service block grant money, state general revenue funds, and state use contracts. Many agencies obtain funding from local United Way organizations, and some obtain private industry or foundation support.

Post-employment services can be provided through the state vocational rehabilitation agency. Personal care services can be funded through the Medicaid program. The availability and procedures for gaining access to these funds varies widely and must be researched in each local situation.

CO-WORKER STIPENDS CAN BE A VIABLE OPTION

Kevin obtained a job with a telemarketing firm, soliciting newspaper subscriptions. The phone numbers were dialled automatically by computer. Because he is blind, Kevin tape-recorded subscription information after each successful call.

A co-worker, a friend who also attended the same church as Kevin, transcribed Kevin's audiotaped information onto subscription forms in the evening, on his own time. Kevin paid the co-worker for each transcription and deducted this sum from his countable earnings as an Impairment Related Work Expense. Kevin feels that the arrangement has strengthened their friendship.

— Rogan, Hagner & Murphy (1992)

Job Sharing

Another ongoing support arrangement without a continuous human service presence is job sharing. In job sharing, two individuals share or split a job position between them. The employer correspondingly splits the salary associated with the position between the two employees.

Two individuals can share a job by (a) each working when the other is not on duty, (b) working together, splitting a job in which coverage is not an issue; or (c) they can split one job into two jobs with overlapping schedules. These forms of job sharing are part of a general movement towards more flexible work schedules that has become increasingly popular as our society accommodates more diverse lifestyles.

Job sharing strategies. Job sharing in which a supported employee receives ongoing as-needed assistance typically involves one individual with a severe disability and one without a disability, who fill at least one full job position. A supported employment agency obtains an agreement from an interested employer, recruits both individuals and matches them to the requirements of a particular position. The employee with a disability is referred and funded to receive supported employment services and the employee without a disability may be recruited through want ads, school placement offices, employment agencies, or from within the company. Each individual performs work for the employer, but the non-disabled employee has some additional responsibilities for providing support to the job sharer with a disability.

Job sharing is an especially appropriate option for individuals with the most severe disabilities who require fairly frequent or specialized ongoing support services in order to maintain employment.

Job sharing payment mechanisms. In job sharing, employers split the salary they would ordinarily pay to one employee between two employees, based on the amount of relative productivity contributed by each job sharer. For example, Joe and Mike share a position at a research laboratory. Joe's job, entering each day's experimental data into a computer, fulfills 80% of the position, and Mike's job, entering the commands to print out hard copies, is 20% of the position. Each receives the appropriate percentage of the salary associated with the position.

The company can pay the job sharers directly as employees or by contracting with the agency which arranges the job sharing. Direct hiring is the more usual arrangement. Wages commensurate with productivity, in accordance with the Fair Labor Standards Act, must be paid to each employee in either case.

In this case, Mike earns $4.62 per hour working 20 hours per week for an annual salary of $4,800.00, and his productivity rating is 40%. (He works half-time to complete 20% of the work.) Joe earns $19,200 per year from the company working full-time to complete the rest of the work (80% of the $24,000 annual salary attached to the position).

Joe's responsibilities also include a number of support functions for Mike, including transportation, setting up the computer, and assisting with toileting and eating. He is paid an additional $400.00 per month by the agency for these responsibilities as a subcontractor. The agency received funding from the state vocational rehabilitation agency to reimburse this expense for the first 18 months, after which funding responsibility for reimbursement shifted to the state disability agency, as specified in Mike's rehabilitation plan.

Although job sharing can be a creative solution for some people, a few cautions are in order. Care must be exercised in the selection and orientation of the non-disabled job sharer, and the possibility that this individual will become a quasi-staff person rather than a co-worker must be considered. The perception of the job sharing arrangement by others within the company must also be monitored carefully. In addition, turnover of either of the parties sharing the position may cause considerable difficulty in recreating the job situation.

The control usually exercised by employers over the recruitment and hiring of employees is diminished or complicated in job sharing. Even when the company hires the two employees, the agency usually recruits and matches them both. Problems also arise if the employer is dissatisfied with one party. Even the logistics of such details as taking a vacation can become difficult to manage. Contracting with the business for both positions makes these complexities the responsibility of the agency but at the same time further weakens the company's sense of ownership and control.

DEALING WITH CONFLICT

Relationships on the job are the essence of social inclusion and the basis for training and support. When relationships are positive, the benefits are mutual. But when workers don't get along, they not only lose each others' support, they set up an antagonistic situation which adds stress, frustration, and anger to the worksite.

This in turn reduces performance and productivity. The employer, who needs an atmosphere of teamwork for cohesiveness and group tasks, will take steps to remedy the situation. This is often done by the quickest solution available — firing the "troublemaker(s)." The employment consultant can head off disaster by recognizing conflict and taking action to defuse a conflict situation in cooperation with the employer and other co-workers.

Recognizing Unsupportive Relationships

Almost everyone has some unsupportive or conflict relationships at work at one time or another. There are usually numerous indicators of conflict. Unfortunately, many times these are hidden from supervisors as from well as employment consultants. Things a consultant should look for include:

- *A change in the setting or routine* — Sometimes adaptations, modifications, or the introduction of someone or something new is seen as threatening by people.

- *Non-verbal signals* — Gestures, body language, or behavior may indicate avoidance, anger, anxiety or other feelings related to conflict.

- *Negative language* — Sometimes tone or semantics, as well as what words are said, can indicate how people feel toward each other.

- *Work avoidance* — If the supported employee begins to have attendance or punctuality problems, or if work performance declines unexpectedly, there may be a conflict involved.

Even if a conflict is not very serious, it is better to explore solutions before a more open exchange occurs. Once a relationship develops a pattern of antagonism, it becomes more difficult to change.

There are several identifiable types of conflict relationships at work (Krupan & Krupan, 1988). Some negative relationships supported employees might encounter are described below.

Difficult supervisor. When the boss has unrealistic expectations, a demanding style or an unpleasant attitude, an atmosphere of fear or distrust can emerge. This could be the result of new demands from management, a new job, misperceptions about the employee or simply a personality mismatch.

Controlling co-worker. Sometimes an individual will try to manage the work environment to his/her personal gain by attempting to "take advantage" of others through manipulation, giving orders or avoiding unpleasant tasks.

Parental co-worker. An overprotective co-worker can be patronizing or overbearing. He or she tends to hover around the person at work, or speak to the person as a child, perhaps in a sing-song tone of voice.

Extra bosses. Too many supervisors, or co-workers who try to act like supervisors, give orders that conflict with one another and overwhelm an employee. This can leave the worker uncertain about whom to respond to and what to do.

Conservative veteran. Every individual will to try to make accommodations in a work setting to fit his own unique strengths and needs. A person who is threatened by an accommodation, especially a perceived significant change, sees innovation and change as disruptions and prefers to keep things the way they've always been.

Unaccepting people. Although rare, some people will victimize others, or harass workers by teasing and joking about disability. These are the people earlier disability advocates attempted to "shelter" people from in special facilities.

Reactions to Conflict

When confronted with a conflict relationship on the job, we all react differently. Responses range from passivity to aggressive confrontation. Responses at either extreme seldom resolve the situation. For the employment consultant, conflict resolution requires a careful balance between advocacy and respect for the culture of a work setting.

The employment consultant must begin by carefully observing the work situation. It is difficult to know all the factors influencing a problem. But the more information you have about the setting, demands, organizational structure and the people who make it up, the more you can help find a resolution.

Resolving Problem Relationships at Work

Consultants can assist in resolving most workplace conflicts through a few simple techniques.

- Model appropriate social behavior at the worksite. Don't contribute to misperceptions of the employee by your own language, posture, materials or tone.

- Convey realistic task expectations to co-workers and supervisors.

- Assist others to spot signs of stress or frustration on the part of the employee if the employee is unable to communicate them.

- Encourage the supported employee to respond to a person during an uncomfortable interaction by stating how the exchange her them feel.

- Don't take on the role of the supervisor and give other employees directives.

- Don't lecture co-workers or supervisors. Act as a resource and suggest strategies that work well for the supported employee.

- Build networks and bridges to those in the work environment who are supportive. Supportive co-workers can act as allies and help defend the employee against unsupportive people.

- Avoid isolating the employee from other workers as a means to resolve social difficulties.

Counseling

Before intervening in a conflict, it is a good idea to sit down with the supported employee to explore his feelings and what seems to be causing them. Sometimes a situation can be changed by selecting a fairly simple coping strategy or making a simple change in a schedule or a routine.

Some steps to use when discussing conflict with a supported employee:

1. Establish supportive communication,

2. Explore perceptions of events and people,

3. Isolate the root causes of feelings,

4. Identify specific behaviors that create conflict,

5. Discuss options for resolving the situation,

6. Select a strategy,

7. Monitor the effectiveness of the strategy over time.

ALLIES ARE KEY TO CONFLICT RESOLUTION

William worked in the processing department at Ace Manufacturing. Pat, a co-worker, was assigned to assist William with pacing his work, because he had difficulty keeping track of time, and with other support needs.

Pat received a report that William was yelling at some co-workers and causing a disturbance, and she went to investigate. Two co-workers had been teasing William and, although they did not intend to be mean, William was having a bad day and he had reacted strongly. Pat talked with William and helped him calm down.

Pat then had a talk with the two co-workers, who admitted that "we were asking for it." She reported to the personnel manager that William "was just sticking up for himself" and that was the end of the matter.

Mediation

If a conflict has advanced to a serious level and interpersonal problem-solving needs to occur, the employment consultant may wish to suggest a meeting between the parties involved with a mediator, possibly the supervisor or an uninvolved co-worker. It is wise for the employment consultant not to act as the mediator, as he/she is not viewed as neutral nor equally influential with the individuals. Some ground rules for mediation include:

- The persons involved commit to fully participate and act in good faith.
- No one is present besides the participants and mediator.
- Each person agrees not to discuss the other before or after.
- The meeting is held in a neutral setting.
- The participants remain calm during discussions.
- The negotiation is confidential except for whatever is jointly decided to share.

The following problem-solving steps are useful during conflict resolution meetings:

1. An agreed time limit is set at the start.

2. Each person briefly states his or her position on a specific issue in conflict. A paraphrase of the other's statement usually is useful to ensure understanding.

3. The participants each explain their situation with relevant and recent examples. Generalizations are not used.

4. The people in conflict jointly set objectives for changing the current situation.

5. They identify obstacles and factors in achieving their objective, both within themselves and in the environment.

6. Each participant suggests strategies for resolution.

7. Proposed resolutions are tested for feasibility and acceptability to each.

8. The people involved select those actions they see as most valuable. They should not agree to any decisions they both cannot support.

9. The work in implementing a solution is divided evenly, taking into account the skill and time required and available.

10. A follow-up meeting to review progress is agreed upon.

When All Else Fails

If a conflict cannot be resolved any other way, an employment consultant can consider direct advocacy at the management level where the required decisions to resolve a dispute can be made. This step should be taken with caution as the strategy may give the advocate a negative reputation among co-workers, and it may also backfire, with the supported employee viewed as the party in the wrong.

If no resolution to a conflict seem possible, assist the employee to determine if the job is worth whatever aggravation is involved. If it is, help the person learn to handle stress through relaxation exercises, stress management or other coping strategies. If a personality conflict is making the supported employee miserable and advocacy efforts are fruitless, review with the employee possible alternatives for an employment change.

Throughout, the employment consultant should try to support the process so conflict is resolved, preferably not at the expense of either party. If the employment consultant joins in the conflict, there will be less of a chance for a negotiation. If the conflict continues, there will be less of a chance for a successful tenure at that worksite. If the consultant can see a solution to a particular problem, it is best to share that strategy with someone at the site who can suggest it to others, or facilitate group problem-solving in which the solution is developed by the group as a whole.

SUMMARY

Correctly learning a job, and even becoming included socially at work, does not mean that support on the job will simply continue to happen by itself. Jobs, situations, and people constantly change, and sometimes external support resources are needed to monitor, facilitate or supplement the internal support available at the worksite. Employment consultants can maintain an active relationship, offering advice and technical assistance as needed to help employers and employees successfully handle situations as they arise. The scope of consultation can sometimes be expanded to include activities which strengthen the department or company as a whole.

Several creative arrangements for ongoing support are available in this effort, including stipends to co-workers, job sharing, and other employer or employee controlled funding strategies. Employment consultants should also pay attention to relationships that may be problematic for the supported employee, as individuals may have difficulty communicating about conflict. A variety of strategies and approaches may be offered to deal with problematic social situations, including counseling, mediation, and problem-solving steps.

CHAPTER 9

Beyond Entry Jobs into Careers

"They always say that time changes things,
but you actually have to change them yourself."
— Andy Warhol

Our career is a journey, sometimes taking directions few of us could have predicted. We have followed our interests, responded to needs, been fired, promoted, or transferred, have quit and started anew, or have pursued multiple fields. And who can tell what lies ahead? Most of us have had a succession of various jobs with a number of different employers. The average employee has worked at about eight different jobs (Wegmann, 1991a).

Many people start their employment careers with what are called "entry level" jobs available in the local economy. Entry level jobs, such as janitorial, dishwashing, food service or retail clerk work, have important uses. They are an exposure to the world of work and help us obtain references from employers for further career moves. They can be stepping-stones to advancement within a company, can test an occupational area or type of work setting without a heavy commitment, or can simply provide income while we define our interests or wait for other opportunities. A few individuals find these jobs satisfying as long-term career options. Most workers, as skills expand and interests crystallize, move out of entry-level employment to positions that provide greater challenges and higher incomes.

Supported employment practitioners sometimes expect a "successful placement" for people with disabilities to lead to an indefinitely long period of employment in that same job. Professional attitudes, agency policies, and funding mechanisms reinforce this expectation. But there are significant advantages to adopting a wider perspective and planning for a succession of supported jobs for each individual. And it is worth exploring how traditional attitudes and policies can be changed.

Establishing a career development perspective, strategies for assessing job satisfaction, and approaches to job change are dealt with in this chapter. The difficult issues that face a person who winds up temporarily between jobs are discussed as well.

A CAREER DEVELOPMENT PERSPECTIVE

People in the field of vocational rehabilitation very often expect one job position to last indefinitely. Ongoing support is designed to support an individual who remains at the same job. Service staff tend to be shocked and discouraged when people lose or quit jobs *they cannot leave any other way*, sometimes blaming the loss on the individual's disability or on their own lack of competence in training and support. Or, vocational personnel may try to influence employees to "stick it out" in a job they have little interest in. Those who do leave or lose their job are at least likely to have a chance of obtaining assistance to find a new job. Less fortunate are those workers who remain marginally employed, socially isolated and unhappy at work while showing up on some human service counselor's program report as a "successful rehabilitation." In today's service structure, employees with severe disabilities who lose their jobs are frequently placed back in sheltered workshops, adding insult to injury. Chubon (1985) termed this the "one shot" approach to rehabilitation. Why do people in supported employment place so much faith in one job? Largely they are operating on a set of outmoded employment myths.

The scientific matching myth. Some people believe in the power of vocational assessment procedures and equipment to generate scientific occupational recommendations that will result in a "correct job match" and long-term job satisfaction. Vocational assessment has been discussed in Chapter 3 and its claims seriously questioned. If someone actually develops an assessment method that provides a valid shortcut to the time-consuming, sometimes heartbreaking, hit-or-miss career development procedure most people use, it will be easy to know about it. People without disabilities will be standing in line to spend their own money to purchase such an assessment, with vocational rehabilitation professionals in the front of the line.

The secondary market myth. Some people may believe that job seekers with severe disabilities are so restricted in their capabilities that there are few jobs they can do. They might view a job that for other workers would be "entry level" and temporary as an end point for a supported employee.

But a lower-skilled job does not have to mean a menial or an entry level job. Using the job creation techniques presented in Chapter 5, positions can be established in all sorts of valued occupations and settings at any given skill level.

Entry level jobs are characterized not so much by the level of skill involved, but by the attitude of employees and employers towards them and in the way they are used in our economy. The segment of the labor market in which pay is low and little or no benefits are involved is sometimes called the secondary labor market. Just as employees have a use for entry level work, companies use the secondary labor market to fill what might be considered "disposable jobs." These jobs are disposable in much the same spirit as disposable pens or disposable razors: They are inexpensive and temporary, and nobody gets too attached to them.

The immunity to boredom myth. There is a common misperception that people with severe disabilities either want or don't object to boring, repetitive jobs. People might say, "I wouldn't enjoy that work, but Bob thinks it's great!" For Bob, compared to what he has been doing, what may be great is simply being in a real business with a real job. That doesn't mean people with disabilities should be eternally grateful for any kind of job. Some work is just plain boring, and whether after ten days, ten weeks or ten months, almost anyone will eventually lose interest in it.

In addition to these powerful myths, some practical organizational realities also function as barriers to implementation of a career development approach. First, agency personnel may put a great deal of effort into developing a job, analyzing and teaching each task, building a relationship with an employer, and performing other job-related functions. Staff may be so overworked finding *one job* for everyone who needs a job that they view career development as an idealistic "frill." These staff members may be quite upset to see that their hard work resulted in a brief period of employment and that now they have to start over.

Second, it can be difficult to establish funding for a job search for a successfully employed individual. The premise behind vocational rehabilitation services is that upon succeeding at a job for two months an individual with a disability becomes "rehabilitated" and his or her "case" will be "closed."

But a one-shot or "wait for failure" approach is incompatible with quality supported employment. Several significant disadvantages can be noted.

- Job choices tend to be made conservatively when avoiding job failure is a prime consideration. While being a chef may be someone's true goal, a dishwashing job may be a reasonable step towards the goal. The danger, though, is that it might be tempting to convince the person that dishwashing is close enough to the goal and stop there. Reaching for a dream can be risky business, and the only sure way to avoid failure is to avoid success.

- As a rule, people similar in age have more in common. Since people move in and out of entry level jobs, an individual who remains in such a job year after year may experience an increasing age difference from his co-workers. Age differences may hinder the development of peer relationships.

- Entry level environments often have weak cultures. In other words, the workers in these settings share fewer social customs and traditions and less camaraderie. Workers are usually not very committed to their job or their employer. They may even distance themselves from their work with statements like "I'm just doing this until something comes up."

- Turnover is often high in entry level positions so people have less chance to get to know each other well.

It is wise to remember that " the customer is always right" in vocational services as in all services. It is not appropriate to resent or blame a person for experimenting and testing out jobs. Nor does it make sense to blame the service providers for not being able to always predict a good job match. People are too complex and jobs are too complex. The most adaptive approach is to expect and plan on a long-term process in which the individual, even though successfully employed, eventually searches out new opportunities and then gives notice and leaves her job on good terms. We call this a career development perspective.

DESIGNING A CAREER

Some people use the terms "job" and "career" interchangeably, but there is an important distinction between the two. A "job" usually refers to a *position*, a discrete productive role occupied by an individual worker: teacher at the Happy Days Early Childhood Center; dispatcher at Fuel Oil Company, and so on. A set of positions that have major tasks in common is an *occupation*, like teacher or dispatcher. Sometimes people use "job" to mean "occupation." A *career* is a series of positions held by an individual worker that are linked together by a consistent theme or pattern.

Joe started his career as a truck driver for a bread company, then switched to ambulance driver for the hospital. Now he is the emergency response dispatcher. A career may consist of a single job, but this is unusual.

It is also possible to change careers, that is, switch to a completely new theme or shift directions radically. For example, a doctor originally interested in building sailboats as a vacation hobby eventually decided to leave the field of medicine and build sailboats as a full-time business. Most common is a pattern of job changes within one overall career pattern: a doctor joins the staff of a hospital, subsequently becomes chief of surgery, then joins the faculty of a medical school.

In our quest for meaningful careers, many workers progress through stages of life, and different career needs and priorities are salient at different stages (Super, 1984). Stages in an individual's career might look like the following:

AGE STAGE	PRIORITIES
15 - 20 *Fantasy and Exploration*	Self-discovery, researching occupations and testing vocations.
20 - 25 *Basic Training*	Learning the ropes, building self-confidence, and establishing a work history.
20 - 30 *Early Career*	Building responsibility, finding a mentor, considering long-term commitment
30 - 40 *Mid-Career*	Judging failure/success, considering the interplay of family/self/work, establishing independence from one's mentor.
40 - 55 *Late Career*	Becoming a mentor for others, exercising wisdom, demonstrating leadership.
55 - 65 *Disengagement*	Exploring new sources of satisfaction, reassessing family life.

| 65- | *Retirement* | Maintaining identity and self-worth and refocusing energies away from employment. |

A shift away from supporting jobs (i.e. positions) to supporting careers for people is an important shift in emphasis for supported employment. It is a more flexible approach because it can accommodate a range of situations, from remaining in the same job for many years to changing jobs many times. This allows workers to explore and experiment without an enormous stake being placed on one position working out.

People with disabilities may find themselves, whatever their age, stuck in jobs appropriate to fantasy, work entry or basic training phases of a career. Providing guidance into the mid and late career phases needs to be a viable part of supported employment services.

While constant job change does not allow for stable career exploration and growth, neither does clinging to the same position for life. There should be a balance between the flexibility needed for personal career development and the stability required to establish a track record as a reliable employee and to develop meaningful relationships with co-workers and supervisors. Maintaining a career development perspective is mainly a matter of thinking of each job as temporary and planning for the day when job advancement will be warranted.

Advancement

Advancement along a career path may be either by changing employers or by changing jobs and advancing within the same business. Most employers are aware of the desire for growth and development on the part of employees as well as the profit-making potential of investing in a stable and skilled work force. Many employees start out with the understanding that opportunities for advancement can be considered once they prove themselves, provided the business thrives. Supported employees are no different. The anti-discrimination provisions of the Americans with Disabilities Act extend to all employment practices, including advancement. Advancing one's career within a company can take a variety of forms (Schein, 1978).

Hierarchical. This is the most traditional way of perceiving career advancement, with an increase in power and influence and movement up a career ladder and with promotion to new job titles and responsibilities.

Technical. As the scope and depth of work deepens, there is an increase in skills, competencies, and a corresponding respect from others due to abilities to get things done well, quickly and/or efficiently. Often, salary increases, enlargement of the scope of one's job or "lateral" moves (to a different but not necessarily "higher" job) signal advancement in technical skill.

Membership. Movement toward the "inner circles" of the workplace social sphere may occur. As key social relationships deepen, one experiences an increase in trust and inclusion with others.

Supported employees may find that they have added responsibilities to their job over time. These should be monitored for the sake of having an up-to-date resume. Added responsibilities also may indicate the need to discuss salary or job title advancement with the employer. Periodic evaluation of performance by one's supervisor provides a good opportunity to discuss advancement. If an employment consultant is assisting with this process, her role should be that of an agent, helping negotiate the best deal for the employee. When no further advancement seems likely or interesting, it may be time to consider a change of employers.

The Job Hierarchy

One's first job, or any one job, rarely has all the elements of a quality working life that an individual is looking for over the span of her working life. Many workers make their first career choices out of economic necessity, or because of the availability of a contact through their personal network. Choice-making and individual expression become more possible with subsequent jobs (Salomone & Slaney, 1981).

Curl and Hall (1990) have suggested that jobs can be usefully viewed as ranging along a hierarchy of levels. A given position will fall on one of five levels.

- A *level I* job satisfies an immediate need for employment but is either temporary or for less than the desired number of hours.

- A *level II* job is a stable job for the right amount of hours but does not really offer the kind of work, social atmosphere, working conditions, or level of pay or benefits that the individual is looking for.

- A *level III* job includes those positions where an individual can exercise her strongest skills and is interesting to the individual but may not have opportunities for advancement.

Figure 9.1: From Job to Job

- A *level IV* job has all these elements but in addition has opportunities for advancement to level V.

- A *level V* job is an optimal match to skills and interests, more than adequate working conditions, pay and/or benefits.

Many individuals begin at one of the first two levels. A personal network job search may initially turn up a job opening that is not the individual's ideal job but nevertheless is a good beginning. These positions should be filled in the same spirit that people without disabilities fill them, as something temporary and a place to start. There should be a regular turnover of people out of lower-level and into higher-level jobs. And even after an individual reaches a level V job, priorities and circumstances continue to evolve as one develops through various stages of life.

Finding and supporting multiple jobs does not require a great deal more effort than finding and supporting one job for an individual, just effort of a different kind. When a person is in the wrong job, or in the right job too long, those providing support become enmeshed in endless, insoluble problems. Most of the time, the situation worsens until the individual quits or loses the job. Meanwhile a vast amount of effort goes into propping up the situation, trying to stave off the inevitable. At some point, it is best to stop and ask yourself "If this was happening to me, would I keep trying to stick it out or would I start looking around for something else?"

And when such a job finally ends, it places everyone involved in the worst of all possible situations: A former employee with a failure experience and possibly a reluctance to try again; an employer whose investment has not paid off, who may not give the individual a very good reference, and who will think twice about hiring the next person supported in the same way; and a frustrated, "burnt out" employment service. By contrast, there is a bright side to helping a person leave a job before dissatisfaction leads to problems:

- The individual receives a positive recommendation from the employer.

- The individual has the experience of making an active choice and pursuing options (one can always pursue a new job lead to the point of getting a job offer, then decide whether to take it or turn it down).

- The previous job provides a rich source of information upon which to base a sound choice about further directions.

- A support organization gets an automatic job lead, being first to hear of the job opening created by the person giving notice.

- The employer has a positive feeling about the experience.

- Since the new job is chosen without the immediate pressure to have an income or be away from the residence, the process of adjustment may be easier.

- If the individual is leaving the secondary labor market, the new setting is likely to have a stronger culture and it will be easier to develop social relationships.

Job Change Funding

Funding requirements can make career development difficult. People who have jobs are presumed to have become "rehabilitated," and ongoing support services are funded at a far lower amount than initial job development and training.

If an employment consultant or organization is supporting several individuals with ongoing support service funding from a state agency or alternative source, then assistance in changing jobs will be one of the ongoing support services. Although funding in most states is far from adequate, the services required to maintain individuals in stable jobs will not be great if every effort has been made to maximize internal sources of support. Dealing with changes in jobs and in support systems on jobs will constitute the bulk of the ongoing support effort.

Individuals who receive services from the state vocational rehabilitation office should be encouraged to consider carefully the goal stated on their written rehabilitation plan. If a goal represents the individual's highest career aspiration, services remain available through earlier jobs that lead up to this goal. An individual's "case" can remain open for funding of job search assistance while initial jobs are used as stepping-stones.

State vocational rehabilitation offices can also reopen a "case" and reintroduce services quickly if the employee and those assisting the individual take the time to understand and follow the various procedures required by the office. Individuals with a record of successful employment are likely to be welcomed as feasible candidates for further services.

HOW DO YOU SPELL "SUCCESS"?

Job tenure, the length of time an individual remains at one job, is a common measure of employment success for employees with disabilities. A "good" job lasts for a long time. One reason for an emphasis on job tenure is that it is easy to measure. Wages earned and hours worked are other common measures of success because they are similarly easy to measure. But in reality, to know whether an individual's work hours indicate job success one has to know how many hours the person *wants* to work. The same is true of income and length of employment.

Features of employment such as job satisfaction, adequacy of the job match, social acceptance, and quality of life, are harder to collect information about. If we make a simplistic assumption that people who stay in their jobs like them, we can simply measure length of time on the job as a proxy measure for success. The trouble is, this is not always a valid assumption. We cannot avoid looking directly at the degree to which a job meets the career goals of the individual.

Assessing Satisfaction

Are you satisfied with air? Probably you consider the question strange. It's not as if you have a lot of options about what to breathe. Some people who have to breathe especially dirty air and who know that cleaner air is possible might be dissatisfied with their air. The rest of us probably don't think about it.

There are two important implications here for job satisfaction. First, satisfaction and dissatisfaction require alternatives. In areas of life where there are no alternatives, they are abstract constructs with little meaning. Second, a lack of dissatisfaction isn't the same as satisfaction. An absence of problems or expressed dissatisfaction on a job should not be taken as an indicator that some final step in career development has been reached. An active approach to job satisfaction is required which allows for multiple approaches to satisfaction and is built around the exploration of options and alternatives.

Steps should be taken to allow any possible dissatisfaction with a job to be brought to the attention of people supporting the individual. Support visits to a worksite can be used to assess satisfaction. Assessment of how an employee feels about the job and the employee's reactions to various elements of the job is an important component of ongoing support.

- Observations, talks with the employee, and talks with the employer should focus both on whether the employer is satisfied and whether the employee is satisfied. The employee might be more comfortable discussing these matters away from the worksite.

- Occasionally review the job specifications that formed the foundation for the job. Does the individual still feel that the job has what she was looking for? There needs to be a credible and trusting relationship so the person feels secure in confiding her concerns.

- Talk realistically about the availability of job search assistance if and when the individual wants to change jobs. Begin to talk with the individual about what new challenges the individual would like to tackle.

- Discuss with the supervisor or employer how satisfactory the individual is to the company and how satisfied the individual appears to be. Employers sometimes have valuable insights about what an individual likes and doesn't like. Satisfaction directly affects productivity, and good managers make it their business to be aware of employee satisfaction.

- Talk to the individual's family or people at the individual's residence who know the individual well. Comments an individual makes while getting ready for work or upon arriving back home, or even the person's facial expression and demeanor, may reveal the person's feelings about the job.

Nisbet & York (1989) have developed an interview protocol that can be used to assess the job satisfaction of individuals who are limited in their ability to articulate their feelings and views. The protocol collects information from four sources: direct observations at work; and interviews with the employee, the employer, and the family or residence. The following questions are important to consider:

- Is the individual learning new skills?
- Does the individual like his supervisor?
- Does the individual like her co-workers?
- What does the person like best and least about the job?
- How does the individual describe what he does? What aspect does he focus on?
- Does the individual talk about work or co-workers at home?
- Does the individual look forward to going to work each day?
- How does the individual react when it's time to begin work, reluctant or excited?
- Has the person grown in self-confidence or other characteristics?

When at least three sources of information agree, in either a positive or negative direction, the information should be given serious consideration.

Testing Career Hypotheses

Each job is an experiment designed to answer two important questions: "To what extent does this job meet my career goals?" and "What should I emphasize or de-emphasize in my next job?"

In supported employment, community businesses are used for assessment and for training. This means that every job site is also an assessment site. In fact, every job can be looked at simultaneously from three different perspectives:

- As an *employment* site, for producing goods or services and earning income,

- As a *training* site, to gain new skills and experiences, and

- As an *assessment* site, to gain information and test out ideas about jobs.

Assistance with the assessment function should not be confined to a brief period at the beginning of a job. It is ongoing throughout an individual's career. The challenge of obtaining satisfying employment is never solved once and for all. People change and businesses change all the time, and a "match" between the two is only a temporary phenomenon. An employee's awareness of what she wants and what she can do also evolves over time. One woman was convinced that she wanted a job with only a few co-workers and very predictable and structured social interactions. When she got a job that met these criteria, she discovered that she missed having opportunities to socialize more freely, and soon became dissatisfied. What is important is the process of assisting people to make sense of what they are experiencing and make their best next decision.

Some secondary school programs provide for a series of job experiences for young adults during the years of 18-21, when many young adults spend time exploring options and gaining new experiences. They assist students to use these jobs to explore their interests and abilities. Whether part of an educational program or an adult career strategy, each job tests an hypothesis of the form "A job with these characteristics in this setting will be satisfying." Strategies that help apply an "hypothesis testing" approach to jobs include:

Maintain job search availability. Mention to the individual that assistance is available to help find other jobs. Be sincere in your offer to help with advancement within the company or a job change at the individual's request.

Continue with career exploration. The fact that a job is successful does not mean that an individual should stop thinking abut the future. Occasional visits to other employers for exploration and information can be arranged during time off from work. Tell the person about interesting possibilities and ask if the individual would like to visit a company or meet an employer.

Offer to convene the career planning team. A career planning get-together to review work goals can be planned, following one of the strategies outlined in

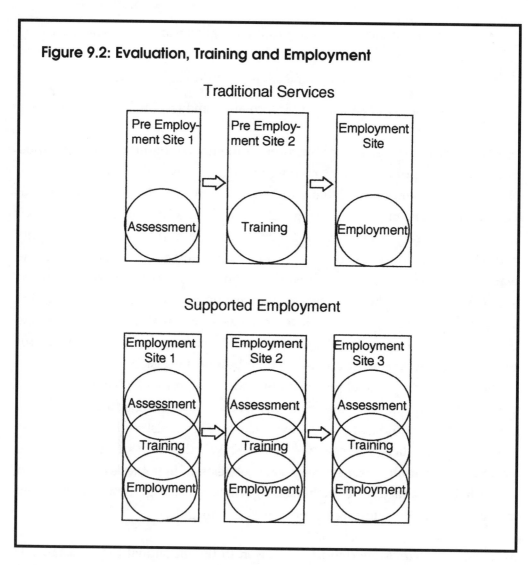

Figure 9.2: Evaluation, Training and Employment

Chapter 3. Work issues might also be dealt with as part of a meeting that also includes other issues. A person might want to invite a trusted and respected co-worker to participate as a member of the team. Care should be taken that any individuals from the workplace retain information in confidence.

View "failures" as learning experiences. Thomas Edison was supposedly asked, after trying out more than two thousand different filament materials for his electric light and finding none very satisfactory, if he was discouraged. His answer was something like "Of course not. I have two thousand fewer things left to try." Every job provides more information, puts more puzzle pieces in place, and lays

THE COMPLETE STORY

Larry found his first job at the Price-Saver Supermarket, returning shopping carts to the store. He enjoyed the job for a few months but gradually began to lose interest, taking overly long breaks. In talking about the job with Larry, the employment consultant found that what Larry particularly disliked was the endless sense of an incomplete job. No matter how many carts he brought in, there were more out there. He wanted a job that could offer more of a sense of completion.

The consultant and Larry agreed that Larry would be more punctual for a while and the consultant would explore alternative possibilities. She met with the manager, and over a period of several weeks helped negotiate a job change for Larry at the store. Larry now is in charge of store displays of "specials." He sets up new displays of advertised items for sale and is in charge of seasonal decorations and in-store presentations.

This job change allowed Larry to gain closure for each task. Once a display was completed, it remained more or less "finished" for some time, and he could point to his work as an accomplishment.

a more solid foundation for the next job search. One of the ways people support one another is by helping them "contain" or "compartmentalize" a failure, and help in the process of learning from it. For example, saying "It doesn't mean you're not a good person or a good employee. It just means that you need a job with more clear expectations" can put a difficult experience into perspective.

Update the resume. Every now and then, perhaps every six months or so, sitting down to review and update a resume is a valuable experience. It is an occasion for discussing one's career path and goals and for adding new accomplishments, new skills learned, new hobbies, or new references. It is also a good opportunity to take pride in one's accomplishments.

Look for messages in problems. A lot of behavior staff label as "challenging" has communicative meaning. Problems may develop on a job that indicate "burnout" or that the job is no longer satisfying. The job may have changed in ways an employee doesn't like, or a personality conflict with someone in the work setting may be making the workplace less desirable. Some behaviors that may be signs of a poor job match include:

- Boredom and lack of interest,

- Poor work quality,

- "Fooling around" and breaking workplace rules or causing trouble for others,

- Reluctance to go to work, excessive time off or feelings of fatigue, and

- Anxiety and stress or frustration with the job.

Employment consultants and other support people should always look for the communicative meaning of behavior rather than only trying to change it or viewing it as the individual's problem. It may simply mean the person doesn't want to be there. It may be difficult to determine whether in an individual case a problem needs to be "given time" or worked through, whether adjustments to the job are called for, or whether it is time to dust off the resume and start looking elsewhere.

Every job is a new test of a new hypothesis, and there is a wealth information to be discovered about how the job impacts an individual's:

- Social life

- Task-related demands

- Environmental concerns

- Supervisory relationships

- Income and benefits

- Family and friends outside of work

- Relationship to life at home

- Leisure and recreational pursuits

- Physical and mental health

This information can be used to create a new hypothesis. With subsequent positions, workers begin to get a sense that they are making choices and getting a chance to discover and develop their true interests.

TEMPORARILY BETWEEN-JOBS

Experiencing success in a community job includes the potential of losing that job. Anything worth achieving involves some risk. People are between jobs some of the time during any career. The problems that result from instabilities in the community job market are the most widely mentioned concerns keeping out-moded sheltered workshop services from fully converting to supported employ-ment. After all, one of the purposes of sheltered settings was as a "secure place to go" for set hours each day. Unemployment is not solved in these settings but is either called something else, such as down time, field trips, or make-work, or it is hidden by stretching out or "featherbedding" the available work.

Unemployment usually lasts 2 to 3 months (Wegmann, 1991b), but individual situations vary greatly. People with disabilities in community jobs have noted that issues related to unemployment are much fewer than was feared. Common sense practices can accommodate most difficulties that do arise. If an individual is supported by service providers at his or her residence, these service providers need to understand and plan for the possibility of periods between jobs, just as for possible times of sickness and vacations. Periodic meetings with individuals involved in providing residential support are good opportunities to reinforce this message.

In the stress and confusion of losing or quitting a job, people sometimes neglect to take some simple helpful steps.

- Make sure the employee has the names, phone numbers and addresses of anyone at the site they liked or who respected their work. Then, assist the individual to keep in occasional touch with these individuals. These colleagues may hear of other job openings, and can give references.

- If the individual is leaving on fairly good terms with at least one person in a management position, ask that individual for permission to use his name as a reference. Obtaining an open letter of recommendation from that individual is a good idea.

- Exit interviews might be stressful but they can also be a source of valuable feedback that employees cannot obtain in any other way. Ask employers if they will agree to meet with the individual and go over the positive and negative aspects of his work with them.

There is no one solution to the difficulties unemployment may pose. An individual who is eligible for Supplemental Security Income should notify his Social Security office so that benefit amounts can be recomputed quickly. The possibility of unemployment insurance should be pursued as well. If the individual's disability will pose a difficulty in finding a new job, the individual will qualify for further vocational rehabilitation services. Most importantly, steps should be taken to minimize the delay in obtaining the next job. Most of these steps can be pursued before a problem arises. While not ideal options by any means, they can be valid responses to difficult circumstances.

Always have a "Plan B". An individual's career planning team should not be "put in mothballs" because a job is begun. The end of a training period, or the occasion of receiving an evaluation or an annual salary increase is a good reason to get together and review the job. Part of the discussion should include "what would happen if...." If lack of a daily planned activity would be a serious problem for the individual, team members should be assigned to develop a back-up plan for daily activity and support.

Create expandable sites or long-deadline positions. Employment support agencies can cultivate arrangements with one or more businesses that are flexible enough to accommodate one or two "extra" workers temporarily. Employees between jobs can move into one of these flexible job positions. While this is not an ideal employment solution or a career step, it offers a safety net of wages and work in situations where having a job to go to is extremely important. The two main types of arrangement are a contract with a business that can absorb an additional individual, and an employer who has one or more low-urgency, long-deadline positions that can be started and ended more or less at an individual's discretion. The probability of weak social inclusion needs to be weighed against the benefits of this kind of arrangement.

Convene an "emergency response" career team. A reevaluation of career desires, expectations and strategies may be indicated following job loss. The individual may have discovered information about work tasks he/she prefers, work settings which are enjoyable or tasks and environments to avoid. An individual can be assisted to convene or reconvene a career team of his or her choice, communicating some sense of urgency to the members, to develop a new plan of action. Team members can take responsibility for specific employer contacts and other tasks.

MORE POWER

An agency gradually downsized what had at one time been a group enclave at Consolidated Power and Light company by helping most enclave members find individual jobs with other companies. Eventually, one individual, John, who enjoyed the work and made close friendships, remained working at the company. His job involved sorting and reclaiming materials from the power line crews. During the summer, John does not keep up with the volume of material brought in, but the company doesn't mind stockpiling it because he catches up during the winter, when line work slows down.

When George lost his job at a bottling warehouse he was unable to remain at home because the residential support he depended on was not available during the day. He needed something right away. The support agency arranged for George to work with John on the reclamation contract three days per week. He spent the remaining two days per week searching for jobs with his employment consultant.

Coordinate and assist in a full-time job search. Finding a new job can be a full-time pursuit. Job hunting activities can include tours of businesses, preparing resumes, meeting with job support staff, calling members of the "social snowflake," going on interviews, reviewing ads, and other activities discussed in Chapter 4. These aspects of job networking are a good investment of time when between jobs. Relationship building is another critical part of job networking. Helping individuals set up informational meetings with local business persons for lunch or coffee is a useful activity which can lead to job possibilities. Sending letters of interest, reworking a resume, or building a reference file are other worthwhile activities which can lead to a new position.

Expand leisure, volunteer or civic activities. Assisting an individual to become involved in volunteer or civic pursuits outside of work hours has a number of benefits. These activities are an important aspect of community participation, and can fill a gap in a person's daily schedule. Leisure or volunteer activities can also expand to cover a larger part of the day if an individual finds himself or herself between jobs. Memberships in clubs, groups and other informal associations are also a good source of new job leads. Support people, family and friends can combine their efforts to develop resources and access to leisure pursuits for someone who is temporarily out of work.

Two jobs may be better than one. Some individuals who do not need employer-sponsored medical insurance may consider two part-time jobs rather than one full-time job. Or, a small part-time job can supplement a full-time job. Many people create a mechanism for a second source of earned income for themselves in some way. In the event the individual loses one income source, there may be a chance of increasing hours at the second. If nothing else, the individual is not without some productive activity and earned income. If this option is used, the cautions in Chapter 5 about the possibility of weaker social relationships at part-time jobs need to be kept in mind.

Use or sponsor a community job club or job seeker support service. Libraries, community colleges, state departments of employment services and community centers often sponsor classes or support groups for job hunters. These can be valuable resources and a source of daily structured activity. If none exist, you can consider inaugurating an "integrated" service of this kind that benefits the whole community.

Investigate community job training programs and community college curricula. There should be no requirement of completing a training curriculum before exploring job opportunities. But tutoring in job success can complement on-the-

---

A FRIEND OF A FRIEND OF ANOTHER FRIEND
Pete attended a bible study group at his church one evening per week, sharing his religious values and thoughts with others with similar interests. When his job suddenly ended, he was left with nothing to do during the day. A member of the group put Pete in touch with a friend, Gene, who had another friend, Lynn, who coordinated a community housing assistance organization. Lynn found a job for Pete clipping and organizing each day's newspaper apartment ads.

— adapted from Schwartz (1992), pp. 18-19.

job training nicely and help with job seeking during times of little or no work. Many communities have job training or retraining programs with six- to twelve-week courses and/or apprenticeship possibilities. Organizations receiving Job Training Partnership Act funds are a good place to start. Virtually all of these organizations are obligated to accommodate their programs so that individuals with disabilities can benefit.

SUMMARY

Career development is an active process. The first job or two an individual obtains are unlikely to be satisfying for long. As we move through various stages of our careers, from the fantasy and exploration, basic training, and early career stages, to our mid-career and late career stage and finally disengagement and retirement, our career needs and interests continually evolve. Developing skills, expanding awareness of work options, and new personal contacts allow us to move out of jobs which meet only a few of our needs to higher level jobs which offer more fulfillment and greater remuneration.

Instead of bowing to pressure for "placement" statistics or operating from a set of outmoded career myths about people with disabilities, high quality career assistance organizations plan for a succession of job changes for the individuals served and establish mechanisms for monitoring job satisfaction over time.

Worksite observations, informal conversations with employees, conversations with those who know the individual best, and periodic reconvening of a career planning process to look at an individual's evolving life dreams are valuable strategies to assess job satisfaction.

Equally important are strategies for insuring that more than one vocational option, and the assistance needed to pursue other options, are realistically available to an individual. For some individuals, these strategies include back-up plans for dealing with time between jobs. With the appropriate mechanisms in place, individuals leaving one job for another can be viewed not as a weakness but as a strength of a career assistance program; not as a failure but as a success for the individual.

Conclusion:
The Challenge of Change

"There are phrases repulsive and obscure to the uneducated,
which yet we cannot dispense with."
— Epictetus

Change related to our understanding of the potential contributions of workers with disabilities to the workforce has occurred at a rapid pace. In Chapter I we reviewed the revolutionary developments which have led to our current system of services, including supported employment and the ideas related to the "natural support" approach to employment support. Not only have recent developments been revolutionary, the pace of change itself seems to have accelerated. New information, more effective strategies, and a new awareness of disability as a human rights issue are challenging the systems, organizations and ideas that seemed "on the cutting edge" only a short time ago.

The Challenge of Systems Change

Organizations respond in a variety of ways to new developments. The need for new ways of thinking about employment services has created a good deal of stress for special education systems, rehabilitation programs, and funding agencies. Changing patterns of services, organizational structures, job descriptions, and funding challenge the existing human service system and create conflict with other programs and services. Reactions to new concepts can range from uncritical acceptance to disbelief, passive resistance, and overt hostility. For example, supported employment has been interpreted by some to mean:

- New opportunities,
- Better wages,
- More friendships,
- Better quality life, and
- Enhanced skills

But for others the same concept has been viewed as:

- Closed facilities,
- Diminished options,
- Fewer jobs,
- Loss of funds, and
- Less security.

As change has accelerated, less and less uniformity can be found across communities. Some communities have extraordinarily innovative and far-reaching projects well underway, and service providers are challenging themselves to open new doors to opportunities for people with disabilities. At the same time, other communities find themselves mired in controversy, debating whether change is good, caught in perennial planning meetings, or struggling to initiate small changes in existing program models.

It is probably inevitable that this would happen, yet the confusion created for individuals with disabilities, their families, and the business community by this mix of approaches and values is unfortunate.

By responding to supported employment more as a threat to what is familiar, rather than as a new opportunity, change becomes personalized into something to be avoided, minimized, or contained. To meet this challenge, people with disabilities, their families, advocates and professionals will need to take risks and provide leadership.

As with any developing movement, today's services are merely one more step in a process whose final stages we cannot imagine. Employers may take on added roles. Families, self-advocacy organizations and others may develop undreamed-of options. It remains to be learned how best to tap into the strengths each of these groups can offer to support and guide individuals with disabilities in the workplace.

Organizations providing services to people with disabilities will have to adapt to new realities. In the present system, the best most prospective employees with disabilities can hope for is that a support agency is available that has:

- ended their commitment to a facility-based, segregated model, or
- begun as a new organization with a consistent philosophy and approach focusing on integrated employment services.

Each of these agencies represents job seekers with disabilities. The agency might have changed its name from something like "Eternal Hope Center" to "Job Connections" to project a contemporary and non-stigmatizing image. It may no longer operate a sheltered workshop and may instead rent a stylish storefront-type operation in town that looks just like a "real" employment agency. But just as workshops can never be real work places, "Job Connections" can never be a real employment agency if it only serves clientele with disabilities. Staff who go out from this organization to contact employers will always carry with them the image of dealing only with a narrow range of job seekers.

Changes in service patterns must be accompanied by corresponding changes in organizational structure. It is no small matter to understand under what auspices supported employment is carried out, what organizations should provide it, and what their image is in the community. We can no longer remain content with a "window dressing" approach to change. Several alternative organizational structures requiring significant planning by current service and funding agencies are clearly possible.

School and adult education-based career assistance. Many high schools are developing, in effect, placement services for graduates who are not college-bound, including many individuals in special education. Employers are asked to consider, not people with disabilities, but young people who are starting out into the world of work. The adult and community education division of many school districts also provides assistance with job maintenance and career development beyond high school. Such assistance could be adapted to the needs of graduates with significant disabilities. Assistance might include directly employing staff members with expertise in supported employment, or helping individuals obtain access to other generic or consumer-directed services in the community.

Specialized services available through community employment agencies. Career services for people with disabilities can join with typical not-for profit and for-profit job placement agencies in the community in a variety of arrangements. These can range from sharing office space, to creating a division within a company specializing in disability support, to full integration of a company's practices so that people with and without disabilities can be provided with employment assistance on an equal basis. Large employment agencies may be currently obligated under the Americans with Disabilities Act to make changes in this direction so that people with disabilities can benefit from their services.

Enhancing or creating apprenticeship programs to include people with disabilities. Apprenticeship programs can to be made available to greater numbers of individuals with disabilities in a wide variety of trades and services, as part of both their education and post-education life. Apprenticeship relationships have the capacity to include training, job placement assistance, and ongoing job support.

Supported employment as part of post-secondary education. A community college can be an ideal location for supported employment services. Career-related courses and job placement offices are already in place at most community colleges. Adapting them to accommodate people with severe disabilities and adding services related to consulting with businesses regarding ongoing support would be well within the reach of most organizations.

"Reverse mainstreaming" in community rehabilitation programs. Disability-focused agencies can broaden the scope of the population they serve by providing career services to people without disabilities. Fee structures similar to those used by typical employment services can be established, with third-party payments for those individuals eligible for funding from a disability agency. Agencies may need to carefully review their articles of incorporation before such an expansion is undertaken to protect a not-for-profit status.

Evolving toward human resource support organizations. Disability agencies can evolve in a different direction, into generic human resource or organizational development consulting firms, or combine forces with generic organizations of this kind. Such firms specialize in assisting a corporation to manage its workforce effectively, including accommodating individuals with different backgrounds and needs as one aspect of diversity management.

Changes in the way services are funded must go hand in hand with changes in the delivery of services. Several states are experimenting with a variety of voucher-type programs through which individuals directly or with help from their families and friends access state agency funds. Some funding agencies issue requests for proposals to provide specific supports to specific individuals. In some communities, a network of self-employed individuals allows individuals with disabilities access to an array of different support styles and resources to choose from.

The Challenge of New Ideas

Perhaps even more difficult than organizational or service system change is the process of changing our thinking about disability. Because our thinking reflects our past experiences, we easily mistake the rear-view mirror for the windshield. This difficulty is compounded by the tendency on the part of many people to quickly adopt the latest "politically correct" language to describe what they do. So for many years we have heard things like, "Oh, yes, we base all our services on a normalization approach," "We've been doing supported employment all along only we didn't call it that," "Sure we use natural supports, " and so on. Some of these statements are more true than others. Like the head of whatever pin angels used to dance on, the "cutting edge" can get pretty crowded.

Sometimes language itself gets in the way of clear thinking or is only useful for a limited time. The word "normalization" caused so much confusion that it had to be retired. "Natural support" is another term that people easily misinterpret. The term can be found used in connection with all sorts of different and even conflicting practices. Three misinterpretations seem to be prevalent.

A laissez-faire approach as "natural support". This can be described by the attitude of "Let's just be natural and let it happen; we should provide only little or no services. People will be taken care of naturally by the community." This is the most serious misconception of natural supports that can occur.

It is easy to imagine why such an inexpensive approach may be favored by people concerned with costs, who ask "Why should I pay for services when natural supports will cost me nothing?"

But as we have seen, facilitating natural support should be an active and involved process. Many people with severe disabilities do require creative accommodations beyond what an employer can reasonably be expected to provide. Formal services are often necessary to supplement those that are naturally available. And natural supports sometimes only occur in any kind of meaningful way as a result of an ongoing, challenging effort to nurture and facilitate it.

Faced with the prospect of inadequate support, and understanding the vulnerabilities of a person with a disability, traditional attitudes about overprotection become easier to understand. If an error has to be made in one direction or the other, overprotection may indeed be the safer error to live with.

Deputizing co-workers as "natural support". Less frequently held, but becoming more common, is the misapplication of facilitating natural supports by turning co-workers into paraprofessional human service workers. We have seen that there are all sorts of problems with "appointing" someone as the expert in charge of the person. Limited relationships form and artificial lines of communication and support get routed through the deputized co-worker.

Providing a structured disability training program and asking co-workers to complete human-service generated forms or use strategies foreign to a business, such as a "time out" behavioral program, is the most common method of deputizing co-workers. But even such subtle practices as setting up physical space so that only one co-worker is available for support can lead to a sense that there is an exception to the work culture for one particular employee.

High quality job coaching as "natural support". Natural support is often equated with "fading" and/or with the "advocacy" function of a supported employment job coach. It is true that effective job coaches use many of the techniques we have discussed, and indeed we learned many of them from job coaches whose practices went far beyond what they had been trained to do. But working together in partnership with employers involves a far broader scope of activities than "fading" and "advocacy". Fading prompts is a specific instructional strategy employed by co-worker trainers as well as by job coaches. Similarly, advocacy is a function that many people can perform, and advocacy sometimes meshes poorly with a skill instruction orientation. Many support arrangements call for pre-faded" job coaches, i.e., job coaches who don't fade because they never enter the picture to begin with. On the other hand, facilitating natural support does not necessarily require that agency staff leave a worksite. Many strategies we have described, such as adopting the role of an organizational consultant, are compatible with a significant continuing on-site agency presence.

Most importantly, calling an external service provider a "job coach" directs attention away from the important "coaching" role played by co-workers and supervisors. "Say what you will," Ludwig Wittgenstein once remarked, "as long as it does not prevent you from seeing the facts. But once you see them, there is a lot you will not say."

It is difficult to find the right amount of "specialness" to apply to a situation to accommodate for a person's disability without adding extra "baggage." An attitude of caution towards using special techniques is difficult to successfully couple with a willingness to use them when they are truly necessary for an individual.

This is made more difficult still by the haste with which professionals hurry to use specialized technology. Part of the allure of technology is the status it confers on the person who applies it. Extra baggage makes a trip seem especially impressive. Some might feel that "natural" solutions reduce their professional stature or the degree of control they feel is necessary.

Any technology can be made to "work," although sometimes at a great price. Ultimately, the people directly affected, with assistance if needed from an informal network of friends and relatives, need to control the decisions regarding when and how specialized technology is applied. As Nisbet (1992) has argued, the concepts of empowerment and natural support are inseparable.

More and more, we need to reject a double standard of "I would never do it that way, but it's tolerable for him or her because of the disability." The methods we use to obtain and learn jobs for ourselves should be considered the "default setting," to be departed from only when and to the extent that we have clear proof that some other method does the job better. We must continually experiment with less direct intervention into people's lives, yet retain the capacity to intervene when people really need us. At the same time, we need to keep people informed about the alternatives available and help people learn about the implications of the choices they make.

The Bottom Lines

Meeting the challenge of new ideas and new organizational structures will not be easy. When we support people well, there is little to point to. When we support people badly, we have something to show. Sheltered workshops and work enclaves have a very real presence that can be reassuring to funders, families, and professionals. We don't easily see the other side: the boredom and monotony of uninteresting work, the drag on our economy created by congregating people on the basis of occupationally meaningless labels, the missed opportunities for friendship and growth for people with and without disabilities.

When we develop the competence of natural systems and provide assistance in small, sometimes indirect ways, there is not much to see. One supported employment service manager who had achieved outstanding success in assisting individuals with complex support needs to obtain employment found it frustrating to bring other professionals to visit a job, only to have them remark "Sure, anybody could achieve success in this situation, with this person."

We now know that separate facilities and special programs — the solutions which appeared so obvious and "natural" to early disability advocates — do extraordinary harm by disempowering communities and fostering social isolation of individuals with disabilities. The task of the present is to remove what is obsolete and unnecessary while retaining the capacity to support inclusion and participation in positive ways. The proper balance between natural supports and support services must be discovered anew each day for each person. The search for "program models" must be replaced by the search for ways to dispense with the need for models. And paradoxically, we know when we succeed not by what we can see but by what we can no longer see.

When supported employees and their co-workers are working together, in one sense nothing special is going on. Disability tends to fade to the background, as a matter of little importance. When employment support organizations and businesses are working together, there is little to show off or even mention. Something has fundamentally changed, but something unnoticed and unremarkable. And that is just the point.

References

Abbott, A. (1989). The new occupational structure: What are the questions? *Work and Occupations, 16*, 273-291.

Amsa, P. (1986). Organizational culture and work group behavior: An empirical study. *Journal of Management Studies, 32*, 347-362.

Aveno, A., Renzaglia, A. & Lively, C. (1987). Surveying community training sites to insure that instructional decisions accommodate the site as well as the trainees. *Education and Training in Mental Retardation, 22*, 167-172.

Azrin, N. & Besalel, V. (1981). *The job club counselor's manual.* Austin TX: Pro Ed.

Baer, J. (1983). *Equality under the Constitution: Reclaiming the 14th Amendment.* Ithaca NY: Cornell Univ. Press.

Bellamy, G.T., Rhodes, L., Borbeau, P. & Mank, D. (1986). Mental retardation services in sheltered workshops and day activity programs: Consumer benefits and policy alternatives. In F. Rusch (Ed.) *Competitive employment issues and strategies.* (pp. 257-271). Baltimore MD: Brookes.

Bigelow, D. (1921). An experiment to determine the possibilities of subnormal girls in factory work. *Mental Hygiene, 4*, 302-320.

Biklen, D., Morton, M., Saha, S. N., Duncan, J., Gold, D., Hardardottir, M., Karna, E., O'Connor, S. & Rao, S. (1991). "I AMN NOT A UTISTIVC ON THJE TYP" ("I'm not autistic on the typewriter"). *Disability, Handicap and Society, 6*, 161-179.

Brown, L., Udvari-Solner, A., Frattura-Kampschroer, E., Davis, L., Ahlgren, C., VanDeventer, P. & Jorgensen, J. (1990). Integrated work: A rejection of segregated enclaves and mobile work crews. In L. Brown, L. Meyer & C. Peck (Eds.) *Critical issues in the lives of people with severe disabilities.* (pp 219-228). Baltimore MD: Brookes.

Callahan, M (1990). "The Vocational Profile Strategy," in M. Callahan (Ed.) *Getting the Job Done: Supported Employment for Persons with Severe Physical Disabilities.* (pp. 31-35) Washington DC: United Cerebral Palsy Associations.

Chubon, R. (1985). Career-related needs of school children with severe physical disabilities. *Journal of Counseling and Development, 64*, 47-51.

Conte, L., Murphy, S. & Nisbet, J. (1989). A qualitative study of work stations in industry. *Journal of Rehabilitation, 55* (2), 53-61

Cook, D. (1983). The accuracy of work evaluator and client predictions of client vocational competency and rehabilitation outcome. *Journal of Rehabilitation, 49* (2), 46-49.

Curl, R. & Hall, S. (1990). *Put that person to Work! A manual for implementors using the co-worker transition manual.* Logan UT: Utah State University Developmental Center for Handicapped Persons.

Curl, R., Lignugaris/Kraft, B., Pawley, J. & Salzberg, C. (1990). *What's next? A quantitative and qualitative analysis of the transition from trainee to valued worker.* (Technical Report #87). Logan UT: Utah State University Developmental Center for Handicapped Persons.

Deal, T. & Kennedy, A. (1982). *Corporate cultures.* Reading MA: Addison-Wesley.

Dileo, D. MacDonald, R., & Killiam, W. (1991). *Ethical Guidelines in Supported Employment.* (Position paper). Richmond VA: The Association for

Persons in Supported Employment.

Dugdale, R. (1877), *The Jukes: A study in crime, pauperism, disease and heredity.* New York NY: G.P. Putnam's Sons.

Dworkin, R. (1977). *Taking rights seriously.* Cambridge MA: Harvard Univ. Press.

Dwyer, J. (1991). Humor, power and change in organizations. *Human Relations, 44,* 1-19.

Edgerton, R. (1967) *The cloak of competence: Stigma in the lives of the mentally retarded.* Berkeley CA: Univ. of California Press.

Evered, R. & Selma , J. (1989). Coaching and the art of management. *Organizational Dynamics, 18,* 16-32.

Fabian, E., & Luecking, R. (1991). Doing it the company way: Using internal company supports in the workplace. *Journal of Applied Rehabilitation Counseling, 22* (3), 32-35.

Fairweather, G., Sanders, D., Maynard, H., Cressler, D., & Black, D. (1969). *Community life for the mentally ill: An alternative to institutional care.* Chicago IL: Aldine.

Feldman, D. (1977). The role of initiation activities in socialization. *Human Relations, 30,* 977-990.

Ferris, G. & King, T. (1992). Politics in human resources decisions: A walk on the dark side. *Organizational Dynamics, 20,* 59-71.

Ford, A. & Knoll, J. (1987). Beyond caregiving: In Taylor, Biklen & Knoll (Eds.) *Community integration for people with severe disabilities.* New York NY: Teachers College Press.

French, W. & Bell, C. (1984). *Organizational development: Behavioral science interventions for organizational improvement.* Englewood Cliffs NJ: Prentice-Hall.

Fullinwider, R. (1980). *The reverse discrimination controversy: A moral and legal analysis.* Totowa NJ: Rowman & Littlefield.

Gabarro, J. (1987). The development of working relationships. In J. Lorsch (Ed.) *Handbook of organizational behavior* (pp. 172-189). Englewood Cliffs NJ: Prentice-Hall.

Garvin, R. (1985). The role of the rehabilitation counselor in industry. *Journal of Applied Rehabilitation Counseling, 16,* 44-50.

Gold, M. (1980). *Did I say that? Articles and commentary on the try another way system.* Champaign IL: Research Press.

Granovetter, M. (1979). Placement as brokerage. In D. Vandergoot & J. Worrall (Eds.) *Placement in rehabilitation: A career development perspective* (pp. 84-101). Baltimore MD: University Park Press.

Greenhaus, J. (1987). *Career management.* Chicago IL: Dryden.

Greenleigh Associates Inc. (1975). *The role of the sheltered workshop in the rehabilitation of the severely handicapped.* (3 vol.). Report to the Department of Health, Education and Welfare, Rehabilitation Services Administration. New York NY: Author.

Hagner, D. (1989). *The social integration of supported employees: A qualitative study.* Syracuse NY: Syracuse University Center on Human Policy.

Hagner, D., Cotton, P., Goodall, S. & Nisbet, J. (1992). The perspectives of supportive co-workers: Nothing special. In J. Nisbet (Ed.) *Natural supports at work, at home, and in the community for people with severe disabilities* (pp. 241-256). Baltimore MD: Brookes.

Hagner, D. & Daning, R. (1991). *Job development in New Hampshire: Employment assistance strategies for people with severe disabilities.* Concord NH: New Hampshire Developmental Disabilities Council.

Hagner, D., Rogan, P. & Murphy, S. (1992). Facilitating natural supports in the workplace: Strategies for support consultants. *Journal of Rehabilitation, 58*(1), 29-34.

Hansen, C, (1969). The work crew approach to job placement for the severely retarded. *Journal of Rehabilitation, 35,* 26-27.

Harold Russell Associates (1982). *A study of accommodations provided to handicapped employees by federal contractors*. Washington, DC: US Dept. of Labor Employment Standards Administration.

Henderson, M. & Argyle, M. (1985) Social support by four categories of work colleague: Relationships between activities, stress and satisfaction. *Journal of Occupational Behavior, 6,* 229-239.

Henderson, M. & Argyle, M. (1986). The informal rules of working relationships. *Journal of Occupational Behavior, 7,* 259-275.

Hirszowicz, M. (1982). *Industrial sociology*. New York NY: St. Martin's.

Hughes, C. & Rusch, F. (1989). Teaching supported employees with severe mental retardation to solve problems. *Journal of Applied Behavior Analysis, 22,* 365-372.

Jackson, T. (1991) *Guerilla tactics in the new job market*. New York NY: Bantam.

Johnston, W. & Packer, A. (1987). *Workforce 2000: Work and workers for the 21st century*. Indianapolis IN: Hudson Institute.

Kahn, W. (1990). Psychological conditions of personal engagement and disengagement at work. *Academy of Management Journal, 33,* 692-724.

Kaplan, E. & Cowen, E, (1981). Interpersonal helping behavior of industrial foremen. *Journal of Applied Psychology, 66,* 633-638.

Karan, O. (1993). *The community revolution in services for persons with disabilities: An interdisciplinary perspective*. Baltimore MD:Brookes.

Kazdin, A. (1979). Situational specificity: The two-edged sword of behavioral assessment. *Behavioral Assessment, 1,* 57-75.

Kiernan, W. & McGaughey, M. (1992) Employee assistance programs: A support mechanism for the worker with a disability. *Journal of Rehabilitation, 58,* 56-60.

Kram, K. (1988). Productivity is often not a training issue. *Personnel Journal, 67,* 117-121.

Kram, K. & Isabella, L. (1985). Mentoring alternatives: The role of peer relationships in career

development. *Academy of Management Journal, 28,* 110-132.

Kregel, J., Wehman, P. & Seyfarth, J. & Marshall, K. (1986). Community integration of young adults with mental retardation: Transition from school to adulthood. *Employment and Training in Mental Retardation, 21,* 35-42.

Krupan, K. & Krupan, J. (1988). Jerks at work. *Personnel Journal, 67,* 68-72.

Laabs, J. (1991). The golden arches provide golden opportunities. *Personnel Journal, 70,* 52-57.

Lamb, H. (1971). *Rehabilitation in community mental health*. San Fransisco: Jossey-Bass.

Langton, D. (1992). Workgroup folklore and its impact on supported employment. *Supported Employment InfoLines, 3,* 1-3.

Lawler, E., Hackman, R., & Kaufman, S. (1973). Effects of job redesign: A field experiment. *Journal of Applied Social Psychology, 3,* 49-62.

Lawrie, J. (1987). How to establish a mentoring program. *Training and Development Journal, 41,* 25-27.

Lebas, M., & Weigenstein, J. (1986). Management control: The role of rules, markets and culture. *Journal of Management Studies, 23,* 259-272.

Lippitt, G. & Lippitt, R. (1984). The consulting function of the human resource development professional. In N. Nadler (Ed.) *Handbook of human resource development* (pp. 5.1-5.16). New York NY: Wiley & Sons.

Lipsky, D.K., & Gartner, A. (1989). *Beyond separate education: Quality education for all*. Baltimore MD: Brookes.

Liptak, J. (1991). The fourth alternative: Leisure search and planning. *Journal of Employment Counseling, 28,* 57-62.

Mank, D., Oorthuys, J., Rhodes, L., Sandow, D. & Weyer, T. (1992). Accommodating workers with mental disabilities. *Training and Development Journal, 46,* 49-52.

Mank, D., Rhodes, L. & Bellamy, G.T. (1986). Four supported employment alternatives. In W.

Kiernan & J. Stark (Eds..) *Pathways to employment for adults with developmental disabilities* (pp. 139-153). Baltimore MD: Brookes.

Martin, D., Elias-Burger, J., & Mithaug, D. (1987). Acquisition and maintenance of time-based task change sequences. *Education and Training in Mental Retardation, 22,* 250-255.

McConaughy, E., Curl, R. & Salzberg, C. (1987, May). *Ecological assessment of business environments.* Paper presented at the 13th Annual Convention of the Association for Behavior Analysis, Nashville, TN.

McGee, J. (1975). *Work stations in industry.* Lawrence KS: Univ. of Kansas University Affiliated Facility.

McKnight, J. (1987). Regenerating community. *Social Policy, 17,* 55-58.

McLaughlin, C., Garner, J., & Callahan, M. (1986) *Getting employed, staying employed.* Baltimore MD: Brookes.

Miller, J., & Labowitz, S. (1973). Individual reactions to organizational conflict and change. *Sociological Quarterly, 14,* 556-575.

Molstad, C.. (1988). Control strategies used by industrial brewery workers: Work avoidance, impression management and solidarity. *Human Organization, 47,* 354-360.

Morey, N. & Luthaus, F, (1991). The use of dyadic alliances in formal organizations: An ethnographic study. *Human Relations, 44,* 597-618.

Mount, B., & Zwernick, K. (1988). *It's never too early, it's never too late: A booklet about personal futures planning.* Minneapolis MN: Governor's Planning Council on Developmental Disabilities.

Murphy, S. & Hagner, D. (1988). Evaluating assessment centers: Ecological influences on vocational evaluation. *Journal of Rehabilitation, 54,* 53-59.

Nisbet, J. (1992) *Natural supports at work, at home, and in the community for people with severe disabilities.* Baltimore MD: Brookes.

Nisbet, J. & Hagner, D. (1988). Natural supports in the workplace: A reexamination of supported employment. *Journal of the Association for Persons with Severe Handicaps, 13,* 260-267.

Noe, R. (1988). An investigation of the determinants of successful assigned mentoring relationships. *Personnel Psychology, 41,* 457-479.

O'Brien, J. (1987). A guide to life-style planning: Using *The Activities Catalog* to integrate services and natural support systems. In B. Wilcox & G.T. Bellamy (Eds.) *A comprehensive guide to the activities catalog: An alternative curriculum for youth and adults* (pp. 175-189). Baltimore MD: Brookes.

O'Connell, M. (1990). *Community building in Logan Square.* Chicago IL: Northwestern University Center for Urban Affairs and Policy Research.

Olson, D. and Ferguson, P. (1992). *Integration at work: Multiple methodologies in research.* Eugene OR: Univ. of Oregon Center on Human Development.

Orth, C., Wilkinson, H. & Benfari, R. (1987). The manager's role as coach and mentor. *Organizational Dynamics, 16,* 66-69.

Parent, W. & Everson, J. (1986). Competencies of disabled workers on industry: A review of business literature. *Journal of Rehabilitation, 52*(4), 16-23.

Pati, G. (1985). The economics of rehabilitation in the workplace. *Journal of Rehabilitation, 51,* 22-30.

Patterson, J., & Kim, R. (1991). *The day America told the truth.* Englewood Cliffs NJ: Prentice-Hall.

Peponis, J. (1985). The spatial culture of factories. *Human Relations, 38,* 357-390.

Pinebrook, S. & Bissonet, D. (1992). Partners in education. *Training and Development Journal, 46,* 69-74.

Pretty, G. & McCarthy, M. (1991). Exploring the psychological sense of community among women and men of the corporation. *Journal of Community Psychology, 19,* 351-361.

Raggins, B. (1989). Barriers to mentoring: The female manager's dilemma. *Human Relations, 42,* 1-22.

Rhodes, L., Sandow, D., Mank, D., Buckley, J., & Albin, J. (1991). Expanding the role of employers in supported employment. *Journal of the Association for Persons with Severe Handicaps, 16*, 213-217.

Richardson, S., Koller, H., & Katz, M. (1988). Job histories in open employment of a population of young adults with mental retardation. *American Journal on Mental Retardation, 92*, 483-491.

Riscalla, L. (1974). Could workshops become obsolete? *Journal of Rehabilitation, 40*, 17-18, 36.

Rogan, P. & Hagner, D. (1990). Vocational evaluation in supported employment. *Journal of Rehabilitation, 56*, 45-51.

Rogan, P., Hagner, D. & Murphy, S. (1992). *Natural supports: reconceptualizing job coach roles.* Unpublished Manuscript.

Royse, D. & Edwards, T. (1989). Communicating about disability: Attitudes and preferences of persons with physical handicaps. *Rehabiliation Counseling Bulletin, 32*, 203-209.

Rubin, S. & Millard, R. (1991). Ethical principles and American public policy on disability. *Journal of Rehabilitation, 57*, 13-16.

Rugg, E. (1983). Limitations of projections of occupational outlook: Users beware. *Personnel and Guidance Journal, 61*, 346-348.

Rusch, F., McKee, M., Chadsey-Rusch, J., & Renzaglia, A. (1988). Teaching a student with severe handicaps to self-instruct: A brief report. *Education and Training in Mental Retardation, 23*, 51-58.

Salomone, P. & Slaney, R. (1981). The influence of chance and contingency factors on the vocational choice process of nonprofessional workers. *Journal of Vocational Behavior, 19*, 25-35.

Salzberg, C., McConaughy, E., Lignugaris/Kraft, B., Agran, M., & Stowischek, J. (1987). The transition from acceptable to highly valued worker. *Journal for Vocational Special Needs Education, 10*, 23-28.

Sandelands, C., Glynn, M. & Larson, J. (1991). Control theory and social behavior in the workplace. *Human Relations, 44*, 1107-1130.

Sathe, V. (1983). Implications of corporate culture: A manager's guide to action. *Organizational Dynamics, 12*, 5-23.

Schalock, R. & Karan, O. (1979). Relevant assessment: The interaction between evaluation and training. In G. T. Bellamy, G. O'Connor & O. Karan (Eds.) *Vocational rehabilitation of severely handicapped persons* (pp.35-54). Baltimore MD: University Park Press.

Schein, E. (1978). *Career dynamics: Matching individual and organizational needs.* Chicago IL: Addison-Wesley

Schermerhorn, J., Gardner, W., & Martin, T. (1990). Management diologues: Turning on the marginal performer. *Organizational Dynamics, 18* (4), 47-59.

Schwartz, D. (1992). *Crossing the river: Creating a conceptual revolution in disability and community.* Cambridge MA: Brookline.

Smircich, L. (1983). The concept of culture and organizational analysis. *Administrative Science Quarterly, 28*, 339-358.

Solomon, C. (1989). New partners in business. *Personnel Journal, 70*, 57-62.

Sonnenfield, J. (1985). Education at work: Demystifying the magic of training. In R. Walton & P. Lawrence (Eds.) *Human resource management: Trends and challenges.* (pp. 285-317). Boston MA: Harvard Business School.

Sundstrom, E. (1986). *Work places.* Cambridge: Cambridge Univ. Press.

Sutton, R. & Louis, M. (1987). How selecting and socializing newcomers influences insiders. *Human Resource Management, 26*, 347-361.

Taylor, S. (1988). Caught in the continuum: A critical analysis of the principle of the least restrictive environment. *Journal of the Association for Persons with Severe Handicaps, 13*, 41-53.

Thomas, J. & Griffin, R. (1989). The power of social information in the workplace. *Organizational Dynamics, 18*, 63-75.

Thomas, R. (1990). From affirmative action to affirming diversity. *Harvard Business Review, 68,* 107-117.

Training and Research Institute for People with Disabilities (1991). *Personal networks and creative supports: Promoting employment opportunities for people with severe physical and cognitive disabilities* (Institute Brief, December). Boston MA: Author.

Turner, J. (1983). Workshop society: Ethnographic observations in a work setting for retarded adults. In K. Kernan, M. Begab & R. Edgerton (Eds.) *Environments and Behavior* (pp. 147-172). Baltimore MD: University Park Press.

Udvari-Solner, A, (1990). *Variables associated with the integration of individuals with intellectual disabilities in supported employment settings.* Unpublished Doctoral Dissertation, Univ. of Wisconsin-Madison.

U.S. Bureau of the Census (1985). *Statistical abstract of the United States: 1986.* Washington, DC: US Government Printing Office.

U.S. Department of Education (1992). The state vocational rehabilitation services program; The state suppported employment services program; Special projects and demonstrations for providing transitional rehabilitation services to handicapped youth; and special projects and demonstrations for providing supported employment services to individuals with severe handicaps and technical assistance projects. *Federal Register, 57* (122), 28432-28442.

Vandercook, T., York, J., & Forest, M. (1989). The McGill Action Planning System (MAPS): A strategy for building the vision. *Journal of the Association for Persons with Severe Handicaps, 14,* 205-215.

Vandergoot , D. (1987). Review of placement research literature: Implications for research and practice. *Rehabilitation Counseling Bulletin, 30,* 243-271.

Virginia Commonwealth University Rehabilitation Research and Training Center (1991). *National supported employment survey data, preliminary report.* Richmond, VA: Author.

Volkemma, R., & Bergmann, T. (1989). Interpersonal conflict at work: An analysis of behavioral responses. *Human Relations, 42,* 757-770.

Wegmann, R. (1991a) From job to job. *Journal of Employment Counseling, 28,* 8-12.

Wegmann, R. (1991b). How long does unemployment last? *Career Development Quarterly, 40,* 71-81.

Wehman, P. (1976). Vocational training of the severely retarded: Expectations and potential. *Rehabilitation Literature, 37,* 233-236.

Wehman, P., Kregel, J., & Seyfarth, J. (1985). Transition from school to work for individuals with severe handicaps: A follow-up study. *Journal of the Association for Persons with Severe Handicaps, 10,* 132-136.

Wesiolowski, (1987) The differences in sizes of social networks of rehabilitation clients versus those of nonclients. *Rehabilitation Counseling Bulletin, 31,* 17-27.

Wolfensberger, W. (1972). *The principle of normalization in human services.* Downsview Ontario: National Institute on Mental Retardation.

York, D. (1991). *Getting the job done: A co-worker training manual.* West Perth, Western Australia: Pro-Em.

Zadny, J., & James, L. (1979). Job placement in state vocational rehabilitation agencies: A survey of technique. *Rehabilitation Counseling Bulletin, 22,* 361-378.

Zey, M. (1988). A mentor for all reasons. *Personnel Journal, 67,* 46-51.

Zivolich, S.(1991). Free market strategies for improving employment services. *Journal of Vocational Rehabilitation, 1,* 65-72.

Zivolich, (1990). *Pizza Hut Jobs Plus Program: Two-year outcome report.* Irvine CA: Integrated Resources Institute.

Index

About the Authors

David Hagner, Ph.D. is Senior Research Associate with the Training and Research Institute for People with Disabilities in Boston MA and teaches in the Rehabilitation Counseling Program at the University of Massachusetts/Boston. He has designed and managed supported employment programs and is the author of many publications related to employment and community integration for people with disabilities.

Dale Dileo, M.Ed. directs the Training Resource Network, a consultation firm which supports the inclusion of people with disabilities in education, home life and employment in their communities. He has provided training, evaluation, and technical assistance to states, corporations and agencies throughout the US and Canada and is the publisher of Supported Employment InfoLines, a newsletter reporting on developments in the fields of integrated employment.